MW00790983

Listening to Art Song

Listening to Art Song

An Introduction

Margaret Olson

ROWMAN & LITTLEFIELD
Lanham • Boulder • New York • London

Published by Rowman & Littlefield
A wholly owned subsidiary of The Rowman & Littlefield Publishing Group, Inc.
4501 Forbes Boulevard, Suite 200, Lanham, Maryland 20706
www.rowman.com

Unit A, Whitacre Mews, 26-34 Stannary Street, London SE11 4AB

Copyright © 2015 by Margaret Olson

All rights reserved. No part of this book may be reproduced in any form or by any
electronic or mechanical means, including information storage and retrieval systems,
without written permission from the publisher, except by a reviewer who may quote
passages in a review.

British Library Cataloguing in Publication Information Available

Library of Congress Cataloging-in-Publication Data

Olson, Margaret, author.
Listening to art song : an introduction / Margaret Olson.
p. cm.
Includes bibliographical references and index.
ISBN 978-1-4422-3020-0 (pbk. : alk. paper) – ISBN 978-1-4422-3021-7 (ebook)
1. Songs–Analysis, appreciation. 2. Songs–History and criticism. I. Title.
MT120.O47 2015
782.42168'117–dc23
2014041734

∞™ The paper used in this publication meets the minimum requirements of American
National Standard for Information Sciences Permanence of Paper for Printed Library
Materials, ANSI/NISO Z39.48-1992.

Printed in the United States of America

For Virginia . . .

Contents

Foreword

John Musto

Words make you think a thought. Music makes you feel a feeling. A song makes you feel a thought. And that is the great advantage.—Yip Harburg

I've been writing songs now, on and off, for over thirty years, and it seems like there is always one more thought to pair with one more feeling, thanks to the wealth of fine poetry in our literature.

Art song (for want of a better term) is really a composer's way of declaiming a poem. Nowadays, poems are so often quietly read from books, magazines, and electronic devices, we forget that by its very nature, poetry is meant to be heard aloud. The song *recital* (and I emphasize the original meaning of that word) is one of the few places one can still experience the sound of a poem.

For a beginning composer, songs are a natural place to start out: they're generally not long, the structure is inherent, and they're easy to disseminate and program. To quote that great purveyor of song, pianist Graham Johnson, "all that is needed is a voice and a piano and a great deal of imagination on both sides of the platform." The challenge: combining the idiosyncrasies of an industrial revolution contraption with the world's oldest instrument. Like anything else, it seems easy when done successfully, and the results are abundantly evidenced by the contents of this book.

There are indeed more popular entertainments than the vocal recital—certainly it's not the stuff of stadium concerts, nor should it be. It's a quiet endeavor, this intimate communion between composer and poem, singer and pianist, and all the above with the audience. And I believe there will always be a place for it.

So long as there are thoughts to be felt, there will be songs.

Acknowledgments

The author would like to extend thanks to Bennett Graff and Gregg Akkerman for their support and encouragement. Thank you to Marilynn S. Olson for her assistance and steadfast support. Thanks to Geraldine Cate, Darlene Lawrence, Bob Spillman, Lee Hoiby, and Julie Simson for being song mentors. Special thanks to Thomas Hampson, John Musto, and Arlene Shrut.

Chapter One

An Introduction to Song

Each song is a world unto itself. The wonder of the human voice, the intensity of poetry, and the diversity of repertory make listening to song a worthy pursuit. An art song is defined as a song written exclusively for the voice and piano. Songs don't always fit neatly into this category. For example, the American spiritual comes from tunes sung without accompaniment and passed down from generations of early Americans. Composers have created songs from previously written material for other instruments or genres. In song, there are as many musical styles as there are composers. Throughout music history some composers were known for writing only song while others wrote for several musical genres.

Every country has songs that reflect its culture. Indigenous traits that are inherent in both the musical and lingual culture of a place come through in song. The sophistication and complexity of the French people is evident in the songs of Claude Debussy. The wide-open harmonic structure and presence of folk tunes in the songs of Aaron Copland are decidedly American. The more familiar a listener is with song, the more quickly he can recognize these traits.

The type of song that will be discussed in this text is often referred to as "art" song or "classical" song. The description of "art" song has been used over the years to distinguish certain songs from popular music. Usually, art songs have been written by composers who write other types of serious music such as instrumental works, opera, choral works, and oratorio.

The idea of classical song defers to a period of music that is long over. It would be appropriate to use the term "classical" to describe the songs of Haydn or Mozart but certainly not the average twentieth-century American composer. "Classical song," like "art song," has traditionally been used to set apart the songs of long-established composers from those of more popular

1

ones. When in doubt of how to refer to a work for voice and piano, it is always appropriate to refer to the songs of any period of composition simply as "song."

THE EXPERIENCE OF SONG

Listening to song is an intensely personal experience. Like with any genre of music, personal preferences will prevail when forming an opinion of a song. Successful songs tend to be the ones that bring about an emotional response in the listener. Many people find song one of the most satisfying ways to enjoy music. Some may wonder how a song for voice and piano can compare to the grandiose nature of a symphonic work or opera. It can, because a song is like a tiny symphonic work. It may be much shorter than an orchestral work in duration, and require only two instruments instead of fifty, but it can be every bit as potent and dramatically and musically satisfying as any symphony.

The best songs are crafted so that there is a distinct beginning, middle, and end. These three sections form the musical and dramatic arc of a song. The arc, or shape, of a song conforms to how a composer expresses dramatic intent. The dramatic intent, or emotion, of a song is what brings about an emotional response in the listener.

WHY SONG?

There are many reasons a composer may choose to write song. Prolific composers, like Franz Schubert, W. A. Mozart, G. F. Handel, and Johannes Brahms, composed songs as a part of a large portfolio of all types of compositions, including symphonic works, chamber music, choral works, and opera. At different times in music history, song composition has been very popular. Its popularity reached a peak in the first half of the nineteenth century with the compositions of Franz Schubert and the "Schubertiad." The "Schubertiad" of the nineteenth century was a very informal evening of music featuring the songs of Schubert. These events usually took place in private homes and often featured Schubert himself at the piano. The audience gathered for these evenings was a combination of society people, writers, artists, critics, and professional and amateur musicians. It is not possible to know exactly what took place at a Schubertiad, but one can imagine Schubert performing as singer and pianist as well as others taking turns at the piano, and Schubert accompanying other singers, even perhaps the lady of the house where the event was hosted. It was typical for a Schubertiad to last until quite late into the evening. Two late nineteenth-century paintings of the Schubertiad show virtually the same scene; a parlor filled to the brim with an audience of formally dressed ladies and gentlemen, with the women seated, and Schubert at the piano. If we are to believe the reality of the paintings, it would seem that the social conventions of the day dictated a somewhat staid environment for listening to music, or perhaps the evenings were sometimes more raucous and informal than the paintings depict.

Another peak period of art song performance was the resurgence of public recital performance in the 1950s, 1960s, and early 1970s when gifted artists such as Gérard Souzay, Elly Ameling, Fritz Wunderlich, and Dietrich Fischer-Dieskau performed entire programs of song in popular music venues across the United States and Europe. This time was a golden age of classical song performance when singers recorded popular albums, were written about and photographed in popular publications, and had a certain degree of celebrity.

As songs were popularized by the artists mentioned previously, a market developed for the amateur musician. Students of music and amateur musicians enjoyed learning songs and created a demand for new composition that has continued to the present day. The existence of music study in higher education has perpetuated the performance of art song by nonprofessional students and kept many editions of song in print. In addition to students, modern-day professional singers still perform song in recital in smaller venues. Singers like Dawn Upshaw, Cecilia Bartoli, and Dmitri Hvorostovsky, among many others, heavily feature songs in their recital performances. The popularity of song has encouraged other composers to create song; composers want their music to be performed. Song's accessibility and popularity can ensure performance opportunities.

Song has also held appeal for composers because it is a relatively short form of music composition. It may take months or years to write a full symphony, but a composer can write a song in just a few days, or in some cases, a few hours. One can imagine the satisfaction a composer must feel when completing a work. If she feels she has created a piece worth performing, it does not matter if the form is a short one. Anyone who has listened to music knows longer is not necessarily better!

THE GENIUS OF SONG

For those of us who know and appreciate song, it is not difficult to see its genius. It is truly miraculous that so much can be musically and emotionally expressed in a two- or three-minute song. A well-written song can encapsulate the genius of a particular composer. For example, Mozart's "Abendempfindung" perfectly demonstrates the graceful harmonies, elegant classical style, and lyrical melodies for which he is known. Listening to this song *is* Mozart; the expression of his style is readily identifiable.

"The Crucifixion" by American composer Samuel Barber is another example of a composer clearly displaying his musical style. Dealing stoutly with the subject matter of the crucifixion of Christ, Barber uses dissonant and unexpected harmonies as well as an open and plaintive treatment in the piano to express pain, sorrow, and suffering. The song beautifully expresses the subject while maintaining the Barber style.

THE UNIQUENESS OF SONG

The art song is a unique musical form because it features the solo voice and the use of text, yet song is a very broad genre. Song encompasses classical or art song, popular music, songs from plays and musicals, and folk music. American song can be loosely divided into art song, national song, spirituals, musical theatre song, and folk song. Popular song includes rock, pop, rhythm and blues, and jazz. How is it possible to distinguish the different types of song from one another? What makes European art song from the nineteenth century any different from Adele's latest song today? If she performs with only piano, not much. Amplification is not used in art song performance. Songs do gain legitimacy over time as they are endorsed by serious artists, teachers, and students and performed often. The songs of composers who write important music in addition to song have staying power. There are duets written for all combinations of instruments; however, piano accompanying voice makes song performance very intimate and personal. A great artist will not attempt to imitate another singer but will find her own musical truth and emotional response to the text. The singer's perspective on the meaning of a text will color the unique performance. The uniqueness of song lies in the uniqueness of the individuals performing it.

The very nature of music is song. Leonard Bernstein often sang along when he was conducting symphonies; he felt the music as song. Most song composers sing their own music when composing; they feel the music as song. Very often, instrumentalists are asked by their teachers to sing a line of music; they are trying to feel their music as song. When someone is asked his favorite music, he sings the tune; he feels music as song. Humans' inherent empathy for the voice leads most of us to closely relate to sung music.

One of the most prolific American composer of song, Ned Rorem, had the following to say while discussing his method of vocal composition: "People say I write graceful vocal lines that singers like to wrap their tongues around; yet I don't think so much about singers as about the very nature of music, which is ALL—so far as I am concerned—inherently song."[1]

NATIONALISM IN SONG

Nationalism, a spirit of and identity with a particular country, is strongly influential in song. It is logical then that each composer brings the traits and traditions of his birth country to his work. His musical sensibilities were shaped by the upbringing he had in a particular country. In western Europe, the songs of the British Isles, Italy, Germany, France, and Spain each have characteristics that can be identified by country of origin. Each of these countries' songs can be further classified according to time period, trends, and place of origin. The diversity of song comes from the variety of composers who write the form. One example of nationalism in song is the German poetry of the nineteenth century. The texts of Heinrich Heine, Eduard Mörike, and Johann Wolfgang von Goethe were set by several German composers and expressed the sentiments of German romanticism.

When listening to song, without knowing the composer, it is sometimes possible to identify the country of origin. Of course, the language of the text may make it obvious; however, some composers write songs in languages other than their own. There are general stylistic traits from times in music history that create an overall style of writing that can be identified as a particular country, or even a region of a country. Of course, the more one knows about the song the easier it is to make these identifications but this is not necessarily always true. Aaron Copland's songs may sound "American" to some as he has set many American folk tunes and melodies in his songs. Twentieth century French composers like Darius Milhaud and Francis Poulenc can perhaps be identified by their French sensibilities that are evident in the sophisticated rhythmic use of the piano that is a natural evolution from Debussy in the nineteenth century. Early Italian song can be identified by the "secco" or dry use of the piano. The accompaniment is more sparingly used in a "recitativo" fashion than in twentieth century Italian song. The experience of identifying the country of origin of a song begins with identifying the composer.

There are particular traits, in addition to language, that can identify song. Italian song often contains melodies similar to those found in opera and emphasizes bel canto and legato singing. German song features a piano part closely integrated with text and largely traditional harmony. It is very often strophic (has verses) and has a clear introduction and conclusion in the piano part. French song can feature nebulous harmonic structure and much pedal in the piano. Twentieth century French song can experiment with harmony and feature more adventurous melodic lines. British song is usually traditional in harmony and structure. Spanish song employs dance rhythms and a sense of drama in the vocal line. Russian song can have a very dense piano part and challenge the singer with the weight and structure of the vocal line. Early American song is traditional and somewhat conservative in structure. Later

American song can be original and individualistic with composers taking risks with melody and harmony and a strong sense of irreverent fun.

It is worth noting that some composers may have a dual or blurred sense of nationalism when composing. Many composers studied music in a country other than their own and from foreign teachers as well. For example, mid-twentieth-century American composer Ned Rorem studied composition in France and has spoken often of the country's influence on his music.

THE ART OF LISTENING

There is an art to listening to song. It may help to think of listening in terms of levels that become more complex. For example, at the top level the ear hears music and text and can assign a specific emotion to what is being heard, at the second level the ear can distinguish the vocal line from the piano and the text from the music, at the third level the ear can follow the vocal line or piano part independently of the other, at the fourth level the ear can hear the elements of the song independently or collectively, and at the fifth level the listener can identify the composer, country of origin, poet, and language and simultaneously interpret stylistic elements of the song and understand how the voice and piano work together musically.

One of these levels is not better or worse than another. Each level has great intrinsic value; however, the levels of listening deepen through experience, knowledge, and critical thinking. Yes, in order to fully appreciate song, critical thinking is essential. Depth of understanding and personal preferences cannot be fully realized without critical thinking. The art of listening should optimally involve not having any preconceived ideas about a song, its composer, or poet when hearing it for the first time. The listener should come to the listening experience with an open mind so she can allow herself to completely experience the composer's intention for the song. This can be very challenging to do! As the listener gains experience and knowledge of song, she will be able to identify the individual style components like tempo, rhythm, and mood.

SONG AS A PERSONAL EXPERIENCE

The experience of listening to song is highly personal. When it comes to opinions about music, each person's perspective is valid. Music often stirs or creates an emotional response from the listener that is related to personal history and experience. Song communicates two languages to the listener at the same time; the nonverbal, music, and the verbal, text. The listener must take in verbal and musical cues simultaneously. The addition of text to music heightens the dramatic effect of song. The addition of text to music may elicit a strong emotional response in the listener or no reaction at all. A listener may not hear the text of a song at all because he is focused on or drawn primarily to the music. Some listeners enjoy the music of a song because they like the poem the composer chose. Other listeners will enjoy the poem because they like the music. The text of a song creates an additional layer of interest for the listener.

A listener's personal reaction to a song has much to do with what is happening in the listener's life at a particular moment. For example, someone who just had an argument with his spouse may not respond well to a song about marital love and devotion. He may not be able to enjoy the song on any level because of the subject matter. Someone suffering from severe illness or depression may not appreciate a song that features a poem about the joys of spring and new life but he may adore a song that features a poem about death and introspection. The personal events and emotions of the listener's life will color the listener's personal experience.

MUSICAL STYLE IN SONG

Musical style is what makes a song unique. Style is made up of several elements that must all fit together perfectly to make a great song. The more familiar a listener is with a composer's musical style, the more he is able to fully form an opinion about that composer's work.

For example, a listener familiar with the orchestral compositions of Aaron Copland will most likely have a good idea whether or not she would enjoy Copland's songs. She would have firm knowledge of his musical expressions from listening to the orchestral works. After listening to a varied sampling of song, a listener will begin to develop a sense of what he does and does not like or prefer in song. Like anything in life, once a definitive opinion is reached about a certain composer's work, it is very difficult to change it. It is to be expected that a listener will not enjoy every song composer's work. He may even find himself not enjoying a composer he expected to like. It is important for the listener to keep in mind that the enjoyment of a particular composer's song does not increase or diminish its value. The diversity and breadth of song composers is far reaching; therefore, different songs appeal to different individuals.

THE VALUE OF A SONG

Those not familiar with song may ask the question: "what makes a song good or bad?" The straightforward answer is: your opinion. The inherent value of any piece of music, including a song, is its meaning to the listener. There are some songs that are considered more structurally complex than others but complexity does not make a song better than a simpler one. For example, who is to say Stephen Foster's "Hard Times" is any less beautiful than Franz Schubert's "An die Nachtigall?" How is it possible to compare songs written on two different continents and forty years apart? The quality of a poem and its worth to a listener also has much to do with an opinion of a good or bad song. If a poem is too pedestrian or crude for one's personal taste, the listener may dismiss the song no matter its qualities.

The expression of an individual opinion of a song is a subjunctive exercise. The ideal method of expressing an opinion of a song depends on the audience. The method that would best support the efforts of someone new to song would be the same used in the academic classroom. The method involves asking yourself questions about why you like or do not like something. Some questions you might ask yourself include: Why does the overall mood of the song irritate me? Is the reason I can't relate to the poem because it does not seem true to me? Is it possible that I do not care for any dissonance and prefer only consonant harmony? In other words, there is usually a specific reason that a song is not enjoyed.

THE SINGER

The experience of listening to song is greatly influenced by the performing singer. The singer performs in partnership with the pianist, communicates the text, and is the central focus of the song performance. The humanity of the human voice is what makes song special among musical forms. Because we are human, we have an immediate response to the sound of a voice. There are many factors that influence the human vocal instrument: age, experience, training, natural talent, voice type, voice size, and type of song repertoire. A listener may strongly relate to and enjoy certain factors of voice production and strongly dislike others. For example, a singer's vibrato (vacillation) rate may be pleasing or disturbing to a listener. A listener can hear two recordings of the same song; one singer with a wide and slow vibrato rate and the other with a faster vibrato rate. He may prefer the wide and slow rate and find that he usually prefers singers with wider vibrato rates.

Some singers have mastery of certain song styles and periods while others do not. It is often the truth that singers can best interpret songs written in their native language, but there are exceptions. Some singers can interpret songs in foreign languages very well but the level of skill depends upon the singer's fluency and familiarity with a composer's musical style.

THE PIANIST

In song performance the pianist is equally important to the singer. In optimal performance, the singer and pianist are working as a cohesive unit to best express emotion and drama through song. Onstage they are truly partners; it is not possible for one to perform without the other, although many singers have multiple musical partners over the course of their careers. The pianist has particular challenges when performing song. She must play the music as the composer intended, employ certain techniques to support the singer, understand the nature of the partnering singer's voice, be aware of the text, control the volume of the piano so the singer is heard, and be musically accurate. The piano parts of songs can be very complex; harmonically, technically, and rhythmically. Master composers who wrote solo pieces for the piano, Beethoven, Debussy, J. S. Bach, and W. A. Mozart, also wrote the piano parts for their songs; but not every pianist can partner a singer. It takes a particular set of skills to perform music in tandem with another musician. In song, a pianist needs to be able to anticipate the breaths of the singer, musically interpret the text of the poem, and conceive his interpretation as a partner to the singer.

THE POEM

The poem is the third instrument, along with the voice and piano, of song. Often with great song compositions, the poem is the inspiration for the song itself. Throughout history composers have written music from the poem, creating a song's musical mood to reflect the meaning and emotion of the words. In some songs, like Francis Poulenc's "Ba, be, bi, bo, bu," the impact of the text is secondary, even insignificant. In a song like Leonard Bernstein's "I Hate Music," the text is impish and clever. In Franz Schubert's "Im Träume," it is atmospheric and transcendent. In William Grant Still's "Grief," the text is political and incendiary. These songs are as different as the words from which they were crafted.

THE LANGUAGE

Songs in a foreign language can create a barrier for the listener if she is not familiar with the language. Hearing a song in a language in which one is completely fluent is quite different from hearing one that is completely foreign. The listener can appreciate the musical language even if he does not understand the verbal language; however, this does limit overall comprehension of the piece. The listener cannot be absolutely sure what he is hearing. The uncertainty makes it impossible for a listener to give himself over to the experience at hand. American singers who study music for many years gain some fluency in at least one foreign language. At the very least, they begin to recognize certain nouns and verbs they use again and again in song, opera, and oratorio. Some singers spend significant amounts of time overseas and gain real fluency in a foreign language. Others study languages apart from their music studies to accelerate learning. For someone in the early stages of learning about song, it may prove useful to follow along a foreign text and its translation while listening. Seeing and hearing the words, and translation, will reinforce comprehension. For example; hearing "In einem Bächlein helle, Da schoß in froher Eil" is quite different from hearing it and seeing the English translation at the same time:

> In einem Bächlein helle, Da schoß in froher Eil
> In a bright little brook, there shot in merry haste
> ("Die Forelle," Franz Schubert, text by Christian F. D. Schubart)

MUSICAL STYLE

Personal taste will directly influence a listener's response to a certain composer. Musical style is how a song composer expresses his individuality. The listener may decide, after some experience, that she prefers twentieth-century American song to nineteenth-century French song, or nineteenth-century Lieder to seventeenth-century lute songs. Again, individual preferences are just that and not a value judgment on the worth of a song. When discussing song with other listeners, it can be beneficial to offer differing opinions and the reasons behind them. An honest exchange about musical preferences is a good use of time. New ideas and views can then be remembered when listening to song next time.

INTERPRETIVE DIFFERENCES IN SONG PERFORMANCE

A song does not come to life until performers take it off the written page. For better or for worse, the composer has very little control over how individuals will interpret his work. Composers make many markings on the written page to communicate their intentions for a song for singers and pianists but those intentions are not always honored. It may seem that clear key and time signatures, tempo and other markings would be enough, but singers and pianists do not always strictly adhere to markings. An authentic performance of a song also depends on the difficulty of the piece and the abilities and limitations of the performers. For example, if a young singer were trying to perform a late Debussy song and had never sung in French, the challenges of the language could prevent her from mastering the nuances of the piece. Vocal deficiencies can draw attention away from the music and to the singer himself; for this reason, it is critically important that singers perform music that is appropriate to their age and abilities. The same is true for pianists.

Personalities of performers play a huge role in song performance. The willingness to work as a cohesive team is not always present between a singer and pianist. Each has to work with the other's ideas and performance habits to create an inspiring performance.

Chapter Two

The Development of Song

It is unlikely that any one country or area of the world can claim the origin of song. Throughout history, the speech sounds and vocalizations of humans have included melodic tunes and songs. Indigenous music of most cultures includes singing or chanting of some kind. In all cultures, songs and tunes are shared, learned aurally, and passed down through generations.

We know from ancient depictions of art that some type of singing and song was often used in celebrations and religious and secular ceremonies of the world's early people. It is logical to conclude that if song was employed for special occasions, it was most certainly found in everyday life. Eventually, tunes and melodies learned aurally over many years were written down and those transcriptions were the beginning of song as we know it today. In every culture, there is some form of lullaby, love song, drinking or celebration song, and song of sorrow or remembrance. Songs, like stories, have always been woven into people's lives.

The precursor to solo song was group song or choral singing. Singing has always been a way for humans of all cultures to express words, ideas, and emotion through chanting or singing in groups. The early music of polyphony (two or more melodic lines sung at the same time) developed into several forms. One example is the fifteenth century Italian frottola form with vocal parts scored for one to four singers and accompanied by one or two instruments. Multiple people singing text at the same time was certainly musical but not ideal for understanding text. In general, performers and composers became dissatisfied with polyphony and its limitations on the expression of the sung voice. The focus on choral music began to lessen as composers gained interest in what the voice could accomplish by itself. In retrospect, the progression from polyphony to the solo song seems like a natural move to a more sophisticated performance style and a medium in which to optimally express text and poetry. Composers had a desire to develop a form of vocal expression that could encompass ornamentation in the vocal line. The kind of ornamentation singers were capable of could not be achieved in group song.

By the sixteenth century, song forms such as the Italian monody, the French air de cour, and the English ayre began to develop and flourish. The forward movement of the solo song was perpetuated by educated amateur singers who enjoyed performing songs at home and in community venues. In certain pockets of society, learning to sing well was considered an essential part of social development.

Throughout the seventeenth and eighteenth centuries, the development of printing and music publications made the distribution of music much easier than in the past. Printed music was more readily available for sale and its distribution led to increased interest in solo song and allowed people to enjoy songs in their homes and communities.

The eighteenth century brought about increased use of the keyboard as a partner instrument to the voice in song. Increasingly, the melodic line began to be set apart within a song's musical texture and the right-hand part of the piano evolved from a supportive chordal structure to its own written-out line. Haydn's canzonettas are an example of how the voice and piano parts of songs were becoming independent entities unto themselves.

ENGLAND AND THE BRITISH ISLES

British song makes up an important portion of the song repertory because of the quality of its composers, their prolific writing, and the significance of their compositions to England's vocal music. Britain's most significant composers were Henry Purcell in the seventeenth century and Ralph Vaughan Williams and Benjamin Britten in the twentieth century.

The popular style of early British song was solo voice with lute accompaniment. These were the first English songs in which accompaniments were carefully composed, even sometimes contrapuntal (two musical lines that are related yet move independently), but in which the tune was the essence of the song and the expression of the text was an important consideration. The vocal line was mostly strophic (repeated verses) and musical units were phrased so that they corresponded to the poetic line. There was usually no introduction by the lute except for a beginning chord. Unlike later British song settings, there was very little or no interlude music. The harmony of these songs was a mix of major and minor tonalities that to the modern ear can sound like an uncentered key signature. The singer's vocal range typically was limited and usually less than an octave in width making lute songs ideal for the beginning or amateur musician. Over time, lute songs were transcribed for harpsichord and later piano accompaniment.

John Dowland (1563–1626) was considered the finest songwriter of his time and had an international reputation as a lutenist and composer. His dominance of the song genre correlated with the "heyday" of English lute songs or ayres. The period of lute song can be traced from 1597 with Dowland's *First Book of Ayres* and the accession of Elizabeth I to the death of James I in 1625. Other well-known composers of lute song were Thomas Morley (1557–1602) and Thomas Campion (1567–1620).

While lute songs were not really designed for formal public performance, the combination of the voice, lute, and intimate poetry was served very well in a more casual performance style. Within the intimate setting of a casual gathering, composers would perform songs themselves as well as accompany other singers.

The royal court set the example of musical patronage. It is difficult to say for sure, but the willingness of the royals to spend money on music surely advanced the development of song in the sixteenth century and beyond. For example, Henry VIII's court employed seventy to eighty working musicians. All ladies and gentleman of the court were expected to be conversant in topics such as literature and art as well as competent in the performance of music. Besides a few dedicated amateur composers and musicians, song performance was usually a decidedly aristocratic pursuit; but, lute songs were not only for the royal court's enjoyment. Even in the lower classes, the folk poetry-infused music tradition was extremely strong. Poetry was most commonly shared and expressed through song and the folk tradition of sung poetry influenced all the literature of the age. The style of the poetry, in contrast to later times, was conditioned by the expectation that it was to be sung; therefore, in general, the quality of poetry used in song was very good. William Shakespeare, Edmund Spenser, Michael Drayton, Sir Philip Sidney, and Ben Jonson were some of the poets set whose songs still endure today. Because the vast majority of the composers, performers, and poets of the day were men, most of the texts were written from the masculine perspective. There are also some songs that are suitable for female performers and in modern performances the distinction between the sexes is rarely made.

Around 1678, composer Henry Purcell (1658–1695) began to dominate the British song genre. Purcell's songs took on attributes of opera and his overall compositional focus was decidedly on the voice. He contributed over 100 songs to the genre and was one of the most influential composers in British history. His work laid a strong foundation for the British vocal composers who would follow.

Eighteenth-century British song did not necessarily live up to the foundation laid in the previous century. The majority of British songs in the eighteenth century were somewhat trivial and their texts focused on themes of the sea, sailors, dancing, and drinking. Songs of this time were often referred to as "ditties." A contributing factor to the plethora of ditties may have been the prevailing influence of Italian music in the London theatres. The themes of Italian opera were mostly based on Greek tragedy and myth and the moods and themes were very serious in nature. The "ditties" provided a welcome contrast. Unlike Italian opera, most British "operas" were dramatic plays with songs interspersed throughout.

There were notable song composers of this time including Thomas Arne (1710–1778) and Joseph Haydn (1732–1809). G. F. Handel was German-born but took British nationality in 1726. He would eventually dominate British music in his lifetime with opera and oratorio compositions. Handel wrote a few solo songs in English and his popular Italian airs were given English words and frequently performed in recital. Toward the end of the century, there was new interest in the songs of Ireland and Scotland and the folk tradition was revitalized.

NINETEENTH CENTURY

The nineteenth century was a productive one hundred years for British song but ultimately not representative of the best of the genre. The Victorian years cultivated the rise of the amateur musician. Affordable sheet music for the rising middle class was an important factor in the creation of the age of the "drawing room ballad." Singers in public concerts still had orchestral accompaniment until the mid-century and many of their ballads were from stage shows and not original songs. Songs from stage shows were published with piano accompaniment like musical theatre songs today. Later in the century, songs were based on the German model and showed an extraordinary care for the inflections of the English language. Composers of the time included Edward Elgar (1857–1934), Hubert Parry (1848–1918), and Sir Arthur Sullivan (1842–1900), who was known for his operetta pieces.

TWENTIETH CENTURY

British song development in the twentieth century was one of the most prolific and exciting times in music history. Ralph Vaughan Williams (1872–1958) was arguably the most significant English song composer before Benjamin Britten. Britten was responsible for the rebirth of the English song in the twentieth century and made immeasurable contributions to myriad musical genres. He is one of the only, if not *the* only, composers whose outstanding work is considered equal in all genres that combine text with the human voice; song, opera, choral music, and oratorio.

ITALY

The majority of music history in Italy has been dominated by the develop-ment of opera. With the development of opera in the seventeenth century, the Italians began to consider the value of the human voice as a solo instrument apart from an ensemble of voices. The style of Italian monody was adapted from ensemble singing and laid the foundation for solo Italian song. Madri-gals and arias were the earliest Italian song forms; however, the aria of this period was not the same as the operatic aria we know today. For example, in early Italian opera, the singer was expected to add to the melody on the page. Similarly to a jazz singer's improvisatory technique, the early Italian singer would have embellished a vocal line in a type of improvisation. The early style of improvisation continued to become more and more ornate before peaking in tandem with the group of male opera singers known as castrati.

The work of Giulio Caccini (1551–1618) set a pattern for solo vocal performance. One of the earliest Italian songs was Caccini's "Amarilli" from *Le nuove musiche* (1602). The song emphasized the expressiveness of text and use of early ornamentation.

In the seventeenth century, another influential composer was Giacomo Carissimi (1605–1674) who influenced Francesco Cavalli (1602–1676) and Marc Antonio Cesti (1623–1669). These years brought about an increased use of the da capo (from the head) aria form and a distinct move from the intimate performance of song to outward and public-oriented performances of song in a larger space. Italian opera developed in full and set the tone for the rest of Europe.

The nineteenth century of Italian vocal music was decidedly focused on opera. Many Italian composers, like Gioacchino Rossini (1792–1868) and Giuseppe Verdi (1813–1901) wrote songs; however, their songs were more like miniature operatic arias than songs.

The twentieth century of Italian song brought about a revival of the earli-est song forms or "stile antico" in contrast to the increased use of atonality and nontraditional harmonies of other countries' songs.

GERMANY

The earliest German songs were performed by Minnesingers, or singers of love, who were mostly of the aristocratic class. As German song developed into the continuo Lied, it related more to folk song than opera. The continuo Lied was typically a strophic song with continuo accompaniment (fully writ-ten out and continuous bass line) and written primarily for amateur perfor-mance. These songs typically avoided musical excesses and were not fully established as a song type until the 1640s.

The polyphonic Lied dominated the fifteenth and sixteenth centuries and representative composers were Heinrich Issac, Ludwig Senfl, and Johann Schein. German composers, like Schein, began to adopt traits of Italian monodic song, which helped to propel the form toward featuring the solo voice. Cities such as Nuremberg and Mainz were locations where there were schools devoted to the study of music and song in particular.

The continuo Lied developed through the mid-eighteenth century and was focused on secular texts. The rise of the middle class and the education of women both contributed to growth of the song genre. The German literary movement of "Sturm und Drang" emphasized ideas about nature and freedom from rules and strongly influenced German musicians and poets. The pre-Schubert era featured the volkstümliches tradition.

The nineteenth century brought about the synthesis of the Lied form. Mozart and Beethoven made early contributions to the Lied. The Lieder of Franz Schubert, Robert Schumann, Hugo Wolf, and Johannes Brahms overshadowed song from other countries during the nineteenth century. Richard Strauss was the Lieder composer that bridged the nineteenth and twentieth centuries. The twentieth century saw German and Austrian composers moving toward a new type of harmonic language with the 12-tone series, also known as serialism. Arnold Schoenberg and his students Alban Berg and Anton Webern took the German Lied to a completely new sphere with their revolutionary compositions.

FRANCE

The earliest French songs were performed by the troubadours of southern France and the trouvères of northern France much like the lutenists in Great Britain. In the early seventeenth century, the solo song forms were the air de cour, bergerette, pastourelle, chanson à boire, chanson à danser, and romance. Song forms were shaped by their environments, composers, geographic locations, performance style, and what was fashionable at the time.

Throughout the eighteenth century, all these song forms converged into what was called the "romance form." The romance became the standard for French song until the distinct shift to something new with Berlioz' song cycle, *Les nuits d'été*, which was later scored for orchestra in 1841 and is still often performed today.

The new French songs were called mélodies. The peak of the French mélodie was parallel to the careers of Gabriel Fauré (1845–1924) and Claude Debussy (1862–1918). Twentieth-century French composers further developed song by integrating new tonal language with older forms and poetry. The musical and literary salon group "Les Six" formed in 1917 and included foremost composers of the twentieth century like Francis Poulenc and Darius Milhaud.

UNITED STATES

The American art song of today can be traced directly back to forms such as musical theatre, vaudeville, blues, spirituals, hymns, and folk tunes. A folk tune is a melody usually passed down aurally through generations and sung in a familial or casual setting. A folk song is an original tune with some kind of accompaniment, usually piano. It can have a piano part that closely follows the melody, a traditional arrangement, or a piano part that is somewhat independent from the voice and written as an original realization of the song.

In eighteenth century America, the colonists arrived in the New World with the tradition of praising God by singing psalms. The singing of psalms, in a religious setting, was a widespread practice among colonists. The psalm-tunes they knew sufficed as sung music until the early part of the eighteenth century when musicians born in America began to compose their own psalm and hymn-tunes. America's first composers were self-taught and viewed music as a functional part of their everyday lives; they were sometimes referred to as "tunesmiths." Located primarily in New England, they collected their music into compilations they called tune-books. The collections were then used to teach others the rudiments of music in singing-schools.

One of the most important and influential song forms of the nineteenth century grew out of the culture of slavery: the spiritual. Folk spirituals were a hybrid of West African and Anglo-American music and ritual.[1] The form became the foundation of the American art song.

Nineteenth-century composers like Stephen Foster and Charles Ives further developed the American song into a cohesive form while ingraining what would become typical American traits such as straightforward poetry full of sentimentality, traditional harmony mixed with experimental tonalities, and snippets of folk tunes utilized within song.

The twentieth century brought about an explosion of song in the United States. Composers like Ned Rorem and John Duke were influenced by European masters and devoted themselves to perfecting the American song form. Aaron Copland, Leonard Bernstein, and Samuel Barber all were prolific and diverse composers who also focused their energies on song composition with great results. Today, William Bolcom, John Musto, Libby Larsen, Ricky Ian Gordon, and many other composers continue to contribute to the genre of American song.

Chapter Three

The Elements of Song

A song is a musical composition written for voice and piano. Song composers' staying power depends on their ability to bring the individual elements of a song together to express musical and dramatic intent. Like a great recipe in which each ingredient is critically important to how the dish tastes, each element of a song is critical to its inherent structure. Composers who are considered "genius" have mastered the ability to weave elements together so that none is outstanding to the listener's ear and all contribute to the enjoyment of a song. In a successful song, each element will have a unique character that is dependent on the composer's musical style. When song elements come together per the composer's vision, style is achieved.

A listener's opinion of a particular musical style depends strongly on personal taste. In addition to style, song elements can be influenced by nationalistic traits. For example, the French composer Claude Debussy used specific piano pedaling to create an impressionistic mood in his songs. He used the same technique in his piano and orchestral compositions and the overall effect greatly contributed to his style. American composer Aaron Copland often built tunes based on hymns, spirituals, and folk music in his song composition. For Americans, there is a sense of familiarity when listening to his songs because some of the tunes are known; it seems as if we have heard the song before. One can hear his use of American folk tunes in his orchestral works as well; Copland famously uses the Shaker tune "Simple Gifts" throughout his *Appalachian Spring* (1943) ballet composition. *Appalachian Spring* was well-appreciated by audiences; Copland won the Pulitzer Prize for the piece in 1945.

One of the most important elements of song is the poem or text set by the composer. The meaning and intention of a poem can significantly color the musical impact of a song. Some composers draw all of their musical inspiration from the text. A composer like Franz Schubert drew musical expression directly from the text and chose the poetry he set to music carefully. The best of his songs perfectly interpreted the dramatic intention of the poet he chose. In his song "Gretchen und Spinnrade" (poem by Goethe), the listener can hear Gretchen at the spinning wheel in the repetitive and relentless note patterns in the piano.

Some of the Italian song composers were, perhaps, less in sync with the poetic idea of their chosen text. While Durante's "Danza, danza fanciulla gentile" is very successful in expressing the whirling of a dancing girl with intense dance rhythms, other Italian songs like "Tu lo sai" and "O del mio amato ben" seem less distinct in how their text is expressed. They do not contain specific musical elements that convey the meaning of the text. In contrast is the nineteenth-century German song from which composers had a rich and sophisticated selection of poetry from which to draw and were focused on text painting. The reason for these differences has much to do with the poet chosen, the composer's feelings about the importance of interpreting text, the nationalistic influences of the time, and the musical style of the composer.

The time period and musical environment in which a song is written also reflects the overall output of a composer. For example, during the "classical" period of music, W. A. Mozart composed his songs in the framework of that style. Mozart's genius is impressive when one considers that he was able to achieve a unique musical style within the confines of an overall classical form.

The American spiritual has elements such as deeply personal text with sometimes hidden meaning, hymn-like or religiously influenced melodies, and traditional harmony. Fortunately, late twentieth-century composers of spirituals have kept those traditions and traits in mind when updating versions of traditional spirituals.

THE ELEMENTS OF SONG

Voice

The voice is the most important element of song. It is what makes song a singular form of musical expression. The voice is the only instrument that can communicate text to the listener. Each individual voice has its own personality. For example, there are certain voices that most people can recognize after just a few notes because the personality and individuality of the voice is so strong. These voices are not necessarily the voices of classical singers but singers with universal appeal because of their exposure in popular culture through venues such as film and television. They are individuals whose voices most people in the world could recognize. Some examples of singers whose voices are universally recognizable and have been especially memorable over the years include Billie Holiday, Judy Garland, Aretha Franklin, Elvis Presley, Michael Jackson, Bob Dylan, Barbra Streisand, and Frank Sinatra and classical artists Marian Anderson, Luciano Pavarotti, and Enrico Caruso. These singers are twentieth-century performers whose voices are unique and memorable for reasons that aren't entirely explained through words. The singing voice can be as distinctive and telling as the spoken voice.

A person's voice is physically shaped by her unique anatomical characteristics. The length and thickness of the vocal folds (cords), the length and shape of the neck and throat, the size and shape of the nose and nasal passages, the arrangement of the facial bone structure, and the shape and size of the mouth and oral cavities all have a large impact on a voice's "personality." A singer's training and vocal technique also affect how the voice physically develops. In describing the human voice, we commonly resort to nonscientific terms. For example, we may describe a high soprano voice as "sparkling," "effervescent," "bell-like," or "shrill"; a bass-baritone voice as "husky," "nasal," "powerful," or "sonorous"; or a tenor as "strident," "lyrical," "rich," or "melodious." Nonscientific descriptions can carry positive or negative connotations. Ultimately there is no right or wrong way to describe the human voice. Descriptive terms based on science or imagery are both valid when discussing the voice.

Before much was known about voice science, human anatomy, otolaryngology, and ear, nose, and throat medicine, nonscientific descriptions were the only options available to teachers and singers when discussing the voice. Fantastic singing was taking place before voice science was fully developed; therefore, a scientific vocabulary is not essential for teachers to communicate with singers or for singers to communicate with their audiences. The resources of science and imagery can increase the quality of singing and aid in the resolution of vocal problems.

Voice Production

The voice has special characteristics that distinguish it from other musical instruments. It is the only instrument that is carried within the human body and thus cannot be seen by the human eye. In addition, the voice is the only instrument that performs a biological function. The act of singing is a physical event that includes the coordination of tone, breath, and support and utilizes the entire structure of the human body.

The voice itself is called the larynx and is made up of one bone (hyoid), cartilages, muscles, ligaments, and membranes. The muscles of the voice work by adducting (bringing together) and abducting (moving apart) the vocal folds. The muscles of the voice are intrinsic and extrinsic. The intrinsic muscles have both muscle ends connected within the larynx while the extrinsic muscles have one end within the larynx and one end outside the larynx. The epiglottis is hinged onto the thyroid cartilage of the voice and functions as a lid for the larynx. The biological purpose of the epiglottis is to protect the airway from food and liquid during swallowing.

When singing, the entire framework of the body supports the voice. The spinal column, sternum, scapula, clavicles, ribcage, and pelvis are the structure of the body and also the voice. Good posture is critical to singing. If the singer is bent forward or slumped in the shoulders, it greatly restricts the ability of the lungs and ribcage to expand and take in a deep breath. It is critical that a singer elongate the spine for optimal voice production.

The breathing cycle has four stages; inhalation, suspension, exhalation, and recovery. The best way for a singer to inhale, or take in breath, is quietly and deeply without involvement of the shoulders or upper body. The inhalation should happen very low in the body. The intercostal muscles move the ribcage outward and inward. The diaphragm muscle is the most critical muscle to the breathing process. When the diaphragm muscle descends and the intercostal muscles open the ribcage, a "vacuum" effect is created that allows air to rush into the lungs. Air enters the mouth and nose, moves down the vocal tract past the larynx, through the trachea, into the bronchi (passageways made of cartilage), and into the lungs. During exhalation, the process is reversed.

Phonation is the production of sound. During phonation, the air passing over the vocal folds causes them to vibrate which creates sound. How does this occur? Immediately before a singer phonates, a pressure (subglottal pressure) builds up underneath the vocal folds and a vacuum-like suction begins vibration. Balanced vocal production is achieved when the singer is not oversinging (hyperfunction) or undersinging (hypofunction).

While singing, resonation (ringing) of the voice takes place. The vocal tract is where resonation takes place. The tract includes the air spaces from the vocal folds to the lips. Included in this area is the inside of the mouth (pharynx) as well as the nasal cavities.

A vocal register is defined as a series of pitches that are uniform in sound and share the same quality.[1] The registers of the female singing voice are most often referred to as the head, middle, and chest registers. While the male voice principally has two registers, the head and chest, it would be acceptable to say that a middle register also exists. The term "falsetto" is often described as a register in the male voice but may also be considered a vocal "affect" instead of a separate register. The castrati singers of Italy sang principally in falsetto.

Singers are distinguished from each other by the method of voice classification. The factors that determine voice classification are gender, timbre, range, tessitura, and register transition points. The four basic categories of

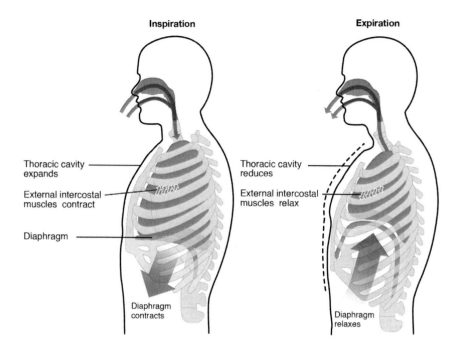

Figure 3.1.   Sketch of the Lungs and Surrounding Structures

voice classification are soprano, mezzo-soprano (alto), tenor, and bass. With-in each of the four main categories are many subcategories. Vocal health is best maintained when a singer is classified correctly and avoids singing song literature outside his vocal classification.

The idea of vocal coordination occurs when all the elements of the voice are working well together to produce a singer's optimal sound. From Dan Marek's *Singing: The First Art*:

"The coordination . . . of the vocal cords becomes a major goal in the training of fine singers. The resulting tone, which is functionally balanced, is said to have *squillo*, or a 'ring.' The ability to control the interrelationship of the breath and the tensing function is one of the hallmarks of great singers. One thinks of the finesse and power of such artists as Adelina Patti, Enrico Caruso, Rosa Ponselle, and Jussi Björling. All were able to sing the softest tones without losing clarity and to swell smoothly to *fortissimo* and back again. This takes a miracle of coordination."[2]

Singers who find success have learned how to care for their voices. The issue of vocal health is critical for professional singers and for anyone who loves to sing. While basic common sense is a good place to start, singers must also take special care of their instruments in several ways:

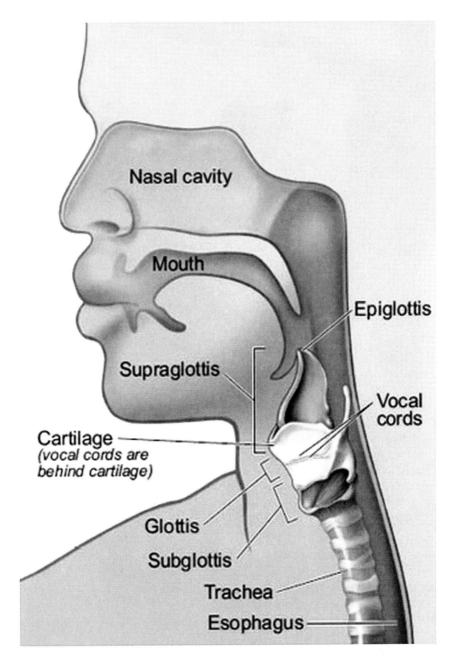

Figure 3.2.   Drawing of the Vocal Tract and Resonators

1. Avoiding misuse of the voice by not speaking too loudly or yelling in crowded or noisy situations,
2. Staying hydrated by drinking plenty of water regularly throughout the day and not just immediately before singing,
3. Not smoking and avoiding second-hand smoke,
4. Washing hands with soap and hot water frequently to avoid germs and avoiding contact with people who are sick,
5. Being aware of the effect of prescribed and over-the-counter medications on the voice,
6. Visiting an otolaryngologist when vocal problems arise,
7. Avoiding foods that cause excessive dryness (like alcohol) or excess mucus (like dairy products),
8. Maintaining general good health.

Piano

The piano is a critical element of song and a partner to the voice in the art song genre. The piano is a powerful instrument and capable of illustrating the musical style of a composer in myriad ways. The pianist can utilize the pedal to amplify or dampen sounds, lower or lift the piano lid to highlight or diminish sound, provide structure to rhythmic patterns by attacking the keys in a certain matter, control volume by adding or lessening pressure to the keys, and follow the markings and tempi of the composer. In the best song performance, the pianist and vocalist have rehearsed extensively and have decided together how to best interpret and present a song. Occasionally, the pianist may be regarded as a *support to* and not *partner of* the singer. This is not acceptable; the pianist is equal to the singer in song performance. In song history, some of the most successful singers have approached performance with a true pianist partner. For example: Pierre Bernac and Francis Poulenc, Leontyne Price and Samuel Barber, Joan Morris and William Bolcom, Dietrich Fischer-Dieskau and Dalton Baldwin, Kathleen Battle and James Levine, Gérard Souzay and Gerald Moore, Harolyn Blackwell and Ricky Ian Gordon, and Amy Burton and John Musto.

The assumption that the two performers are not equal could be made from observing a song recital for the first time. On stage, the pianist is in a sitting position and the singer is standing; visually the pianist is in a weaker position than the singer. The pianist plays her part from printed music on a stand in front of her while the singer most often performs from memory. The pianist must look at the singer to follow breaths and receive musical cues. All of this may make the pianist appear subservient to the singer or as a follower rather than an equal. An ideal performance situation is one in which the pianist and singer are equally aware of each other onstage and perform as a team. To that end, many performers experiment with the placement of the singer and pianist in a variety of positions onstage in an attempt to equalize the visual plateau.

Pianists who accompany singers are very accomplished musicians in their own right. Not only are they fluent pianists, but they have also mastered the skill of collaborative piano, which is very different from playing solo piano. A collaborative pianist usually plays with singers in a variety of venues such as schools, churches, community centers, performance halls, private homes, and other places. A professional collaborative pianist may be familiar with art song but also opera, oratorio, musical theatre, operetta, popular music, standards, and other genres. Some genuinely enjoy working with singers and may have coaching experience as well. A vocal coach will help a singer find the optimal way to perform a song that makes the most of the music and text. The coach will have a deep understanding of the composer's style and the text at hand and can help the singer with language pronunciation and musical style. The coach will help the singer with difficult rhythms, entrances, and pitches (notes) and can share performance traditions with the singer, especially in operatic literature.

Text

Text is a critical component of song performance. A musical form that includes text makes vocal performance both unique and challenging. When an oboe, violin, or trumpet is played, the listener has to only listen to musical sounds. The music expresses a mood, of course, but its palette is a blank one on which the listener can make his own colors. When a singer performs, text is just as prevalent as music to the listener's ear. The words of the poem cannot be ignored.

The meaning of the text takes away freedom of interpretation from the listener and gives an emotional and logical context in which to listen to music. Just as the poem chosen by the composer influences his music, it influences the listener. The context of word meaning in a song hugely influences the listener's experience.

Language

Songs are composed in many different languages. This book is focusing on the languages of Western Europe but there are songs composed in every language on the globe. Not all of these songs may be written down, but every culture has an aural history that includes tunes and melodies. As we have more and more access to the world's cultures, we are learning more about the songs of Asia, Eastern Europe, and Africa. There are thousands of songs in the main vocal repertory that are not addressed in this book. They include songs of Russia, Scandinavia, Spain, Central America, and Eastern Europe.

The personality of a language will greatly affect the listening experience. Each language has traits that influence singers' vocal production. While in music school, singers devote a large portion of their study to foreign language diction or the study of the enunciation of speech sounds. Singers use a tool called the International Phonetic Alphabet or "IPA." The IPA is a set of symbols used to notate speech sounds and was created by linguist scholars in the late nineteenth century. The IPA symbols remain consistent from language to language.

Singers memorize a different set of rules for each language using the alphabet of IPA symbols. If a singer does not know a particular language, he can learn the rules and transcribe the foreign text into IPA symbols. He then learns the text of the song from the symbols. Many singers eventually do not need to use IPA once they are familiar with a language. Some singers have fluency in a language from extensive study or living overseas. Some singers do not learn the IPA at all and familiarize themselves with foreign languages by imitating singers on recordings. A singer's foreign language skills depend on nationality, education, opportunity, and desire.

As the birthplace of opera, Italy's vocal music flourished in no small part due to its imminently singable language. The Italian language contains seven basic vowel sounds. The consonants can be pronounced as single (quickly) or can be doubled (exaggerated). Consonants are quick and clean in articulation with the exception of doubled consonants and rolled "r." Italian is well-established as a favorite language of singers because the majority of sung sounds in that language are vowels sounds. Vowels are sustained by the voice unlike consonants which cannot be sustained by breath flow. The sustained vowels allow for true legato (smooth) singing and optimal vocal quality and expression. All of the sounds in Italian are made closer to the front of the mouth than the back. This trait makes voice production easier.

German is a very different language from Italian. German vowel sounds include "mixed" vowels in which two sounds are pronounced at the same time. One sound is produced with the tongue and one with the lips. Mixed vowels are marked with an "umlaut" (ü) symbol. There are many consonant clusters (two or three consonants together) that contain consonants pronounced with different parts of the mouth. There are even sounds that are produced from the back of the throat which are known as "guttural" sounds.

The French language adds another dimension to the challenges of sung diction. The French have mixed vowels but also sounds known as "nasals." Nasals are vowel sounds pronounced using the nasal resonances. Some French sounds require a somewhat closed or fully rounded aperture (mouth) for correct pronunciation and can be challenging because they restrict sound. Some consonants in the French language are silent and their pronunciation depends on what letters they adjoin. The language also uses "elision"; the end of one word blends into the beginning of the next word sometimes dropping the final consonants as a result.

English is a complex language in which to sing. It is especially difficult if it is not a first language. Many words in English and French are not pronounced the way they appear, for instance: knead, receipt, island, soften, and thumb. Other words have the same pronunciation but different spellings and meanings: right and write, see and sea, threw and through, sew and so, eight and ate, aisle and isle.

CHARACTERISTICS OF SUNG FOREIGN LANGUAGES

Poetry

The composer's chosen poem is a critical element of song. Without poetic inspiration, most song composers would have no context in which to write! A poem provides the inspiration, mood, context, emotion, drama, and storytelling to a composer. It can also dictate musical and rhythmic cues for compositions. Elton John composes songs from poems written by Bernie Taupin. Mr. Taupin writes and Mr. John creates music from the texts. Elton John has said their individual writing processes are completely separate from one another; they do not work together in the same room. This is similar to the way most classical song composers have written. They take the words of a preexisting poem and create a song. The poems are usually about themes and ideas that appeal directly to the composer. Traditionally, composers tend to gravitate toward the same poets many times in their careers. Sometimes songs are written as a commission in which the composer may or may not have selected the texts himself. Sometimes the poet is a friend of the composer as in the case of lyricist Anne Hunter and Joseph Haydn. There is also the possibility that the individual commissioning the work has written the text herself, as in the case of Frederica von Stade and Jake Heggie. The famous mezzo-soprano commissioned Mr. Heggie to write songs based on her text in honor of her daughter, Lisa Elkus. The resulting work, *Paper Wings*, a cycle of four songs, premiered in 1997 at the University of California at Berkeley with Ms. von Stade singing and Martin Katz at the piano.[3]

The quality of poetry used in song varies greatly. The quality can depend on the time and place in which the song was written. For example, the poetry of the German period of Romanticism in the late eighteenth century and early nineteenth century is generally considered some of the best ever set to song. By focusing on themes of introspection, nature, and the lows and highs of every emotion, poets like Johann Wolfgang von Goethe created poetry that reflected themes that are deep, meaningful, and thought-provoking to most and set to song by many composers.

Table 3.1.   General Language Traits

	Italian	German	French	English
Vowels	• Seven vowel sounds • Open and closed "e" and "o" • Diphthongs (two consecutive vowel sounds)	• Mixed vowels (umlaut [ü]) • Diphthongs	• Mixed vowels • Nasals (vowels produced with nasal resonance [õ, ã] occur next to nasal consonants like "n" or "m")	• Long and short vowels • Diphthongs
Consonants	• Dentals (pronounced with the tongue touching the teeth) • Single consonants pronounced quickly • Double consonants pronounced with exaggeration	• Guttural "r" (pronounced in the throat) • Consonant Clusters (Schmertz)	• Silent consonants • Nasal consonants (n, m)	• Consonants not always pronounced how they appear

Other times in history have not always produced songs with deep meaning. Much of the poetry of eighteenth century English ballads was somewhat banal and often based on shallow themes such as drinking and carousing.

Similarly to music, the poetry of a time and place is subjective to its circumstances and those of its poets. As with music, the quality of poetry is highly interpretive and subjective and determined by the individual.

Mood

The mood of a song is an intangible but essential element of musical expression. Not every composer is able to achieve a discernible mood in a song. Mood is a delicate combination of text, melody, piano, and all the elements of song. Certain elements, like harmony, play a large part in creating a mood. The combination of harmony and rhythm can have a profound effect on mood. For example, a song with a minor tonality and *slow* tempo can express a mood of sadness or reflection while a song with minor tonality and an *upbeat* tempo can express something else, like anger. The combination of two elements can create one type of mood, also substituting one element for another can greatly alter the mood of a song.

In a well-conceived song, the mood is integral to the poetry. The listener should be able to make sense of and easily reconcile the text of the poem with the mood of the music. All the elements of the song should reflect the intention and emotion of the poem. There is a delicate balance to achieving a clear mood that often evades composers. In addition to the work of the composer, the singer has a special responsibility to assist in creating the mood of a song in performance. A good singer will strive to honor the music and intention of the composer rather than instilling his own style upon the listener. For example, a composer may write a vocal line that is quite high and indicate that the voice should be soft and airy to reflect the mystery of the poem. A singer may decide to ignore the composer's intention and sing the notes quite loudly because he or she thinks their voice sounds best at a loud dynamic. This choice will most likely take away from the mysterious mood of the song and confuse listeners. Singers sometimes make performance choices out of ignorance or ego, but most do their best to serve the music. When the intention of the singer and pianist is to serve the music, and not themselves, the result is usually very successful.

Melody

Melody is an essential element of song; a song does not exist without a melody. The vocal part of a song is the melody. Parts of the melody can be incorporated into the piano part. The shape of a melody is how the composer controls what he wants a singer to do and how he wants the voice utilized within a song. There are many ways a composer can construct a melodic line. A melody can be melismatic (several notes sung on one syllable), syllabic (changing notes with each syllable), lyrical (sweeping, romantic lines), static (not much motion or movement), patter-like (rapidly changing syllables and pitches), or conversational (melody closely following speech patterns). A song can have one melodic characteristic throughout or mixed characteristics. Often a changing melody mirrors changing harmonies.

Motive

Song composers sometimes use motives. A motive is a short melodic pattern that repeats throughout a song. It can be repeated once or several times. A motive can be heard in the voice alone, the piano alone, or in both the voice and piano. The use of motives in song serves as a unifying factor. A motive can be an anchor for the melody or tie in the voice and piano at a critical moment in the text. Sometimes within a song cycle (a group of songs with a unifying element), a motive from an earlier song can appear in a later song as a recapitulation or repetition of a musical idea. Robert Schumann utilized this technique in his song cycle *Frauenliebe und leben*.

Harmony, Rhythm, and Tempo

Harmony and rhythm make up the structure and framework of a song. If a song were a house, the harmony would be the foundation and the rhythm would be the structure on top. Composers create harmony to serve the text of a song and to express an emotion or mood. The key signature in music provides a harmonic structure in which the composer can write. An example of a key signature is C Major, e minor, or A flat Major. Each key signature has a parallel minor (that is, C Major and c minor, E Major and e minor). Key signatures have different musical personalities. Some composers have favorite key signatures they use when they want to express a specific mood. Harmony can be tonal (with a center) or atonal (without a center). Atonal compositions tend to be present post–nineteenth century. Harmony can be consonant (clear harmony) or dissonant (less clear harmony). Harmonic structure can move from major to minor and back again within one song, or even one phrase. Keys can modulate (change) within a song.

Rhythm is another device composers use to express music with intention. The construction of rhythm in a phrase can greatly affect a listener's understanding and belief of the text. For example; in Stefano Donaudy's "Spirate pur, spirate," he uses a long series of even eighth notes to express the gently moving breeze. A dotted, or jagged, rhythm would not convey the same ease of the breeze. In Franz Schubert's "Die Forelle," the composer perfectly employs a rolling and almost syncopated rhythm to bring to life jumping fish.

It is a brilliant use of rhythm and the listener becomes accustomed to the moving fish in the introduction before the singer makes a sound.

Meter is the time signature of a song; it indicates how many beats are allotted per measure. For example, a time signature of 3/4 indicates that there are three beats per measure and the quarter note value gets one beat. A time signature of 2/2 indicates that there are two beats per measure and the half note gets one beat. Time signatures can be simple, compound, or irregular. The tempo (time) marking of a song or section of song is different from the rhythmic structure but strictly related to it. A tempo is the overall rhythmic feel of a song or a smaller section of a song. For example, a section of song can be marked "largo" (slow), or "con passione" (with passion). Editorial metronome markings used by the composer can also indicate tempo.

Form

Songs are written in different forms. At times in western music history, certain song forms were very popular and at other times, composers created new forms in which to write. Not all songs fit neatly into a specific "form," but most do. One common type of song form is "strophic." This form is made up of multiple verses that repeat melodic material with different text, very much like a traditional hymn. A through-composed, or the less commonly used term "durchkomponiert," is a song that does not have repeated material. Songs can also be in binary or ternary forms; two or three main parts.

Range and Tessitura

Vocal range encompasses all the notes in between the lowest note and highest note a singer sings within a song. The range of notes in a song tends to be mostly high, mostly medium, mostly low, or a combination. Songs are usually written in one key and then transposed to many other keys so singers of differing voice types can access them vocally. Tessitura is the section of the range where most of the melody is written. It also refers to the part of the scale with which a singer is most comfortable.

SONG PERFORMANCE

Throughout the centuries, song has been performed in many different ways and venues. Both formally and informally, song has been integrated into the lives of people belonging to every socioeconomic class. Songs were sung by musicians in the royal courts of Europe for daily entertainment and to embellish important occasions and events. Troubadours, lutenists, folk singers, and minnesingers have sung songs in the out-of-doors as part of village life in the country and on the streets of towns and urban centers. Amateur and professional singers have enjoyed songs in every language within their homes and in front of audiences both personal and critical. Music salon afternoons and evenings, in which musicians and audiences enjoy music in private homes, have served to showcase the songs of composers while often incorporating the composers themselves into the performances. These gatherings in the homes of high society matrons, musicians, and humble music-lovers alike have done much over the years to perpetuate the lively stories about musicians and the romance of song. Salon evenings have brought artists, writers, musicians, entertainers, politicos, and literary and philosophical figures together for some of the most truly unique mixes of people in history. Musical salons were very popular in eighteenth and nineteenth century Germany and France.

The role of the composer in performance is most often a non-issue. In the majority of performances throughout history, the composer has not been a part of the performances of his songs. Currently, the composer is most often no longer with us and his music is being performed posthumously. It is possible that a song composer like John Duke or William Bolcom, who held teaching positions for many years, had more opportunities to hear renditions and performances of their songs by students and faculty than a composer like Hugo Wolf, who was not teaching full-time. Of course, the composer of a song is always present in spirit during a performance. The music of a song is the language of the composer. The singer is only a conduit of the material; the composer is the creator. Each time a song is performed and listened to, with an earnestness of spirit, the composer is present. Today, more and more composers are actively performing their songs with various singers.

There are some very lucky audiences who have been in attendance when composers are premiering their own works. Three classic American song premieres with the composers performing took place in New York's Town Hall. The composer Samuel Barber and his frequent collaborator, soprano Leontyne Price, debuted Barber's *Hermit Songs* in 1954. Ms. Price would later sing the title role in Barber's Lincoln Center debut *Antony and Cleopatra.*

American composer Aaron Copland debuted his *Old American Songs* with baritone William Warfield at Town Hall in 1951. Another premiere was with composer Leonard Bernstein at the piano and mezzo-soprano Jennie Tourel singing Bernstein's song cycle *I Hate Music!* in 1943.

In song performance, the roles of the singer and the pianist are inextricably linked. The preparation of song performance requires work of the participants individually and together. The singer is responsible for learning the vocal part of the song (the melody), how it interacts with the piano part, the pronunciation of the text, the translation of any foreign language text, and the markings and requirements of the composer. Once the fundamentals of the music are mastered, the singer will then work to align his personal technique with the required style of the piece, depending on the specific genre of song. The singer will also decide how he will interpret the poem of the song and how to express emotion and dramatic intent when performing. Throughout the process, the singer is memorizing the song for performance.

The pianist has just as much song preparation as the singer. The pianist is responsible for learning the piano part of the song in the appropriate style of the composer and style period. If she is not familiar with the song or composer, she will listen to various recordings of the song to better understand how it is usually interpreted. The pianist must learn the vocal line as well as her own part so she fully understands where the melodic phrases begin and end and internally hear the voice and language. She must also, and perhaps most importantly, know where the singer will most likely want to take a breath and make adjustments accordingly. Once the pianist has all the pitches and fingerings learned, she will begin to fully incorporate the style of the piece and the markings of the composer including dynamic markings, tempo markings, and pedal points. An experienced vocal collaborative pianist will read and translate the poem so she has the same knowledge as the singer as to the meaning of the text. Even though the burden of text expression is on the singer, who is facing the audience, the pianist must incorporate emotional expression into the piano part as much as possible.

Once the singer and pianist have done their preparation work individually they are ready to come together for rehearsal. The purpose of the rehearsal is two-fold; the singer and pianist must learn the song with the alternate piano or voice part integrated and the pair will discuss and implement ideas for performance style and musical and dramatic expression. There are as many different kinds of song performing teams as there are people. Some pairs include; student and coach, student and student, equal professionals, husband and wife, and singing star and famous conductor/composer.

The most traditional kinds of song recitals performed today fall into four categories of vocal performer; well-known singer, professional singer, amateur singer, and student. At the top of the song recital pyramid are the most famous singers in the world. The category could include singers like Jessye Norman, Cecilia Bartoli, Thomas Hampson, Dawn Upshaw, Kathleen Battle, Dmitri Hvorostovsky, and Natalie Dessay. The singers in this group are usually famous for singing opera roles and also frequently perform song recitals for packed audiences. They record song as part of their discography and usually artistically gravitate toward a certain genre of song. For example; Natalie Dessay and Debussy, Cecilia Bartoli and eighteenth-century Italian song, Thomas Hampson and Copland, and Jessye Norman and Strauss. When famous singers perform song it is almost always in a high visibility performance venue and usually recorded for commercial purposes as well as posterity. The singers are sometimes invited to raise the profile of a performance series or venue and can be the highlight of a season. These types of recitals are one of the most effective methods of art song promotion in today's competitive classical music climate. Famous singers often deal with certain audience expectations that other singers don't necessarily experience. For example, if a singer has had a long career, it is unavoidable that comparisons of how they "used to sound" will take place. Famous singers' song recitals are usually reviewed in the press and sometimes the stakes are very high. A singer who is reviewed by a critic at the *New York Times* can expect millions of people to have access to the review.

There are many professional singers who are not famous who perform art song as a regular part of their repertoire. Some of these performances may have a paying audience and some may not. These performers sing in venues both high and low profile and most likely specialize in a certain genre of song or song performance. This group includes teachers of singing who are on the faculty at a college, university, conservatory, or community school who have a career that bridges teaching and performing. Many singers who primarily teach as a career also keep up active performing schedules, either working with other professionals, professional management, or creating opportunities in their own communities. The singers in this group will not have large expectations from the audience as to repertoire and therefore have more freedom in choosing their programs of song. These singers may also perform art song as part of a competition or professional audition. Singers who interview for teaching positions at universities and colleges are usually expected to sing art song for the selection committee at the time of the interview. Singers who teach are exposed to song literature on a daily basis and tend to have a good idea of what repertoire is new, popular, or newly published. Singers may also know composers who may ask them to debut their new songs.

Amateur singers who perform art song are usually excellent musicians who choose to earn a living in a field other than music. They probably do not charge admission for their performances but may offer a musical performance through their church, community venue, or home salon concerts. Amateur singers do not have the pressure of having to sustain themselves financially from their singing careers and have the luxury of choosing what song literature interests them and in what situation they would like to sing. Amateur singers who perform are usually individuals who have studied song intensely at some point in their lives. They may or may not be working with a teacher.

Students in the United States and abroad make up a large portion of the singers performing songs today. Students of singing at colleges, universities, and conservatories are required to learn various genres of song as part of their education. Young singers, especially, will most certainly start their professional studies in school with song before moving onto the more vocally demanding operatic, oratorio, and symphonic literature. Students are very enthusiastic about song because most of it is new to them and the breadth of the genre seems endless. There is truly something for everyone. The songs students sing in their years of training will be of great importance to their future musical lives and the foundation of how they approach song literature as fully formed musicians.

The art of planning a successful recital is possibly even more important than how well the music is performed! There can be a certain brilliance to putting together songs in a way that is fresh and exciting or never before considered. When not limited by requirements or great expectations, artists can use their imaginations in creating a cohesive program of song that may not even be related by decade of composition, language, or composer. There are several important points to consider when planning a recital program. Perhaps the most important is the type of audience to which you are singing. Is the audience made up of students? Will the audience include young children? Will the audience include a professional music critic and other professional musicians? Is there a good chance that the audience will expect a certain genre of song or a certain composer's works? Is there some type of song that the audience will particularly enjoy? And if the singer is famous, what songs will be expected and hoped for on the program? For example, if Cecilia Bartoli is performing a recital and has just released an album of French song, it is logical to think that the audience will expect to hear her sing some French song. If an amateur singer is performing in an art song competition and one of the judges is a song composer, the singer may consider including one of the composer's songs on his list. If a student is giving a song recital as part of her degree requirements, she will be expected to perform songs that lie within the parameters of her school's academic requirements. If a singer is performing a song recital at a German Lieder symposium, it will be expected that songs by German composers are included on the recital. A singing teacher performing a recital in front of her students may take care to include songs that her students are not currently studying or songs that are unknown to students.

Certain performance venues require special consideration by performers. A singer presenting a recital at Constitution Hall in Washington, D.C., or in Alice Tully Hall in New York would be well-served to know a little bit about the history of performances in those spaces and to take them into consideration when selecting repertoire. There are practical issues of venues that affect performances as well. The size of a space, the quality of the acoustics, the sight lines to and from the stage, and the backstage layout and access can all influence the performance. A singer must always consider the type of venue in which his or her voice will best be featured. Not every voice is appropriate to every venue. The size of the instrument and the acoustic power of the voice is best served in the correctly sized venue. Not all performance halls and spaces are constructed for nonamplified performance; in fact, most are not.

Consideration of the city and country in which a song recital is performed is also part of the planning process. For example, an American singer performing a recital in Berlin, Germany, will want to make sure their German language skills are excellent. The level of preparation for a Lieder recital in Germany may not be as high as for the same recital in Iowa. When performing a recital in New York City, where song is frequently performed, a singer may consider including lesser-known or new songs on a program. This tactic is perhaps more important in New York City than on a recital performed in a city or town where song is not frequently performed.

Song recitals can be planned according to composer, country, style, time period, language, poet, or theme, or a combination of all the above. While recitals of songs all by one composer are somewhat rare, they are a great musical insight into a composer's life. Today, this type of recital would most likely be a performance of one or two song cycles by the same composer such as Franz Schubert or Robert Schumann. Recitals that celebrate one composer are often included in symposiums or festivals that are honoring the anniversary of a composer's birth or death. A song recital made up of songs by composers from the same country or songs of all the same language is also worthy of an audience. Language-themed recitals are very effective, especially if they are in the language in which the singer is most comfortable and able to focus on expression and musicality without the added barrier of foreign language. A recital in all French or English, if one is from France or the United States, provides the singer with the opportunity to explore musical nuances that may be harder to discover when singing foreign songs. Songs grouped for performance by years of composition can make a thought-provoking program. For example, a song recital made up of a few of the 150 songs Robert Schumann composed in 1840, his *Liederjahr* (song year), would be a fitting tribute to a seminal year in song. An American song recital featuring songs composed between 1940 and 1960 could be an interesting study of American music history, especially when accompanied by program notes. Throughout music history, song recitals have been performed according to a theme, but the popularity of these types of recitals rises and falls. It is particularly unfortunate when a "theme" recital does not demonstrate sufficient forethought or logic of the singer to the audience. A theme recital should not be about a catchy title, but rather, a comprehensively planned program that is shaped to the theme of choice. The theme of a recital can be a historical period or movement, an artistic period or type, or a theme directly relating to the texts of the songs. For example, "love" is one of the most common recital themes, or some variation thereof. There is more than enough repertoire to build a recital of songs about love, spring, nature, death, despair, and many other themes. More subtle poetic ideas take more effort to uncover but the choices for themes are only limited by the performer's imagination.

Anyone who has attended a vocal recital has probably noticed that there are often selections from opera, oratorio, and musical theatre included on some programs. If the definition of art song is a song written especially for voice and piano, how do these other genres of singing fit into the song recital? There are different schools of thought on the issue. The individual who is a purist believes the song recital should only include art song or songs intended by the composer to be performed by voice and piano. Others think that there is no harm in including selections from other genres that feature the voice. Perhaps a performance including additional vocal genres could be considered a "vocal recital" and a program of all song a "song recital." A common practice is for established opera singers to present programs that include operatic arias mixed with songs, but it is becoming increasingly acceptable to perform a recital of all song with an aria included only as an encore selection. Matthias Goerne and Natalie Dessay are two singers who have practiced this method in performance. As musical theatre becomes more popular as a subject of academic study, recitals featuring musical theatre are becoming more common. Cabaret and theatre performers will sometimes intersperse musical theatre song selections with text to create an original cabaret show and some classical cabarets intersperse art song with more popular genre songs and a script to tie all the elements together.

The standard song recital mantra of "stand and sing" is changing as singers are exploring new ways to perform and interpret song. Increased use of media and technology have also affected all stage works, including recital, and technology is being incorporated into recital performances similar to what the Metropolitan Opera has done with text translations. Translations, or lyrics, can be projected to audiences during song recitals as they are for opera performances. For example, the Brooklyn Academy of Music is pushing boundaries with its innovative programming of song titled "Lieder-palooza" and "21st century liederabend." The genre of song performance will continue to evolve as restrictions lessen and expectations change.

One of the most critical parts of planning a recital is the selection of repertoire. Not all songs are appropriate for all voices for a variety of reasons. Most singers do not sing equally well in Italian, German, French, and English. The vocal writing and musical style of some composers may be too advanced for some singers. In addition, there is the intangible magic of finding the best songs for a specific voice. The personal taste of the performer is also a real issue. If a student is performing a recital, he will plan the program with his teacher. Amateur and professional singers alike usually plan a program with a teacher, vocal coach, or pianist. Established singers may perform the same songs many times or never perform a song twice. There are as many songs and composers as there are skill levels of singers.

The wonderful thing about song is that there is a vast amount of repertoire from which to choose. There is a certain presentational style in presenting song recitals that has been in existence for a long while. It consists of a conservative and straightforward approach to performing, coordinated entrances and exits by the singer and pianist, and not a great deal of physical or stage movement. As mentioned earlier, it is becoming more acceptable to try new things in song performance and the traditional performance style should be considered, a foundation on which to build.

SAMPLE RECITAL PROGRAMS

Undergraduate Student Soprano

I Attempt from Love's Sickness	Henry Purcell (1659–1695)
Man Is for the Woman Made	
Sound the Trumpet (duet)	
Sento nel core	Stefano Donaudy (1879–1925)
Spirate pur, spirate	
O del mio amato ben	

—Pause—

Frülingsglaube	Franz Schubert (1797–1828)
Du bist die Ruh	
Heidenröslein	
An die Musik	
I Hate Music!	Leonard Bernstein (1918–1990)
My Name is Barbara	
Jupiter Has Seven Moons	
I Hate Music!	
A Big Indian and a Little Indian	
I'm a Person Too	

Undergraduate Student Tenor

Ideale	Paolo Tosti (1846–1916)
'A vuchella	
La serenata	

Mai	Reynaldo Hahn (1874–1947)
L'heure exquise	
Paysage	
Le printemps	

—Pause—

Come Away, Death	Roger Quilter (1877–1953)
O Mistress Mine	
Weep You No More, Sad Fountains	

Come Ready and See Me	Richard Hundley (1931–)
Sweet Suffolk Owl	
The Astronomers	
Moonlight's Watermelon	

Professional Mezzo-Soprano

Quattro liriche: Antica poesia popolare armena	Ottorino Respighi (1879–1936)
No, non è morto il figlio tuo	
La mamma è come il pane caldo	
Io sono la Madre	
Mattino di luce	

Chants d'Auvergne	Joseph Canteloube (1879–1957)
La pastoura al camps	

Bailero
Trois bourrées
Pastourelle
L'Antouèno

—Pause—

Mother Goose Lyrics   Richard Faith (1926–)
Where Are You Going To, My Pretty Maid?
Jenny Wren
The Queen of Hearts
I Saw a Ship A-Sailing

Cabaret Songs   William Bolcom (1938–)
Waitin
Love in the Thirties
Toothbrush Time
Song of Black Max
Amor

Professional Tenor

Dichterliebe   Robert Schumann
                                                        (1810–1856)

Im wunderschönen Monat Mai
Aus meinen Tränen spriessen
Die Rose, die Lilie, die Taube, die Sonne
Wenn ich in deine Augen seh
Ich will meine Steele tauchen
Im Rhein, im heiligen Strome
Ich grolle nicht
Und wüssten's die Blumen, die kleinen
Das ist ein Flöten und Geigen

Hör' ich das Liedchen klingen
Ein Jüngling liebt ein Mädchen
Am leuchtenden Sommermorgen
Ich hab' im Traum geweinet
Allnächtlich im Traume
Aus alten Märchen
Die alten, bösen Lieder

—Pause—

Seven Sonnets of Michelangelo	Benjamin Britten (1913–1976)

Sonetto XVI: Sì come nella penna e nell'inchiostro

Sonetto XXXI: A che più debb'io mai l'intensa voglia

Sonetto XXX: Veggio co'bei vostri occhi un dolce lume

Sonetto LV: Tu sa' ch'io so, signior mie, che tu sai

Sonetto XXXVIII: Rendete a gli occhi miei, o fonte o fiume

Sonetto XXXII: S'un casto amor, s'una pietà superna

Sonetto XXIV: Spirto ben nato, in cui si specchia e vede

Graduate Student Soprano

Der Hirt auf dem Felsen, D. 965   Franz Schubert (1797–1828)

Twelve Poems of Emily Dickinson   Aaron Copland (1900–1990)
Nature, the Gentlest Mother
There Came a Wind Like a Bugle
Why Do They Shut Me Out of Heaven?

The World Feels Dusty
Heart, We Will Forget Him
Dear March, Come In!
Sleep is Supposed to Be
When They Come Back
I Felt a Funeral in My Brain
I've Heard an Organ Talk Sometimes
Going to Heaven!
The Chariot

—Pause—

Chansons de Bilitis   Claude Debussy (1862–1918)
La flûte de Pan
La chevelure
Le tombeau des naïades

Six Elizabethan Songs   Dominick Argento (1927–)
Spring
Sleep
Winter
Dirge
Diaphenia
Hymn

Undergraduate Student Soprano

Though you are young and I am old   Thomas Campion (1567–1620)
Harke all you ladies
What is a day, what is a yeere?
Your faire lookes enflame my desire

Breit' über mein Haupt   Richard Strauss (1864–1949)

Nichts

Morgen

Ständchen

—Pause—

Quatro Madrigales Amatorios   Joaquín Rodrigo (1901–1999)

¿Con qué la lavaré?

Vos me matásteis

¿De dónde venís, amore?

De los álamos de vengo, madre

A Horse With Wings   Ricky Ian Gordon (1956–)

My Sister's New Red Hat

Song for a Dark Girl

Joy

Undergraduate Student Baritone

Per la gloria d'adorarvi   Giovanni Bononcini
                                                 (1672–1750)

L'esperto Nocchiero

Lunghi da te

Now Sleeps the Crimson Petal   Roger Quilter (1877–1953)

O Mistress Mine

It Was a Lover and His Lass

Hey, Ho, the Wind and the Rain

—Pause—

From *Die schöne Müllerin*   Franz Schubert (1797–1828)

Das Wandern

Morgengruß
Tränenregen
Mein!

The Gambler's Songs   John Jacob Niles (1892–1980)
The Rovin' Gambler
The Gambler's Lament
The Gambler's Wife
Gambler Don't You Lose Your Place
Gambler's Song of the Big Sandy River

Undergraduate Student Tenor

Vergin, tutto'amor   Francesco Durante (1684–1755)
Danza, danza fanciulla gentile

Die Forelle   Franz Schubert (1797–1828)
Die Nachtigall
Lied der Mignon
Jägerlied

Tel jour telle nuit   Francis Poulenc (1899–1963)

—Pause—

Blue Mountain Ballads   Paul Bowles (1911–1983)
Heavenly Grass
Lonesome Man
Cabin
Sugar in the Cane

From *Old American Songs*   Aaron Copland (1900–1990)
At the River

The Dodger
Simple Gifts
I Bought Me a Cat

English Song Recital

Now Sleeps the Crimson Petal	Roger Quilter (1877–1953)
Weep You No More, Sad Fountains	
The Faithless Shepherdess	

Come You Not from Newcastle?	Benjamin Britten (1913–1976)
Sweet Polly Oliver	
The Deaf Woman's Courtship	
Oliver Cromwell	

Loveliest of Trees	John Duke (1899–1984)
I Can't Be Talkin' of Love	
i carry your heart	
Shelling Peas	

—Pause—

Five Street Songs	Charles Ives (1874–1954)
Old Home Day	
In the Alley	
A Song of a Gambolier	
Down East	
The Circus Band	
Shadow of the Blues	John Musto (1954–)
Silhouette	
Litany	
Island	
Could Be	

Chapter Four

How to Listen to Song

There is no correct way to listen to and interpret a song. Every individual's method and opinion is valid. The language of song is the language of music and music is for anyone who would like to listen. A listener's opinion of a song is subject to her musical experiences, knowledge of the mechanics of music, understanding of foreign language, an appreciation for poetry, and personal taste. The experience of listening to song is a reward in itself but there is no question that increased knowledge of the genre will enhance the art of listening. For example, it may benefit a listener to know that Berlioz's "Villanelle," performed by voice and piano, was also composed for voice and orchestra and is part of a group of songs knows as *Les nuits d'été*. A listener may appreciate Aaron Copland's "Shall We Gather by the River" more by knowing it is an updated folk tune and not an original composition. Mr. Copland's two volumes of *Old American Songs* are the perfect example of folk tunes that become fresh and interesting when conceived as solo songs with piano. Improved knowledge of song is similar to knowing how a painting by Gauguin fits into the progression of modern art. The knowledge makes the experience of music or art more interesting and pertinent to self.

The listening experience of the American spiritual is greatly enhanced once it is understood that there is a rich subtext underneath the sung words. The words of sung tunes were often used as code among slaves to communicate danger or information about the Underground Railroad. Because slaves did not have the freedom to communicate, they used songs to share information.

In spite of the examples above, a listener does not need to have historical or factual knowledge about song composition to enjoy or understand a song. It is the listener's prerogative to place value on a particular song. There are going to be differing interpretations of a Monet painting between an art

49

historian and someone who knows nothing about art. It does not diminish or negate the inexperienced person's enjoyment of the painting.

One of the truly unique properties of song is that it is usually a short musical form. The average length of a song is about three minutes, although some songs can be much shorter or longer than that; Ned Rorem's thirty second "I Am Rose" is one example of an extremely short song while Richard Strauss' "Im Abendrot" is about seven minutes in length. The limited duration of most songs places a dramatic impetus on composers. A song composer only has a short amount of time in which to create a complete story for the listener. A composer needs to create a full-scale three-act drama within a relatively short amount of time. A great song should have a clear beginning, middle, and end both musically and dramatically. It should have dramatic and musical cohesiveness and stylistic interest created by the composer.

The short form of song can be a benefit or a liability for a composer. As a benefit, the form allows composers to communicate musical style and poetry in short bursts of creativity that can be very effective. As a liability, the form is so short that it may be difficult for the composer to complete his musical thought or intention and for the listener to absorb all the nuances of the style. For these reasons, there are very few composers who have mastered song composition. Certainly, song composition has not historically been the first choice of genre for many serious composers. Some composers such as Ralph Vaughan Williams only focused on song in the early part of their careers.

The listener has a choice in *how* to listen to a song. He may try to hear it as a cohesive whole and pay attention only to the overall mood of the piece, he can focus on one or two separate elements of the piece, or he can focus on the text to the exclusion of other elements. He may be drawn to or repelled by the quality of the voice and unable to listen objectively. In some cases, the composer makes the decision of how to focus the listener's ear. For example, in "Erlkönig," Franz Schubert directs the listener's attention to the bass line of the piano as a startling motif is relentlessly repeated throughout the song. In Samuel Barber's "The Crucifixion," the harmonic dissonance conveys the crucifixion of Christ and dominates the musical landscape. Another Schubert song, "Gretchen und Spinnrade," employs a pianistic technique, called perpetual motion, that draws the ear directly to the relentless spinning of the wheel.

LISTENING TO THE VOICE

The listening experience begins with the interpretation of individual song elements. The singer's voice is the most critical element of a song and the one most likely to illicit a strong response from the listener. It is very challenging to hear the individual elements of a song if the quality of a voice is distracting or difficult to tolerate. If a listener does not enjoy the sound of a large, operatic voice, he may not enjoy listening to Jessye Norman interpret Richard Strauss songs. If a listener cannot tolerate straight tone or the tenor voice, she will not enjoy Peter Pears performing Benjamin Britten songs. Sometimes, the personal history of a singer can positively or negatively influence an individual's feeling about music. For example, it may make a difference for a listener to know that the German soprano Elisabeth Schwartzkopf's career was negatively affected by her affiliation with the Nazi party during the Second World War.[1] Despite her grace and talent, her personal revisionist history about her involvement with the Nazis threw a shadow over her career in later years and even after her death. This knowledge may influence one's enjoyment of her singing or lead the listener to other singers.

An individual's national origin may inform musical choices and preferences as well. It makes good sense that an American might enjoy songs in English more than songs in German, if he is not fluent in German. The comprehension of language can certainly facilitate enjoyment of song. A person from Spain may prefer Italian song to German or French song, because the Italian language is more similar than the others to his own. The wonderful thing about song is that there are plenty of choices for everyone. A listener's personal and musical history will determine his song preferences.

The human voice is the most unique of instruments. There are no two voices exactly alike and there are as many types of voices as there are people. The voice is what makes the genre of song the most special of any musical form. Only in song, can an instrument (the voice) convey text, and therefore specific emotion, feelings, and dramatic intent. Instrumental music can only *imply* emotion, but song can offer words with *actual* meaning. When emotional intent is added to those words, the song becomes a very powerful instrument in itself.

Voice types that interpret song include soprano, mezzo-soprano, tenor, and bass, and also countertenor, contralto, light lyric tenor, basso profundo, coloratura soprano, and many more. Because there are so many song composers, and so many songs, voice types of all kinds are utilized in song performance. Voices that might not shine in opera can be masterful in song. When it comes to song performance, the art of choosing the right song for the right voice is the secret to success.

Soprano—the higher category for female voices

• Coloratura soprano—bright, flexible voice with an extended upper register
• Lyric soprano—lyrical, bel canto technique
• Dramatic soprano—a full, large-size voice

Mezzo-soprano—the lower category for female voices

- Lyric mezzo-soprano—strong legato line and flexibility
- Dramatic mezzo-soprano—somewhat darker sound than the lyric mezzo-soprano, good size instrument
- Contralto soprano—similar to the dramatic mezzo-soprano, but with an extended lower range, a highly unusual voice type

Tenor—the higher category for male voices

- Tenorino—small tenor voice
- Lyric tenor—lyrical, bel canto technique
- Dramatic tenor—large size voice with excellent lower register

Bass—the lower category for male voices

- Baritone—flexible voice with a good upper register
- Bass-baritone—good size voice with a good range from top to bottom
- Bass—darker color than the bass-baritone, good lower range

Countertenor—the male singer who exclusively uses his falsetto register

- Sopranist—or male soprano, a countertenor with a soprano vocal color who focuses on soprano vocal literature
- Mezzist—countertenor focused on repertoire in the lower range of the voice

The appeal of a specific voice to a listener is highly indicative of whether or not she will enjoy a song. Qualities of the human voice that influence the listener include; timbre, resonance, tessitura, vibrato rate, color, and vocal technique. Sometimes in music history, certain vocal affectations were in vogue. For example, many singers of popular songs in the 1940s had very fast vibrato rates. A fast vibrato rate can be referred to as "goat-like" or "bleating," but it was very popular for a time. In the 1960s and 1970s, the performing partnership of Benjamin Britten and Peter Pears resulted in a style of singing that was largely reliant on straight tone and absence of vibrato. The trend influenced singers to think that all British music had to be performed with a straight tone!

LISTENING TO THE PIANO

In performance of art song, the piano is the duet partner to the voice. In great song performance, the two instruments are really one entity. When writing song, the composer must conceptualize his song composition as much for the piano as the voice. How the piano is used in song varies greatly; historic period, nationalistic elements, and musical style all contribute to the overall effect. Claude Debussy often used pedal effects of the piano to create a lushness in song. Claudio Monteverdi's compositions of seventeenth century Italy reflect a different approach. His song compositions most often used the "stile recitativo" (writing for voice that mimics speech) style.

His songs consisted of melody with underlying chordal support that provided harmony but allowed the singer to embellish with freedom. Because the voice ornamentation was an important part of the melody, the piano took a less florid role in performance. Franz Schubert truly understood how to use the piano to reflect the meaning of the text. He drew inspiration from his chosen poems and used pianistic stylistic effects to aid the voice in bringing the text to life. In his "Die Forelle," listen for the trout leaping out of the piano!

LISTENING TO THE TEXT

In song performance, a singer's native language is often the one she is able to perform best. That is not to say that singers cannot perform well in languages different from their own, but one only has to watch and hear Luciano Pavarotti singing in Italian to understand the benefit of a singer performing his own language. The difference is imperceptible, but extremely effective.

All of the aspects involved in listening to song may not always be in the forefront of a listener's mind nor do they need to be. As an individual's knowledge of song increases, he will be able to hear more elements at once and solid opinions and ideas will begin to form. The listener will develop specific tastes and will be able to seek out the composers and singers he prefers. It is the building of a library of recordings and the growth that comes from experience and careful listening that will enable the casual listener to best appreciate the vast and entertaining genre of song.

LISTENING TO THE DRAMATIC INTERPRETATION

An important component of any vocal performance is the singer's dramatic interpretation of the textual and musical language of a piece. In truth, there is not much difference between interpreting an opera aria and a song. The advantage, or disadvantage depending on one's imagination, of interpreting an operatic aria is that it is part of a larger story, the details of that story are created for the singer by the librettist, and the character singing has already been created and is in existence. The aria is part of a bigger story and, even when performed alone, cannot be separated from its story. Of course, operatic arias are often performed in recital or concert apart from the rest of the opera. In these cases, the singer still has to consider the character from the opera in his interpretation.

Interpreting a song requires the same techniques used in an opera excerpt with a few additions. The singer must create a character out of the poem at hand and the musical setting as well as the character's point of view. He must understand the character's emotional viewpoint and the reason he is singing the song. The singer should have specific emotions to interpret based on careful analysis of the text presented. The singer needs to create a dramatic arc in his performance that has a clear beginning, middle, and end. The singer must ensure that his physical movements match his emotional intent and also that any physical habits that are tied to his vocal technique do not distract from the performance. In addition, the singer must take care to not venture too far into emotional abandon so that his vocal production is affected. For example, expressing anger might lead to tension or clenched muscles and the singer cannot let his instrument become constricted in any way. Just like actors have to keep a layer of reality firmly underneath their performances in order to maintain balance, singers must not let real emotion affect their techniques.

There are several acting techniques that singers use to help them project emotion to the listener of song; subtext, substitution, and visualization are a few examples. A subtext consists of the words that lie directly underneath the text of the poem. The subtext is what the character is *truly* thinking. For example, when an actor speaks a line of dialogue in a play his words have a meaning. "I am going to the store to get some milk." The character is telling us he is going to the store to get some milk. But perhaps he is saying the line to his wife, with whom he has just had a huge fight and is very angry. His character's subtext may be "I hate you and am going to kill you when I get back home." The subtext expresses the character's emotion and that is what infuses the original line, "I am going to the store to get some milk," with real meaning. A spoken line delivered without subtext means nothing. A song performed without subtext is just a musical exercise; it is certainly not worthless, but not completely alive either.

It is difficult for singers to express a single emotional idea throughout a song. For example, a singer may think "I will express joy in this song." That idea is not specific enough for the singer to stay emotionally engaged throughout a song, even if it is only two or three minutes. It may be much more effective for the singer to think of a specific subtext; "I am so, so happy to see my daughter for the first time in five years." The more specificity the singer can conjure the more the listener and audience can respond to something real.

Substitution is an acting technique singers can use when preparing a song interpretation. Substitution means taking an experience from one's personal life that closely relates to the emotion and motivation needed in performance, and substituting the personal experience for the character's experience. It does not have to be exactly the same emotion the character in the song is experiencing but an approximation. Substitution is something to practice until it becomes a layer of the performance. It can be a useful and effective technique. For example, if a singer is preparing Dominick Argento's song "Come Away, Come Away, Death" and is not connecting with the fear of death needed by the character, he may think of an occasion associated with the death of someone he cared about and how he felt at that time. He can then use the memory of that event and those emotions in his performance.

Visualization is a technique singers use to make songs come to life. It is particularly helpful when singing a text that is difficult to relate to, highly illustrative of a particular time period, or evocative of a certain location. An example would be singing about a location in nature like a grassy field, tree, or stream. Many song texts are set in nature; singers can create a specific visual tableau in their imaginations and make the text more alive with that visual image.

LISTENING TO THE SONG

There are different ways to listen to a song. You can listen individually or with other people. You can listen to a live or recorded performance. You can listen to a live performance in a formal setting by a professional singer or a casual setting by an amateur singer like a student. You can listen while following a printed score (written out music) or not. You can choose a recording that is not technically advanced, but historically significant or a more modern recording that uses state-of-the-art technology. There are many options from which to choose when seeking out listening opportunities. With digital music available everywhere, almost the entire song repertory is available online and can be played on smart phones, laptops, iPads, and tablets of all kinds.

USING THE PRINTED OR DIGITAL SCORE

The usefulness of following a printed (hard copy of music) or digital score when listening to song may depend on the listener's ability to read music. If the listener cannot read music, there are still benefits to seeing the score. The score will tell you several things about the piece. It will show the text and how the text is set to the melody. It has the piano part written out with the left and right hand each on its own stave. The composer or editor's markings will be in the music and give insight into the intended performance style. Dynamic markings will be in the piano and voice parts. The composer and poet's

56   *Chapter 4*

names and probable birth and death dates will be at the top of the score and the composer may have a dedication on the first page or other personal notes written somewhere on the page, usually at the conclusion of the piece.

Depending on the listener's purpose for studying song, the score is not an absolute necessity. Young singers should definitely be studying scores while listening to song and non-singers could benefit from seeing music written out as well, especially if they read music or play another instrument. Musical scores are available online and directly from stores that sell printed music. Individual songs can be easily downloaded from music websites. The public library may also obtain scores from interlibrary loan. If one lives near a university or college with an active music program, that library would have scores as well.

LISTENING EXERCISE TO HELP IDENTIFY ELEMENTS OF SONG

1. Select a song presented in this book or any song of interest.
2. Find a good recording of the song online, or in your own music library.
3. Note the name of the song, whether it is from a group or cycle, the composer, and poet. It is helpful to start familiarizing yourself with this information as you build your listening experiences.
4. If you have a copy of the poem or text, read it through for a basic understanding of the words. If the song is in a foreign language, follow a translation of the poem while listening to become familiar with the text and better understand the composer's musical choices. A good online source for song translations is http://recmusic.org, search by composer's last name. Translations are available in many places and "recmusic" is a good place to start.
5. Listen to the song straight through one time. Try distinguishing the melody from the texture of the piece, then the text, then the piano. Try to hear each of these three elements individually.
6. Take a moment to reflect on what was heard. Think about your opinion of the quality of the song, the poem, and the voice.
7. When listening to the song again, choose certain elements to focus on as discussed in chapter 3 such as: voice, piano, poem, mood, melody, motive, harmony, rhythm, tempo, range, form, tessitura, and song performance. Each time you identify and consider an element of song, you are increasing your listening skills and refining your knowledge of song.
8. Voice: what voice type is the singer—soprano, mezzo-soprano, and so on? Does the quality of the voice add to or detract from the song

performance? What qualities does the singer have that enhance the song?

9. Piano: is the pianist a good partner to the singer? If yes, how does he support the singer in performance? Are the dynamics of the instrument well-balanced with the voice? Is the piano part supplemental to the melody or independent of the voice? Are there extended introductions, interludes, and postludes in the piano part? If yes, what purpose do they serve? Does the pianist use any special effects or devices to highlight the meaning of the text? What are they?

10. Poem: if the poem is in the listener's native language, is it clearly understood? Is the singer's diction effective? If the poem is in a foreign language, is it possible to pick out certain words that are familiar? What traits of the language affect the overall mood of the song or the singer's vocal production? Are the sentences cohesive thoughts? Has the composer honored the poet by setting his poem in an appropriate manner? If yes, how has he achieved this? Does the composer use text-painting to emphasize words or emotional ideas in the poem?

11. Mood: what is the overall mood of the poem? Is there one prevalent mood or does it change during the performance? What elements of the song create the mood? Is the mood created by pianistic effects, the quality of the voice, the tempo, dynamics, or something else?

12. Melody: is the melody written in a way that reflects the meaning and emotional intent of the text? Is it syllabic, meaning every syllable has a new pitch, or is it melismatic, where several notes are sung on one syllable, or is it a combination of both?

13. Musical Motive: does the song contain a short musical phrase that is repeated throughout the song? If yes, is the motive in the melody or the piano? How does the motive serve the mood, emotional intent, or meaning of the text?

14. Harmony: is the harmony mostly major or mostly minor? Is it tonal or atonal? Is there a key change that relates to a new section of the poem? Is there dissonance or chromaticism? If yes, how does it reinforce the meaning of the text?

15. Rhythm: does the rhythm serve the melody and meaning of the text or does it represent an independent component? How does the rhythm shape the melody and piano part?

16. Tempo: is the tempo steady throughout the piece or does it change? Does the composer's chosen tempo relate to the meaning of the text? If there are shifts in tempo, are they directly related to the emotional intent of the song?

17. Range: is the singer using his voice in the middle of his range, the lower part of his range, the upper part of his range, or a combination of

two or three? Is there a reason the melody is set in a certain range? If yes, how does it serve the meaning of the text?

18. Form: what is the form of the song? Are there verses where the entire melody repeats (strophic)? Is there no repeated melodic material (through-composed)? Is the song in three sections where the first and last section are the same (ABA)?

19. Tessitura: what part of the voice does the singer use the most throughout the song? The tessitura will relate to the voice type; for example, a tenor or soprano will use their upper range more than a baritone or mezzo-soprano.

20. Song Performance: how is the quality of the song performance? Is the acoustic balanced? Does the musical style serve the composer's intentions? Does the mood the performers create concur with the emotional intent of the text?

LISTENING TO LIVE PERFORMANCE VERSUS RECORDINGS

Most song purists would probably say that the best way to listen to song is in live performance. They would say that there is no substitute for sitting in a perfectly sized hall watching and listening to a seasoned singer and pianist perform their favorite songs by Strauss or Purcell or Fauré. For many years this would have been true; there is no substitute for the full experience of song in live performance. In today's world, there are many developments that have taken audiences out of performing venues and put them in complete control of their own access to song. Videos of famous, professional, amateur, and student singers performing song are readily available on YouTube and other streaming websites. The quality of many of these videos is exceptional and there are some outstanding historical performances available that have not been available in the past. Digital music downloads allow listeners to pick and choose the songs they want to buy and have taken away the concept of an "album." This has most likely encouraged people to purchase more music as they search for the songs they really want to hear. The videos with audio and the audio recordings alone can be enjoyed on any number of wireless devices instantly. Many find this kind of access difficult to leave behind for season tickets, waiting in line, crowds, parking, and a coughing and sneezing audience during the pianissimo final note of Cecilia Bartoli's eighteenth century Italian song.

In addition to logistics, there is a definite musical perfection that can be achieved by the artists and recording technicians in the studio. Singers can repeat sections of songs as many times as they like, sing the same song three days in a row and pick the best take, and compile snippets of song from different takes to utilize the best high note, and technicians can make the music seamless and perfect. The result is a stunning recording but not really a live performance. Also, the singer most likely does not have the adrenaline and nerves that are present before and during live performance and the extra energy and raw power from excitement is also absent.

Live performance has its own risks. Words can be forgotten, notes can be missed, singers can be distracted, and audience members can make annoying noise. Even the most accomplished singers have made mistakes in performance for many different reasons. If these human traits can be overlooked, live song performance can bring thrilling moments to the audience. The energy from the audience helps the singer to stay fully present and engaged in expression and the exchange between audience and singer buoys the singer. Under the pressure of being on stage, singers can reach heights not always found in the recording studio.

Live song performance and song recordings each have a place for the listener who appreciates song. The secret is balancing the two venues and finding opportunities to hear live singers that are appealing to one's individual taste.

LISTENING TO SONGS WITH ORCHESTRA

Symphonic concerts are one of the few music performance staples in today's restrained cultural climate and even they are in danger of extinction. Symphonies from Austin to Baltimore to New York are experimenting with and expanding programming to include repertoire and formats that appeal to a wide audience. Symphonic composers have always transcribed songs for singer and orchestra. Sometimes the songs are written specifically for orchestra and sometimes they were originally conceived for voice and piano and transcribed for orchestra. Inversely, many songs that have been conceived as orchestral pieces are popular for voice and piano alone. It is much easier logistically to sing with piano alone instead of with an entire orchestra. Some songs written for or transcribed for orchestra include: Hector Berlioz' *Les nuits d'été*, Gustav Mahler's *Kindertotenlieder*, *Lieder eines fahrenden Gesellen*, and *Des Knaben Wunderhorn*, Richard Wagner's *Wesendonck Lieder*, Aaron Copland's *Old American Songs*, Richard Strauss' *Vier letzte Lieder*, Andre Previn's *Honey and Rue*, and Joseph Canteloube's *Songs of the Auvergne*, to name a few.

LISTENING TO SONGS AS CHAMBER MUSIC

Many song composers have expanded their writing for voice and piano to additional instruments. Some of the resulting works are frequently performed and others are not. Ralph Vaughan Williams wrote *Ten Blake Songs* for voice and oboe alone. Franz Schubert wrote *Der Hirt auf dem Felsen* for soprano, piano, and clarinet, and Louis Spohr wrote *Six German Songs* for soprano, piano, and clarinet as well. Clarinet is just one instrument that has often been featured with voice by song composers.

Vocal chamber music includes cantatas by Italian composers like Alessandro Scarlatti and Claudio Monteverdi and twentieth-century works like George Crumb's *Ancient Voices of Children* and Schoenberg's *Pierrot Lunaire*. Current twenty-first-century works include Maria Schneider's *Morning Walks* and Crumb's *The Winds of Destiny: Songs of Strife, Love, Mystery and Exultation.*

HOW TO START SINGING

For some, interest in song may lead to an interest in learning how to sing. One may or may not have experience with singing, but it is certainly something that can be gained and no age is too late to start. Probably one of the simplest ways to start is to join a choir. Every community has a choral group of some kind. Churches and community groups have choral programs that are usually open to anyone who would like to volunteer. If there is uncertainty or tentativeness, speaking to the choral director should allay any fears. Most groups welcome new members, even if they are inexperienced. Some choral groups require an audition. These would most likely be groups that perform frequently with orchestra or have a performance season of their own. Depending on one's vocal abilities and the willingness of the director to take inexperienced singers, it may be possible to join these types of groups as well. The most important point is to find a place that is comfortable.

Choral singing is not the same as solo singing but the skills practiced in group singing can greatly accelerate a beginning singer's progress. In the choral ensemble, one will learn vocal exercises to warm up the voice and build a technique, how to read music, how to follow a score, how to understand musical cues from the conductor, and how the voice part fits into the overall structure of the piece. All of these skills will translate beautifully to any work on solo song.

The highly motivated beginning singer could augment his choral singing with regular practice at home. The same vocal exercises from choir can be practiced individually at home and the vocal range will begin to extend as the vocal folds begin to acclimate to new demands. A hymnal or folk songbook will provide plenty of tunes to begin singing as practice. After vocalizing, and learning the tunes of songs alone or with assistance, the singer can practice the tunes applying the same voice production practiced at home and in choir.

As the singer gains experience, she will begin to note what part of her vocal technique needs the most attention. If a singer wants to continue singing and focus more on her individual technique, private voice lessons may be a good idea. Finding a good teacher can be a daunting and difficult process. One of the best ways is to speak to people who are singers or take singing lessons about who may be a good teacher for a beginner. It can also help to ask a choral director or church musician if they know of a fine teacher. The National Association of Teachers of Singing (NATS) has a national database of teachers online. The address is www.nats.org and a search can be made by state and zip code to find a teacher in a convenient location.

Once you decide to try a teacher, it is important to let him know when setting up the lesson that you would like a trial lesson. A singer is not under any obligation to make a commitment for several lessons before trying a session with the potential teacher. The teacher may offer a reduced fee for a trial lesson or may not charge at all. If the singer is not comfortable with the potential teacher or does not enjoy the lesson, she should try other possibilities until she finds a good fit.

The purpose of individual voice lessons is to build the vocal technique while eliminating bad habits and incorrect vocal production. The lesson typically is in two parts; the vocal exercises sung mostly on vowels and the repertoire study that focuses on applying the technique to a song.

Chapter Five

Italian Song

No one country can claim to have invented song. Singing, in one form or another, has been present since the beginning of man. If one country had to be selected as leader of the development of singing in the history of music it would be Italy. Italy is the undisputed birthplace of opera, a vocal art form which many believe to be supreme above all others. Before the development of opera in the very early seventeenth century, vocal music was present in many secular and sacred venues. The church, and more importantly, its patrons, played a large part in financially supporting church composers who wrote music for use in cathedrals and churches across Europe. Secular songs developed among the people and in the streets of cities and songs were performed informally among family and friends by amateur musicians. Most music was likely not written down but passed on from aural memory. Italian song developed out of secular and sacred madrigals and later was influenced by opera.

Each country has singular traits or characteristics relating to their culture and traditions. The same holds true for song. Songs from Italy have different characteristics than songs from Spain. Russian songs have an abandon and fierceness that is different from the sophisticated restraint of German song. American songs have personality as varied as the musical genres that influenced them—blues, jazz, classical, spirituals, and folk tunes to name a few.

One of Italian songs' most unique characteristics is its language. Most professional singers agree that the Italian language is ideal for singers. It tends to be one of the easier languages to perform and because of its quick consonants and long vowels it is ideal for voice production and achieving optimal sound. The voice has more time to phonate when vowels are emphasized and consonants are quickly pronounced.

The Italian language promotes true legato for the same reasons its language is easy to sing. The legato, or smoothness, comes from singing vowel to vowel and lends itself to uninterrupted sound. Uninterrupted sound is ideal for singing. The vowel sounds in Italian are the same sounds that singers use in vocal exercises. The vowel sounds are mostly open and not "mixed" like the German umlaut (ü). For this reason, Italian is usually the first foreign language vocal students attempt.

Italian song has always emphasized vocal production above all else. Its song forms were developed by composers out of a deep understanding of opera and how to write for the voice. The development of opera required superior singing and Italy cultivated a culture of excellence in development of the voice. Voice teachers and composers wrote ornate and detailed "solfeggios" (singing exercises) that required students to fully develop and practice all aspects of voice production. The teaching and opera traditions created extraordinary singers and positively influenced song composition.

While reading about the song composers of Italy, and other countries, certain similarities about the composers' lives may become evident. It is impossible not to notice the personal traits and characteristics many of the composers share. For example, most song composers come from families where their parents, siblings, or other relatives play musical instruments. Most composers start learning the piano or other keyboard instrument from a very early age and many also learn a stringed instrument like the violin or cello. Many song composers study composition at a university or conservatory before beginning their professional careers. Almost all composers worked in auxiliary music jobs like teaching, conducting, church music, and commissions while composing music. Many composers did not achieve financial security in their lifetimes or even critical or popular recognition. Some song composers suffered from health and mental health issues that greatly affected their personal and professional lives. Many composers lived very short lives that greatly reduced their contributions to all genres of music.

SEVENTEENTH CENTURY

Terms used to describe early Italian song included madrigal, frottola, stile rappresentativo, arioso, and aria. The term aria (solo song) has a very different connotation in the seventeenth century than the operatic aria we know today. Before the development of opera, it referred to a secular song based on dance rhythms. Song styles grew out of ensemble singing, the madrigal, and the reduction of many voice parts to one. These early songs were closely related to dance and its rhythms.

The early seventeenth century brought about the birth of opera with Peri's *L'Euridice* (1600) and Monteverdi's *L'Orfeo* (1607). Early opera was usually written at the bequest of a royal court for a specific purpose. These early composers started a tradition of writing songs as well as opera. Monteverdi, Bellini, Rossini, Donizetti, and Puccini are all Italian opera composers who wrote songs.

Around the same time as early opera, solo songs began to appear. One of the first groupings of songs to appear in Italy was called *Le nuove musiche*. The songs, translated as "new compositions," were published in Florence in 1602.[1] The composer was Giulio Caccini (1551–1618). Caccini referred to these songs as "madrigals." His songs should not be confused with choral madrigals. Caccini spent a great deal of his life at court and was very well known as a performer and teacher. He had an affinity for teaching and working with singers. Because of the time in which he lived, and his involvement with the royal court, Caccini would have taught the first singers of opera.[2] "Amarilli, mia bella" is a song from *Le nuove musiche* that exemplifies the musical traits of early song.

Song Title	Amarilli, mia bella
Year of Composition	1602
Composer	Giulio Caccini
Language	Italian text
Poet	Guarini
Text	Features the name of Amarilli; the object of the singer's affection
Voice	Beginning level, medium range
Piano	Continuo to indicate chords
Mood	Two distinct moods, quiet and still, then more intense
Form	AB, and repeated material
Melody	Meant to be ornamented
Harmony	Melancholy
Tempo	Slow, with spirit
What to listen for	There are many versions of this teaching staple available. Listen for the many ways singers ornament Caccini's melody and how the ornamentation is or isn't successful. How does the ornamentation emphasize or detract from the meaning of the text?

Claudio Monteverdi (1567–1643) was an important Italian composer of many genres including operas, masses, songs, and madrigals. He wrote one of the earliest operas in existence, *L'Orfeo* (1607). He was brought up with sacred music and in the church environment. Monteverdi worked in the Court of Mantua as a string player and later as a conductor. He eventually held the prestigious maestro di cappella (master of the chapel) position at St. Mark's Cathedral in Venice. He became a Catholic priest later in life after his wife died.

ALESSANDRO SCARLATTI (1660–1725)

Alessandro Scarlatti is considered the founder of the Neapolitan school of eighteenth-century opera. He was a prolific composer of opera and revitalized the culture of opera in Naples with the popularity of his work. He held the position of "maestro" of the Royal Chapel in Naples. In addition to opera, Scarlatti wrote oratorios, masses, motets, church music, and over 600 cantatas, most for solo voice and continuo.

"O cessate di piagarmi" is a lament that is as tragic as it is perfectly formed. Scarlatti uses a minor key to convey a feeling of desperateness throughout.

Song Title	O cessate di piagarmi
Year of Composition	Unknown
Composer	Alessandro Scarlatti
Language	Italian text
Poet	Unknown
Text	Praying for the end of torment
Voice	The voice hangs in the upper middle register
Piano	Dotted rhythms in left hand and syncopated patterns
Mood	Mournful
Form	Strophic
Melody	Still, with little movement
Harmony	Minor
Tempo	Not too fast, but agitated
What to listen for	The voice and melody are sustained over syncopated rhythms in the piano. The voice is required to linger in the upper middle register; a challenging range for singers. The repetitive text presents opportunities for dynamic variation. Scarlatti has not written out

embellishments in the melody but they can be incorporated by performers to emphasize the melancholic text.

"Toglietemi la vita ancor" is an excellent contrast to the previous song. Scarlatti uses syncopation and sophisticated rhythms to great effect as well as interplay between the voice and accompaniment.

Song Title	Toglietemi la vita ancor
Year of Composition	Unknown
Composer	Alessandro Scarlatti
Language	Italian text
Poet	Unknown
Text	"I cannot live without love"
Voice	Short and intense phrasing
Piano	Rhythmic sixteenth-note phrases interspersed with chords doubling the voice
Mood	Intense
Form	Strophic
Melody	Short phrases with rhythmic accents
Harmony	Some dissonances
Tempo	Steady and very dramatic
What to listen for	The song is unique for its very non-Italian-like phrasing which is neither legato nor bel canto. The short phrases may be jarring at first but provide much drama and rhythmic contrast. The voice always begins on the offbeat in each phrase. The staggered rhythm creates a symmetry in the piece. Different modern editions contain markings that may not be original to Scarlatti. It is essential that singers mark their interpretations by gaining inspiration from the text.

FRANCESCO DURANTE (1684–1755)

Francesco Durante came from a musical family and studied violin and music fundamentals professionally as a youth. Durante was unusual for an eighteenth century Neapolitan composer in that, unlike his contemporaries, he did not focus on opera composition. Instead, he focused his career on composing church music and teaching. He composed a small number of songs that remain teaching staples to this day: "Danza, danza fanciulla" was originally conceived as a "solfeggio" (vocal exercise) and the piano part was added in the nineteenth century.

Song Title	Danza, danza fanciulla
Year of Composition	Unknown
Composer	Francesco Durante
Language	Italian text
Poet	Unknown
Text	Enchanting subject of a dancing maiden
Voice	Utilizes sustained and melismatic passages
Piano	Realized and modernized bass line continuo that accents the dance rhythms of the piece
Mood	Lively and exciting
Form	Through-composed
Melody	Syllabic phrases interspersed with sustained and melismatic phrases create interest
Harmony	Traditional, some dissonance
Tempo	Vivo, fast
What to listen for	Durante introduces the whirling and dancing described in the poem from the first note of the piano part. The melodic line is sweeping and almost constantly moving up or down to emphasize the movement of the maiden dancing on the beach. The inherent dance rhythms throughout are reinforced by syncopation between the voice and piano.

The early Italian song style of sparse accompaniments placed emphasis squarely on the singer. The emphasis on the voice, the explosion of opera, and the demand of the church all led to the creation of the castrato singer. Women were banned from singing in church and high voices were needed to complete the choir. The church came up with the solution of young castrati singers. The typical castrato was a prepubescent boy with an affinity for music who underwent castration to preserve his high voice. This is far from the god-like status of castrati in music lore. His family most likely did not live in the city but in a rural area. He would have had a family that wanted the best for him and believed that sending him to the city for a music education would keep him in health and comfort for his entire life. The family most likely did not completely comprehend the complexities and sacrifices of the physical transformation that was required of him. The chosen boy would move to a city center and begin musical training. He received the best comprehensive musical education possible with studies in singing, piano, violin, theory, and history.

In addition to castrati performing in church, eventually opera composers wanted the high voices of castrati on their opera stages. Castrati gained a cult status as a direct result of the Italian demand for ingenuity and brilliance on the operatic stage. The phenomenon has been well dramatized in the film *Farinelli*. Castrati cultivated the Italian people's great interest in singing. Their interest and continued demand for opera directly led to more writing for the voice. The castrato singer is vital to Italy's music history and to song. There is one known recording in existence of the last living castrato, Alessandro Moreschi (1858–1922).

EIGHTEENTH AND NINETEENTH CENTURIES

The eighteenth and nineteenth centuries of Italian singing were solidly devoted to the genre of opera. There was a large output of operatic works by Italian composers such as: Vincenzo Bellini (d. 1835), Gaetano Donizetti (d. 1848), Gioacchino Rossini (d.1868), Giuseppe Verdi (d. 1901), and Giacomo Puccini (d. 1924). All the Italian opera composers devoted some time to the song genre. Their compositions were sometimes devoted to personal friends or patrons. The songs were sought out by amateur singers and elevated to salon performances in private homes. Composer's songs had the benefit of maintaining a composer's style, but in a shorter and more accessible form that the operatic aria.

GIOVANNI PERGOLESI (1710–1736)

Giovanni Pergolesi showed great musical promise as a child and studied violin in Naples from an early age. In 1731, he completed his education and almost immediately started receiving prestigious commissions and opportunities to write opera, masses, and instrumental works for organizations such as the Teatro San Bartolomeo.

He is most significant as a composer for his great contributions to comic opera of the eighteenth century. Pergolesi wrote serious operas (opera seria); his comic operas (opera buffa) were best received by audiences. His comic opera, *La serva padrona*, is still often performed today.

Pergolesi was embraced by Naples' royal families and their support greatly aided his financial well-being.[3] His success is all the more impressive when considering that he only lived a short twenty-six years.

The nineteenth century brought about the development of the "bel canto" style. Bel canto, or "beautiful singing," was a large part of the teaching vocabulary of Italian singing teachers. It refers to legato phrasing and faultless vocal technique.[4] The term bel canto has gone through many permutations over the centuries. The meaning has changed over time depending on its context and usage. For some, the term is most closely associated with nineteenth-century opera composers like Donizetti, Rossini, and Bellini due to their emphasis of the long legato vocal line. Italian teachers of singing used the term to describe what they considered the uniquely Italian way to sing; legato (smoothness) above all else to emphasize beauty of tone. A singer who has achieved bel canto is singing with absolute legato, able to easily ornament the vocal line, and capable of utilizing her most beautiful voice.

Vincenzo Bellini (1801–1835) did not live a long time but made an invaluable contribution to romantic opera. One of his most well-known and respected musical traits was his sense of melody. His melodic writing made his operas stand out in Italy and other countries. His use of melody contributed greatly to his song output which is much beloved. His style reflects the ability to marry melody with dramatic interpretation of text and emotion. His songs are didactic; singing teachers regularly use them as teaching tools, especially for students who show an affinity and vocal skill for operatic music.

"Vaga luna che inargenti" is considered a song but has some traits of an operatic aria. The singer has some freedom in the interpretation of the tempo as the piano part is arpeggiated and mostly follows the voice. Bellini has provided several moments for the voice to linger above the staff on held notes (fermatas).

Song Title	Vaga luna che inargenti
Year of Composition	1833
Composer	Vincenzo Bellini
Language	Italian text
Poet	Unknown
Text	Common themes of love and nature
Voice	Featured in an almost operatic presentation
Piano	Arpeggiated chord progressions
Mood	Highly romantic

Form	Strophic
Melody	Syllabic yet lyrical
Harmony	Traditional
Tempo	Andante cantabile
What to Listen for	Bellini introduces the melody in the right hand of the introduction. He engages a dotted rhythm from the first note the voice sings as if to emphasize its entrance. Notice how Bellini emphasizes certain notes in the melody with the occasional tenuto (emphasis, but not a stop) and fermata (stop).

TWENTIETH CENTURY AND BEYOND

Italy neglected the solo song during the prolific period of opera composition in the eighteenth and nineteenth centuries. The country experienced a renaissance of song starting in the mid-nineteenth century. Composers such as Ottorino Respighi brought back Italian musical forms of the past and added a romantic interpretation.[5] The form is sometimes referred to as "stile antico."

Italian song of the early twentieth century was created from the established traditions of French impressionism and German chromaticism.[6] The composers of this time were also composing opera, that for many was considered the highest art form for the voice. One composer from this group, Alfredo Casella, was instrumental in the forward movement of Italian music and was involved in organizations that supported new music, such as the International Society for Contemporary Music and the Venice Festival of Contemporary Music.

OTTORINO RESPIGHI (1879–1936)

Ottorino Respighi learned piano and violin at a young age and attended the conservatory in Bologna. The early part of his career was spent as a performer of the viola and violin, including with an orchestra in St. Petersburg, Russia. He later worked as a professor of composition in Rome at the Conservatory of St. Cecilia, where the singer Cecilia Bartoli studied many years later. Respighi had much success with orchestral compositions like *Fontane di Roma* in 1915.

He contributed about sixty songs to the repertory with texts in Italian and French. His understanding of the voice is evident in the way in which it is written as an integral part of a song.[7] Respighi and his wife, former Conservatory student Elsa Olivieri Sangiacomo, performed often together with Elsa interpreting his songs. Mrs. Respighi wrote a biography of her husband titled *Ottorino Respighi*, published in 1962.

"Notte" is an example of the revised stile antico style and is one of Respighi's best-known songs. It reflects his mature style as a composer and demonstrates some influence of impressionism on his compositions.[8]

Song Title	Notte
Year of Composition	1905
Composer	Ottorino Respighi
Language	Italian text
Poet	Ada Negri
Text	Reflects images of nature
Voice	Requires long lines and excellent breath control
Piano	Dense texture with constant motion
Mood	Mysterious
Form	ABA with coda
Melody	Challenging and a high tessitura
Harmony	Traditional
Tempo	Lento tranquillo
What to listen for	Respighi has created a piano part to support the mystery and ethereal quality of the text. At the end of the piece, the effect of moving from forte (f) to triple pianissimo (ppp) is very striking.

The term stile antico or stile antiche (old style) has broad meaning throughout Italian music history. It usually refers to a previously used or historical style or old-fashioned musical features.[9] The old style concept was renewed in the twentieth century and in tandem with the resurgence of the neoclassical style. Stefano Donaudy's group of thirty-six songs *Arie di stile antico* is one example.

STEFANO DONAUDY (1879–1925)

Stefano Donaudy was Italian-born and studied at the Palermo Conservatory. He was somewhat of a prodigy who wrote his first opera at age thirteen. He worked as a teacher, pianist, and coach to earn a living while also working as a composer. In addition to his thirty-six songs written in the old style, he composed a few operas that have not been a part of the modern operatic repertory.

Donaudy's brother, Alberto, wrote the texts to many of his works. His songs are still performed today by accomplished singers and are a standard part of the teaching literature.

"Spirate pur, spirate" is one of his more frequently performed songs and a good song for beginning singers as it requires the mastery of medium length melismatic phrases within a short vocal range. "O del mio amato ben" is a clear demonstration of Donaudy's use of the older style melodic writing.

Song Title	Spirate pur, spirate
Year of Composition	1918
Composer	Stefano Donaudy
Language	Italian text
Poet	Alberto Donaudy
Text	Lighthearted description of breezes carrying messages of love
Voice	Combination of legato and flexibility required
Piano	Balanced texture that emphasizes the text
Mood	Buoyant
Form	ABA
Melody	Graceful with triplet figures and much movement
Harmony	Traditional
Tempo	Allegro mosso
What to listen for	There is clear text painting on the word "spirate" (waft) as the voice wafts between pitches. Donaudy has made many dynamic and emphatic markings on the held pitches. The singer should never be stagnant on a held pitch, but always changing and moving through the interpretation.
Song Title	O del mio amato ben
Year of Composition	1918
Composer	Stefano Donaudy
Language	Italian text
Poet	Alberto Donaudy

Text	Brokenhearted, lovesick, forlorn
Voice	Requires urgency and passion
Piano	Much use of pedal adds to romanticism
Mood	Passionate
Form	Strophic
Melody	Graceful with triplet figures and much movement
Harmony	Traditional
Tempo	Andante quasi adagio
What to listen for	Donaudy has written out embellishments of the melody that sound spontaneous and integrated into the texture. The piano incorporates the melody into the interludes. The combination of the pedal in the piano, the varied dynamics, and the embellished melody create a very romantic mood.

Palermo, Italy: The audience at the Palermo Conservatory in Italy is greatly anticipating a rare performance by the composer Stefano Donaudy. Donaudy himself will be accompanying voice students at the conservatory. His brother and frequent lyricist, Alberto, is in the audience. The audience has heard that the songs are written in the "stile antico" or "old" style and are looking forward to hearing what Donaudy has done to re-create the beloved style. Many listeners present are familiar with his opera compositions but have not heard his songs. Donaudy begins to play "Spirate pur, spirate" and the audience is immediately drawn into the brisk chordal introduction. The young singer takes a deep breath and begins to sing. The inherent charm of the poem, the idea of sending wishes of love wafting on the breezes, the traditionally structured song form, and Donaudy's lyrical and bright melody conspire together to seduce the audience into giving themselves over to the experience of song.

PAOLO FRANCESCO TOSTI (1846–1916)

Paolo Francesco Tosti is a well-known composer of the early twentieth century. Unlike many other Italian composers, Tosti's principal mode of composition was song and he was prolific with some 350 compositions.

Tosti enjoyed an extensive education at the Naples Conservatory and was taken under the wing of an experienced composer, Sgambati, who helped him gain credibility in Rome and across Italy. He was endorsed publicly and privately by a royal, Princess Margherita of Savoy, and became her singing teacher and curator of the court music archives.[10] He later moved to London and became singing teacher to Queen Victoria's children. He was an integral part of the royal household and in charge of vocal concerts at the palace.

"La serenata" and "Ideale" are representative of Tosti's ability to write lyrical vocal lines. The piano parts do not distract from the melody but retain their own personalities.

Song Title	La serenata
Year of Composition	1888
Composer	Francesco Tosti
Language	Italian text
Poet	Giovanni Alfredo Cesareo
Text	Romantic
Voice	Sustained legato floating above the active piano
Piano	Festive and almost dance-like rhythms
Mood	Joyous
Form	Modified strophic
Melody	Legato and occasionally imitative of the piano
Harmony	Traditional, with unexpected shifts
Tempo	Steady
What to listen for	The dynamic and engaging piano catches the attention of the ear from the opening notes. There is a subtle yet distinct tonal shift that is a surprise. Tosti has marked many dynamics throughout to keep the singer in a state of dynamic transition throughout.

Song Title	Ideale
Year of Composition	1882
Composer	Francesco Tosti
Language	Italian text
Poet	Carmelo Errico
Text	Romantic
Voice	Sustained feeling
Piano	Triplet rhythm in the right hand throughout
Mood	Pensive and romantic

Form	Strophic with a coda
Melody	Small stepwise and intervallic movement, small range
Harmony	Traditional
Tempo	Even
What to listen for	Tosti uses triplet motives in the voice and piano parts. He has many specific markings for the voice like "con anima" (with movement) and "ritardando" (slow) to help shape the melodic line. The ebb and flow of the melodic line, the changing dynamics, and the pensive text create a very romantic piece.

Washington, D.C.: It is March 26, 1981, and a fortunate few people are invited to attend a command performance for President Ronald Reagan at the Ford's Theatre. On the program is tenor Luciano Pavarotti, one of the greatest singers of all time and, in 1981, at the peak of his vocal gifts. He is introduced and walks out on the simply dressed stage to take his place in front of the black grand piano. He is dressed in white tie and carries his signature white handkerchief. The applause is electric with anticipation as he walks to the piano. The audience is expectant and ready to love whatever he will sing. His face is open and obviously pleased with the audience's reception and obvious affection. He announces his selection simply: "From Paolo Tosti, the first song I will sing is called La serenata." Pianist John Wustman begins the charming piano accompaniment with rolling chords and lightness of touch. As Pavarotti begins to sing, his voice eclipses the piano. Bright, yet full of depth, with absolutely pure legato and grace, Pavarotti's voice is a joy to hear. It fills the entire width and depth of the hall and has so much vibrancy and color that the audience can actually feel the buzz his vibrato creates. It is thrilling that the audience knows and understands they are in the presence of an artist doing something that very few people can do and better than anyone else. It is unlikely that they will ever hear the Tosti song sung that well again in their lifetimes. As Pavarotti concludes with a diminishing dynamic and a smile on his face, the audience bursts into loud and sincere applause.

The most significant second-generation Italian song composers of the twentieth century are Mario Castelnuovo-Tedesco and Goffredo Petrassi.[11] Mario Castelnuovo-Tedesco (1895–1968) was born in Florence, Italy. He studied piano and composition with Pizzetti. Like the American Ned Rorem, Castelnuovo-Tedesco was both a musician and writer. He had many essays on music published throughout his career.

Like many musicians before him, he suffered persecution due to his Jewish faith through cancelled performances and banned music. He left Italy in

1939 and settled in California where he composed music for film as a career. He composed in other genres such as opera, instrumental works, and songs. He taught at the California Institute of the Arts and was a highly valued source for students interested in music for film, including John Williams and André Previn. In song, his musical style was firmly rooted in the idea of expressing emotion and text meaning. He did not classify his style according to any established schools.

Goffredo Petrassi (1904–2003) enjoyed a traditional education in Rome in the sense that he was studying at the Conservatory of St. Cecilia and the music of established composers. He was also experiencing the movement of music away from the established opera status quo. Soon after Petrassi began composing, his music was noticed and received acclaim. He was a prolific and highly visible composer of many forms and also known for being an effective teacher. Among Petrassi's composition students was Peter Maxwell Davies.

WELL-KNOWN ITALIAN SINGERS AND THEIR SONGS

There are some singers in the history of Italian music who are distinctive. The singers listed below each contributed something unique to the genre of song. Recommended recordings of highlighted singers are also listed below.

CARLO BROSCHI (1705–1782)

Carlo Broschi, stage name Farinelli, was not the typical castrato singer. He was one of the most acclaimed and famous Italian singers of all time and stands alone as a singular performer in the history of opera. His family was not poor, but well supported, by the head of the family Salvatore Broschi. It was only after his father's death at a young age that the decision was made by the rest of the family to put Carlo on the path to becoming a castrato singer.

After his education in Naples, he started performing in Rome around 1722 and quickly gained a reputation as being a special talent. He is said to have had a voice of great flexibility and power and was able to sing ornamentation in a way that was both technically masterful and highly entertaining. He has been described as having a large and full chest and it is thought that the combination of pure lung power, great talent, and the unusual ability to master ornamentation all combined to create an unforgettable performer. The public of Italy and all of Europe were in awe of him and he became a very famous and public figure. He earned high fees for performing in public and private venues.

Farinelli eventually left the public opera stage and became a court musician of King Philip V of Spain in 1737. He was active in the court for over twenty years, performing opera, organizing and directing musical events, and teaching and singing with the royals. While he was not thought to have political interests, he did very well at initiating himself in the court life and surviving comfortably there. Farinelli retired to Bologna where he died in 1761. Today, the Farinelli Study Centre in Bologna continues to preserve and research the artifacts of Carlo Broschi's life. In 2005, the Centre held an international symposium about Farinelli to mark the 300 years since his birth.

Carlo Broschi's life was dramatized in the well-known fictionalized film *Farinelli* in 1994. While reviews and ideas are mixed about the authenticity of historical accounts in the film, there is no question that the musical sequences are highly entertaining. The vocal fireworks in the film, in an attempt to recreate Farinelli's voice, were produced by mixing two modern voices together. Ewa Malas Godlewska, coloratura, and Derek Lee Ragin, countertenor, are the singers whose voices are utilized to great effect in the film. Farinelli did not focus on song in most of his performing, however, he most likely performed songs during his singing career especially while in service to the royals and in more intimate settings than the opera stage.

There are no recordings in existence of Carlo Broschi, but the soundtrack of the film Farinelli *gives a historically accurate performance of how he may have sounded. There is one known recording of the last living castrato, which is also listed below.*

RECORDINGS

Farinelli: Il Castrato, Film Soundtrack, Auvidis Travelling Label, 1995
The Last Castrato: Complete Vatican Recordings, Alessandro Moreschi, castrato, Pearl Label, 1902 and 1904

ENRICO CARUSO (1873–1921)

Enrico Caruso is one of the most famous Italian tenors of all time who had the rare distinction, similar to Luciano Pavarotti, of crossing over from classical music into popular culture and gaining general renown. Caruso was born in the musical city of Naples, Italy. He studied singing locally in Naples and began performing opera in the city in his early twenties. Caruso quickly gained a career as a professional opera singer and eventually performed at Covent Garden, La Scala, and the Metropolitan Opera. He became well-known to American audiences through his role of Dick Johnson in Puccini's opera *La fanciulla del West* in 1910. He had a long career at the Metropolitan Opera performing most of the important tenor roles in the repertory.

Caruso had the good fortune to be at the peak of his vocal powers around the same time the gramophone was gaining popularity as a way of listening to recorded music at home. The combination of his Metropolitan Opera radio broadcasts and the availability of recordings of his music made him a household name. For the first time, individuals could enjoy and appreciate the genre of opera in their homes.

Listening to his grainy recordings today it is still possible to hear the gorgeous legato, natural grace, and supple vocal qualities that made his career. His vocal background as a baritone, combined with a very capable upper register, made for a unique vocal talent.

Caruso was certainly one of the very first singers to popularize song recordings. The inclusion of Italian song in his repertory and discography has preserved authentic performances of popular Neapolitan songs for audiences to enjoy for generations.

RECORDINGS

In Song, Enrico Caruso, tenor, RCA, 1965
Italian Songs, Enrico Caruso, tenor, RCA, 2002
Neapolitan Songs and Romances, Enrico Caruso, tenor, Butterfly Italy Label, 2008

LUCIANO PAVAROTTI (1935–2007)

Luciano Pavarotti, born in Modena, Italy, was the most famous tenor of the twentieth century. He cultivated a successful operatic career by focusing on the composers who suited his voice best; Puccini, Donizetti, and Verdi. He sang in all the major opera houses of the world and appeared frequently in recital. He often sang art song, usually Italian song, on the recital stage. Pavarotti in many ways typified the idea of an opera singer; the Italian birth, generous girth, white handkerchief as stage prop, and grandiose performing style. Through that veneer there was a straightforward and heartfelt personality that audiences responded to and embraced.

Along with Plácido Domingo and José Carreras, Pavarotti took classical singing to new heights with the "Three Tenors" franchise. Their concerts were broadcast from huge stadiums all over the world to international audiences. Recordings from these concerts became best sellers and broke many sales records. The Three Tenors often included songs in their performances.

Pavarotti was televised in opera performance, notably in the Metropolitan Opera's *La Bohème* and on popular shows like *Saturday Night Live* and *Sesame Street.*

Because of his great fame, Pavarotti brought special attention to art song whenever he sang it. He frequently performed the songs of Bellini, Respighi, and many others from the world's stages to great acclaim. His song recordings are an important part of the Italian song library.

RECORDINGS

O Sole Mio: Favourite Neapolitan Songs, Luciano Pavarotti, tenor, London Decca, 1990
O Holy Night, Luciano Pavarotti, tenor, Decca, 1990
Volare: Popular Italian Songs, Luciano Pavarotti, tenor, Decca, 1990

CECILIA BARTOLI (1966–)

Cecilia Bartoli is a professionally and commercially successful mezzo-soprano. She was born in Rome and studied singing with her parents who were professional singers. She also studied at the National Academy of St. Cecilia in Rome. Bartoli possesses the combination of an unusual voice that is equally gorgeous in the lower and upper registers with an amazing extension, as well as an animated and enthusiastic stage persona that is appealing to audiences. She has performed many opera roles, specifically those of Mozart, Donizetti, and Rossini at the Metropolitan Opera in New York, the Royal Opera House, Covent Garden, in London, La Scala in Milan, the Salzburg Festival, and the Zurich Opera House.

Bartoli has augmented her opera career with recording projects that are usually best-selling albums. She has focused on music of the baroque and early classical eras and enjoys working with original instruments and orchestrations in her performances. Bartoli has been recognized with several Grammy wins and the prestigious Herbert von Karajan Music Prize.

Her contribution to the song repertory is reflected in her many recordings. Song is a regular part of her performing repertoire. She has taken the unusual step of recording many songs that have long been considered a critical part of the teaching repertoire but are not usually recorded or performed by established singers. Her attention to these songs, specifically songs from the literature of eighteenth century Italy, has legitimized their worthiness to countless students of singing the world over.

RECORDINGS

Cecilia Bartoli: An Italian Songbook, Cecilia Bartoli, mezzo-soprano, London Decca, 1997
If You Love Me: 18th Century Italian Songs, Cecilia Bartoli, mezzo-soprano, London Decca, 1992
Live in Italy, Cecilia Bartoli, mezzo-soprano, Decca, 1998

It would be impossible to list every Italian song in existence. The list below is a starting point for those interested in listening to a variety of Italian song.

SONG LIST

Franco Alfano

Antica ninna-nanna partenopea
Felicità
Tre liriche
    Perché, allo spuntar del giorno
    Finisci l'ultimo canto
    Giorno per giorno
Tre poemi di Rabindranath Tagore
    Mamma, il giovane Principe
    Egli mormorò: Amor mio, alza i tuoi occhi
    Parlami amor mio
    Nuove Liriche tagoriane
    Perché siedi là
    Non nascondere il secreto
    Corro come il cervo muschiato

Vincenzo Bellini

La farfalletta
L'abbandono
L'allegro marinaro
Quando incise su quel marmo
Sogno d'infancia
Torna, vezzosa Fillide
Tre ariette
    Il ferivido desiderio
    Dolente immagine di Fille mia
    Vaga luna, che inargenti
Sei arietta
    Malinconia, Ninfa gentile
    Vanne, o rosa fortunata
    Bella Nice, che d'amore
    Almen se non poss'io
    Per pietà, bell'idol mio
    Ma rendi pur contento

Giovanni Bononcini

Per la gloria d'adorarvi

Giulio Caccini

Al fonte, al prato
Amarilli, mia bella
Occhi immortali
Udite, amanti

Antonio Caldara

Alma del core
Come raggio di sol
Sebben, crudele

Giacomo Carissimi

Vittoria, mio core

Alfredo Casella

Tre canzoni trecentesche
    Giovane bella, luce del mio core
    Fuor de la bella gaiba
    Amante sono, vaghiccia, di voi
Quattro favole romanesche di Trilussa
    Er coccodrillo
    La carità
    Er gatto e er cane
    L'elezzione der presidente

Mario Castelnuovo-Tedesco

Stelle cadenti (selections from 12 songs)
    La barba bianca
    L'Infinito
    Stelle cadenti
    Tamburino

Francesco Cavalli

Son ancor pargoletta

Stefano Donaudy

Ah, che odor di buono
Ah, mai non cessate
Amor mi fa cantare
Amor mi tiene in pugno
Amor s'apprende
Amorosi miei giorni
Certo un po' di cielo colse
Come l'allodoletta
Cuor mio, cuor mio
Date abbiento al mio dolore
Dormendo stai
E Filli m'ha detto
Freschi luoghi, prati aulenti
Luoghi sereni e cari
No, non mi guardate
O bei nidi d'amore
O del mio amato ben
Ognun ripicchia e nicchia
Or che le rèdole
Perché dolce, caro bene
Perduta ho la speranza
Quand' il tuo diavol nacque
Quando ti revedrò
Quella labbra non son rose
Se tra l'erba
Se volete un servidore
Se vuoi ch'io mora
Sento nel core
Sorge il sol! Che fait tu!
Spirate pur, spirate
Tempo è alfin di muover guerra
Tregua non ho
Vaghissima sembianza
Venuto è l'aprile
Vorrei poterti odiare

Gaetano Donizetti

L'amor mio
La conocchia
Giuro d'amore

La zingara
Preghiera

Francesco Durante

Danza, danza fanciulla
Vergin, tutto amor

Giuseppe Giordani

Caro mio ben

Giovanni Legrenzi

Che fiero costume

Antonio Lotti

Pur dicesti, o bocca bella

Gian Francesco Malipiero

Il sonneti delle fate
    Eliana
    Mirinda
    Melusina
    Grasinda
    Morgana
    Oriana infedele
Tre poesie di Angelo Poliziano
    Inno a Maria Nostra Donna
    L'eco
    Ballata

Benedetto Marcello

Il mio bel foco

Giovanni Paisiello

Nel cor più non me sento

Giovanni Pergolesi

Nina

Se tu m'ami, se sospiri

Goffredo Petrassi

Alla sera
Benedizione
Coro di morti
Invito all'Eràno
Io qui vagando
Lamento d'Arianna
Noche oscura
Tramontata è la luna

Ildebrando Pizzetti

I pastori
Il clefta prigione
La madre al figlio lontano
San Basilio
Passeggiata
Tre canzoni
    Donna lombarda
    La Prigioniera
La pesca dell'anello

Giacomo Puccini

E l'uccellino

Ottorino Respighi

Canzone sarda
Cinque canti all'antica
Cinque liriche
Contrasto
Due liriche
E se un giorno tornasse
Invito alla danza
L'ultima ebbrezza
Lagrime
La donna sul sarcofago
La funtanelle
La musica
La statua

Luce
Notturno
Tanto bella
Miranda
Notte
Nebbie
Nevicata
Scherzo
Stornellatrice
Stornello dall'opera
Quattro rispetti toscani

Gioacchino Rossini

Il rimprovero
La danza
La pastorella dell'Alpi
La regata veneziana
    Anzoleta avanti la regata
    Anzoleta co passa la regata
    Anzoleta dopo la regata
La serenata
L'invito

Francesco Santoliquido

Nel giardino
Riflessi
Tre poesie persiane
    Quando le domandai
    Io mi levai dal centro della terra
    Lo domandai
Tristezza crepuscolare

Alessandro Scarlatti

Già il sole dal Gange
Le violette
O cessate di piagarmi
Se Florindo è fedele
Sento nel core
Son tutta duolo
Toglietemi la vita ancor

Alessandro Stradella

Pietà, Signore!
Se nel ben sempre inconstante

Giuseppe Torelli

Tu lo sai

Francesco Paolo Tosti

Addio, fanciulla
Aprile
'A vucchella
Chitarrata abruzzese
Ideale
Il pescatore canta
In van preghi
La mia canzone
La serenata
L'ora è tarda
L'ultima canzone
Luna d'estate
Malia marenchiare
Mattinata
Non t'amo più
Penso
Sogno
Tormento
Tristezza
Vorrei

Ermanno Wolf-Ferrari

Quattro rispetti
　Un verde praticello senza piante
　Jo dei saluti ve ne mando mille
　E tanto c'è pericol ch'io ti lasci
O sì che non sapevo sospirare

Chapter Six

German Lieder

German Lieder, or song, makes up the largest portion of European song literature mainly due to the prolific writing style and abilities of German composers. The quality and variety of German poets like Johann Wolfgang von Goethe and Wilhelm Müller greatly influenced song composers and helped to inspire song composition. For example, Franz Schubert alone composed over 600 songs. His career corresponded with the height of German Lieder in the nineteenth century.

In each of the chapters about songs of a specific country certain similarities about composers to be revealed. While not all song composers have similar upbringings, educations, and lifestyles, many of them do. Some composers have much in common in spite of their differing nations of birth such as Germany, Italy, France, England, or the United States. Almost all the composers included in this study of song began their musical educations at an early age and usually on a keyboard instrument. Sometimes they studied the violin in addition to piano. Also, it is common for song composers to benefit from early exposure to classical music from a parent or family member. Most composers showed gifted tendencies toward composition earlier than other musicians. Song composers have often sought out educational opportunities with already established or older composers and have gravitated toward urban centers with myriad musical venues and activities. Song composers have started foundations, institutes, or more informal groups to study and perform others' music. Many composers enjoyed performing song in front of other composers in informal settings. Unfortunately, some composers endured terrible illnesses related to their lifestyles or bad genetic luck. Oftentimes, these illnesses prevented them from working on music and interrupted their performing and composing opportunities. Some composers suffered from mental illness at a time when treatments were limited and medical professionals did not know enough to help them find relief. Many had to struggle to see their music performed and printed for distribution; in fact, struggling was much more common that not, and most did not achieve commercial success even though their work is cherished and revered by subsequent generations.

The characteristics of German Lieder have similarities and differences to songs of other countries. For example, poetry was of critical importance to the Germans as to the French. German composers had many outstanding poets from which to choose, including Johann Wolfgang von Goethe, Richard Dehmel, Joseph von Eichendorff, Heinrich Heine, Eduard Mörike, Rainer Maria Rilke, Friedrich Rückert, and Friedrich Schiller.

The German school of composers cultivated and perfected the song cycle, in which a composer conceives a group of songs to be performed together, often with a common theme and texts by one poet.

The compositional form of the Lied is often strophic (verses) and German composers called their through-composed (no repetition) songs "durchkomponiert."

PRE-EIGHTEENTH CENTURY

Before the nineteenth century Lied that we know today was established, German song was sometimes referred to as "Lied," but it was a different genre. It is important to note that throughout music history and as the art song evolved, it was known by many different names depending on the country of origin and the trends of the day. If a piece was conceived for voice and keyboard, it was a song.

There are basically three periods of German song before the eighteenth century; the eras of the minnesingers and meistersingers, the polyphonic Lied, and the continuo Lied.

The "minnesingers" or "love singers" began as early as 1156 and were the first German folk singers. They were the counterpart to the French troubadours. Minnesingers were knightly poet-musicians who sang about love, nature, and the romance of the traveler/wanderer. Wolfram von Eschenbach is a noted minnesinger who lived from about 1170–1220. Walther von der Vogelweide (1170–1230) was one of the most gifted minnesingers. He clearly recognized the charms of middle and lower class women in addition to women of the upper class. He wrote in Middle High German; the language of his time.[1]

The meistersingers developed throughout the fourteenth, fifteenth, and sixteenth centuries and included musicians who were not necessarily aristocratic. Middle class tradesmen and artisans took advantage of the new opportunities for working musicians. Ironically, the more commonplace people who joined the ranks of the meistersingers resulted in less expressive and free songs than the minnesingers.

The polyphonic Lied of the fifteenth and sixteenth centuries was usually written in four parts with the composer's intention that a solo voice would sing the top part, or melody, with the other three parts serving as instrumental accompaniment. Composers of the polyphonic Lied included Heinrich Issac, Ludwig Senfl, and Johann Schein. German composers, like Schein, began to adopt traits of Italian monodic song, which helped to propel the form toward featuring the solo voice. The importance of song in cities like Nuremberg and Mainz was evident in the establishment of special schools in the sixteenth century whose purpose was to teach and cultivate the composition of texts and melodies. [2]

The continuo Lied developed from about 1620–1750 and was written for voice with continuo and occasionally an ostinato instrument. The form displayed a closer relationship between the voice and poetry than previous song forms. The continuo Lied was usually written in verses and focused on secular, rather than sacred, texts. The subject matter of the texts was light-hearted and included opines on dancing, singing, nature, and being in love. Composers intended for the songs to be performed in casual settings by lay or amateur musicians.

Martin Opitz (1597–1639) was a German poet who led the way for the development of the German continuo Lied during the seventeenth century. [3] His poetic reforms that inspired the continuo Lied began the modern era of German poetry by using High German spelling and pronunciation, regularizing meters, and writing in strophic form. Johann Nauwach (1595–1630) was a court composer and one of the first to set Opitz' poems.

The development and popularity of the Italian cantata and German opera contributed to the demise of the continuo Lied. In the late seventeenth century the music became increasingly difficult for the amateur.

EIGHTEENTH CENTURY

The eighteenth century was a very active time in German song development and many factors contributed to the growth of song. Two critical developments in music history were the invention of the piano in Florence in 1709 and the invention of music printing in 1756, which made it possible to distribute music on a mass scale. Increased printing capabilities brought about an explosion in the growth of literacy and the popularity of literary journals. Other factors included the rise of the middle class and the education of women.

Throughout the eighteenth century, poets of the day were involved with the "Sturm und Drang" movement, which had a great effect on the direction of song composition. The movement featured ideas about nature, religion, freedom from rules, and reforms of the German language.

The most typical song form of the pre-Schubert era in Germany was the "volkstümliches" or folk tradition. Johann Reichardt (1752–1814) is a well-known composer of the volkstümliches tradition. Additional song forms were the singspiel, arietta, ballad, and romance.

It is a common practice in music history to retroactively name a group of composers, poets, or writers who shared common interests in music, literature, and art. In France, there was "Les Six" and "the symbolists." In German music history, there are two "Berlin Schools" that represent a group of composers and a specific musical style of a period. The First Berlin School existed from 1750 to about 1770. The composers emphasized simplicity of form and poetry. The songs were usually short and folk-like. There were two innovators of the school that were not typical composers.

C. P. E. Bach (1714–1788) and C. G. Neefe (1748–1798) personified two distinctive movements in German music history. C. P. E. Bach wrote about 300 songs and was ahead of his time musically. He embodied the idea of "Empfindsamer stil" or "sensitive style." He also focused on bold harmonic progressions and independent accompaniments. C. G. Neefe exemplified the musical equivalent of "Sturm und Drang" or "storm and stress," meant to shock with emotional fullness of feeling and melodic inventiveness. He influenced a young Ludwig van Beethoven.

The Second Berlin School existed from approximately 1770 into the early nineteenth century. Major composers of the school included J. A. P. Schulz, J. F. Reichardt, C. F. Zelter, C. F. D. Schubart, and J. R. Zumsteeg. The school is associated with the term "volkston," which is a compositional style influenced by folk music. The characteristics of volkston include singable melodies written in a linear fashion with no ornamentation and texts that are plain spoken in nature. The purpose of the volkston style was enjoyment of music. Composers strove to create enjoyable songs for the middle class community from which they came. Poets like Johann Herder (1744–1803) helped create interest in volkston poetry and he influenced later poets like Goethe and Eichendorff.

In volkston, or any folk song composition, there are three basic methods of utilizing folk melodies; use of existing folk melodies (like Brahms), use of folksong texts with new melodies (like Quilter), and use of new melodies that are separate from the volkston tradition (Mahler).

The composers and work of the First and Second Berlin schools and the styles that came before are important precursors to the development of Lieder. In the nineteenth century, Franz Schubert would serve as the catalyst in which all these styles were synthesized into the new Lied. Schubert's compositional style was a strong contrast to the volkston composers as he was a professional musician and volkston composers wrote music as a secondary career.

JOSEPH HAYDN (1732–1809)

Joseph Haydn is a unique song composer. He did not begin composing song until he was fifty years old. Perhaps song composition was not a priority to him as a composer; he was very prolific in other forms. He was born in Vienna and enjoyed being appreciated and celebrated as a composer during his lifetime. Haydn was known as the "father" of the symphony, yet he also excelled in the genre of song, contributing about forty-seven songs (twenty-four of them Lieder) to the repertoire. He published fourteen songs in English known as "Canzonettas."

"The Mermaid's Song" is a good example of Haydn's charming compositional style. It epitomizes a graceful melody, light-hearted but tender text, and an evocative and classical piano part. The following song chart provides details of the song.

Song Title	The Mermaid's Song
Year of Composition	1794
Composer	Joseph Haydn
Language	English
Poet	Anne Hunter
Text	Playful and evocative of the sea
Voice	The voice must maintain lyricism within a syllabic structure
Piano	Long introduction, overall texture is dense, and utilizes sixteenth note triplets
Mood	Playful and enticing
Form	Strophic
Melody	Rhythmic variety, requires much vocal flexibility
Harmony	Tonal and traditional
Tempo	Moderately quick, but not rushed. The piano part moves a great deal, so the voice should stay steady
What to listen for	The playful words Anne Hunter contributed to the song create a mystical world of the mermaid. Haydn's piano writing epitomizes the classical style of writing.

The right hand of the piano doubles the vocal part
while creating harmony in thirds. The long piano
introduction is unusual for an art song and sets up the
spirit of the song very effectively.

"She Never Told Her Love" is an example of a Haydn song strongly influenced by operatic elements. The melodic line is written to feature the flexibility of the voice and to allow for melodic embellishments.

Song Title	She Never Told Her Love
Year of Composition	1794
Composer	Joseph Haydn
Language	English
Poet	Shakespeare
Text	Somewhat dark
Voice	Operatic structure
Piano	Varied treatment, aria-like
Mood	Dismal
Form	Through-composed
Melody	In service to the text
Harmony	Tonal
Tempo	Varied, movement is stopped by Haydn's markings for effect
What to listen for	This short piece is full of vocal ornamentation and pianistic decoration which both serve the nature of the text. The piano often expresses a word after it is sung, "patience," "grief," "smiling."

Wolfgang Amadeus Mozart (1756–1791) is one of the most well-known and prolific composers of all time. His works span opera, church music, string quartets, masses, piano concertos, wind and string quartets, and song. His life was dramatized in the popular film *Amadeus*. In spite of his frequent commissions and jobs, Mozart had financial difficulties and had to teach and give private performances in order to survive. His songs epitomize the classical period and endure today.

Mozart's songs often resemble ariettas. He contributed about thirty-five songs in Italian, German, and French to the repertory. His songs were meant to be vocal showpieces and mostly intended for entertainment and home use. Mozart wrote brilliantly for the voice and his songs reflect the same melodic gift and empathy for text placement as his operas. Mozart understood that vocal music must fully incorporate text. He said, "Poetry should always be the handmaiden of music."

LUDWIG VAN BEETHOVEN (1770–1827)

Ludwig van Beethoven is a famous German composer. His major compositional output was not song, but he did contribute about eighty songs to the repertory. His critical role in the history of song is the contribution of his song cycle *An die ferne Geliebte* (1816). The cycle of six songs is related structurally, thematically, and textually. Often referred to as the first song cycle, it is an important precursor to the nineteenth century song cycles of Schubert and Schumann.

POETRY OF THE EIGHTEENTH CENTURY

One of the most famous poets of all time is Germany's Johann Wolfgang von Goethe (1749–1832). He was a poet and intellectual figure in Germany and had a special affinity for drama and writing texts specifically for song. He wrote about two hundred books and was accomplished in several professions, including philosophy, acting, and theater directing. He wrote poetry with the intention it would be used for song. He regularly included songs and references to songs in his plays and novels.

Goethe had a compositional period of "Sturm und Drang." The idea of "storm and stress" manifested into a period of about twenty years in the late eighteenth century. It was reflected in the literature and music of Germany when emotionalism was at its height. In tandem with the movement, Goethe's poems moved away from conventional to new spontaneity and emotional power.[4]

His most famous works include the novel *The Sorrows of Young Werther* (1774), which was later made into an opera by Massenet titled *Werther*, and *Wilhelm Meister's Lehrjahre* (learning year) (1795), which is a series of six books.

Another poet, Joseph F. von Eichendorff (1788–1857), used his poetry to glorify the idea of "Wanderlust." Wanderlust was an expression of the desire and intention to "wander" toward resolution in one's life. It could also be

connected with the religious idea of praise of the gift of wandering, or travelling, and how it is God's special gift.[5]

NINETEENTH CENTURY

The nineteenth century was an exciting time in song history. The first half of
the century brought about the refinement of the Lied and the height of romanticism in Germany. The nineteenth century Lied developed from its precursor, the ballad, which was the dominant song form at the start of the
century. The typical ballad text was a narrative focused on supernatural or
historical subjects. The ballad tended to be longer than the Lied and was
more like cantatas than songs. Johann Rudolf Zumsteeg (1760–1802) was a
German composer of the ballad, among other genres. His success with the
ballad form had a clear influence on Franz Schubert. While Schubert would
later dominate German song, his earliest pieces were directly modeled on
Zumsteeg's settings of the same poems.[6] Another master of the ballad form
is Carl Loewe (1796–1869).[7]

The nineteenth century included the development and culmination of the
Biedermeier style from about 1815 to 1848. The Biedermeier style reflected
a life influenced by art. The term Biedermeier has been used to describe art,
literature, music, architecture, and design. During this period in Germany,
the salons of middle class families became cultural centers. As there was a
move away from symbolism to realism in poetry and writing, art of the time
focused on home life and realism over perfected images. What was happening with the art scene of the time was reflected in music performance and
enjoyment in the home. Composers would often write ballads and early
Lieder with this particular audience in mind: the salon milieu. Biedermeier
composers include Felix Mendelssohn (1809–1847), Robert Franz
(1815–1892), and Peter Cornelius (1824–1874).

FRANZ SCHUBERT (1797–1828)

Franz Schubert personifies the height of the romantic movement in song. His
work represents a melding of the meaning of text with emotion. Schubert is
known for being one of the most prolific composers of all time. He is certainly the most prolific *song* composer with over six hundred songs written
during his short life. Schubert showed musical promise from an early age and
auditioned for the composer Antonio Salieri as a young child. He was accepted to and attended a highly respected boarding school in Vienna and
began composing in earnest as a young teen. For example, he composed 150
songs during his eighteenth year (more than one every three days).

His songs are organized by opus numbers and it is interesting to note that they reflect the date of publication and not the date of composition. The year 1815 included his first important songs.

Melody in song was of utmost importance to Schubert and he considered the poetry less critical than the vocal line. Within the melody, he widened breadth of phrasing in a way not previously seen in song and he also experimented with rhythms. His use of harmony was innovative for its time.

Schubert's accompaniments continued in the direction of the Second Berlin School whose composers had started the trend of using representational motifs for objects and events in nature. The motifs were used as devices to connect emotions to the human world. The work of Beethoven had an influence on Schubert's piano writing. Schubert tended to focus on one poet at a time and he would write a group of songs drawing on one poet's works.

Social occasions where music was performed and enjoyed by a small group of friends and family, and which featured the music of Franz Schubert, were known as "Schubertiads." These occasions were very popular in the nineteenth century and existed in some form in other countries as well. The English had the drawing room ballad and the French had Chausson's and Renaldo Hahn's salons.

In January of 1821, Joseph Huber wrote about his experience at a Schubertiad: "Last Friday, I was excellently entertained . . . Franz Schober invited Schubert and fourteen of his close acquaintances for the evening. Schubert sang and played a lot of his songs by himself, lasting until about 10 o'clock in the evening. After that we drank punch offered by one of the group, and since it was very good and plentiful the gathering, already in a happy mood, became even merrier; it was 3 o'clock in the morning before we parted."[8]

In his very short life of thirty-one years, Schubert rarely left Vienna and never married. He was the first great composer to be completely financially independent and one of the first composers to devote most of his attention to song. He died in November 1828 never having bought or owned a piano of his own.[9] His death has been attributed to syphilis by several historians. He was taken care of by his family at the end of his life. The only public concert of all his own music that he put on did not happen until the last year of his life.

"Die Forelle" is a light-hearted and entertaining song by Schubert that exemplifies the idea of text-painting, or using the piano or voice part to fully realize the meaning of the text, in this case, the movement of the trout.

Song Title	Die Forelle
Year of Composition	1819
Composer	Franz Schubert

Language	German
Poet	C. F. Schubart
Text	Themes of nature
Voice	Requires a lightness and ability to move freely
Piano	Schubert uses the right hand part to paint the trout leaping out of the water and the left hand represents the rapidly moving brook
Mood	Bright
Form	Modified ABA
Melody	A wide range with chromatic leaps
Harmony	Tonal
Tempo	Animated
What to listen for	Schubert's mastery of text-painting in the piano part. The brightly animated accompaniment is a perfect counterpoint to the legato melody. The varied rhythm of the piano part creates a interesting counterpoint throughout.

Schubert's "Gretchen und Spinnrade" is one of the clearest examples of text-painting in the song repertory and also one of the most emotionally intense songs by Schubert.

Song Title	Gretchen und Spinnrade
Year of Composition	1814
Composer	Franz Schubert
Language	German
Poet	Goethe
Text	Painful reality

Voice	Requires maturity of technique and approach to the theme
Piano	The piano is clearly representing the spinning wheel
Mood	Bright
Form	Modified ABA
Melody	A wide range with chromatic leaps
Harmony	Tonal with dissonances
Tempo	"Like the wind"
What to listen for	Schubert keeps the piano moving constantly throughout the piece to symbolize the desperateness of Gretchen's feelings. The final section speeds toward resolution with a fury not usually found in song. The postlude is the spinning wheel coming to a stop.

SCHUBERT AND THE SONG CYCLE

Schubert was the first composer to fully develop the song cycle as a mode of art song performance. *Die schöne Müllerin* and *Winterreise* were some of the first cycles of major status. *Die schöne Müllerin* was composed in 1823 and consists of a group of twenty songs. Schubert employs a piano motif throughout that is reminiscent of a brook and acts as a unifying device.

In contrast to *Die schöne Müllerin* is the cycle *Winterreise*. *Winterreise* is a significant work in Schubert's career. The twenty-four songs with poems by Müller, were published in 1828, the last year of Schubert's life. The songs display extreme emotional despair and bleakness that act as a unifying factor. Some accounts describe him proofing copies of these songs for publication days and hours before he died. The piece is arguably Schubert's masterpiece and he personally considered it his best work; perhaps because it was one of his last works. He was not in good health when writing these songs and his feelings of despair and hopelessness are well expressed in the music. In fact,

Schubert is thought to have corrected proofs of the unpublished *Winterreise* in the last days of his life from his deathbed.[10]

The first song of Schubert's *Die schöne Müllerin* is "Das Wandern." It symbolizes the beginning of the protagonist's journey.

Song Title	"Das Wandern" from *Die Schöne Müllerin* (The Miller's Beautiful Daughter)
Year of Composition	1823
Composer	Franz Schubert
Language	German
Poet	Wilhelm Müller
Text	Introduction of the cycle's protagonist, syllabic text setting
Voice	Requires a steady approach with a bouncy feel
Piano	Arpeggiated chords that clearly imitate walking
Mood	Jolly
Form	Strophic
Melody	Has movement, but relaxed
Harmony	Tonal
Tempo	Animated, moderately fast
What to listen for	Listen for the optimism and excitement that is in the singer's voice as he anticipates the beginning of his journey. Schubert has created the motion of walking in the piano part.

"Der Lindenbaum" from Schubert's cycle *Winterreise* (Winter Journey) is a good example of the angst felt by the singer throughout the group of songs.

Song Title	"Der Lindenbaum" from *Winterreise*

Year of Composition	1827
Composer	Franz Schubert
Language	German
Poet	Wilhelm Müller
Text	Themes of nature and deep emotion
Voice	Haunting quality
Piano	Triplet motive throughout
Mood	Contemplative
Form	Strophic
Melody	Has motion, but relaxed, small intervals and range, for minimal movement
Harmony	Tonal
Tempo	Moderate
What to listen for	The pleading triplet figure translates to the voice and represents the introspective longing of the singer. Listen to how Schubert uses the postlude to bring the song to a quiet and touching conclusion.

ROBERT SCHUMANN (1810–1856)

Robert Schumann brought innovative stylistic traits in addition to the 250 songs he contributed to the genre. He was a champion for the piano and its role in song performance. He was able to elevate the piano accompaniment as an equal partner to the voice. He believed that the piano was as critically important to the interpretation of a song as the voice. Schumann achieved equality by writing extended preludes, interludes, and postludes for the piano. There is no doubt that his extended piano writing in song was largely due to his interest in writing for the piano as a solo instrument.

Surprisingly, and unlike Schubert, melody is not the most important element of Schumann's style. The melding of voice and piano takes precedence. Harmonically, he made use of "floating" harmony in which there is no clear beginning or closing cadence and utilized frequent key changes. When it came to poetry, Schumann tended to choose poets he knew personally or poets who shared his political views.

"Die Lotosblume," written during Schumann's Liederjahr, is a fine example of his ability to write lyrical melody for the voice and fully incorporate the piano part with the voice.

Song Title	Die Lotosblume
Year of Composition	1840
Composer	Robert Schumann
Language	German
Poet	Heinrich Heine
Text	Very romantic, the "Lotus flower" representing the woman
Voice	Legato and pensive
Piano	Chordal throughout
Mood	Tender
Form	Through-composed
Melody	Very lyrical
Harmony	Tonal
Tempo	Moderate, somewhat slow
What to listen for	Musically, Schumann creates a push and pull feeling with the tenderness of text and the emotions that the singer feels when she realizes love will bring pain. The pianist and singer work in tandem to ebb and flow with a feeling of freeness within the structure of the rhythm.

"Du bist wie eine Blume," also written in the Liederjahr, incorporates the romanticism of the symbolism of the flower into the melody of the song.

Song Title	Du bist wie eine Blume

Year of Composition	1840
Composer	Robert Schumann
Language	German
Poet	Heinrich Heine
Text	Use of nature image, flower, as a symbol for woman
Voice	Legato and requires excellent breath control
Piano	Chordal and steady, doubles the voice, the postlude is reflective without being heavy-handed
Mood	Romantic
Form	Through-composed
Melody	Long, languid phrases
Harmony	Tonal, subtle dissonances
Tempo	Langsam (slow)
What to listen for	Schumann has captured the rhythmic flow of the poem exquisitely with this song. It personifies simple elegance and German restraint.

LIEDERJAHR

The year 1840 was a very special time in Schumann's career. 1840 was known as his "Liederjahr," or "song year." He composed 150 songs in 1840 alone, including his beloved song cycles *Frauenliebe und leben* (in just two days) consisting of eight songs and the cycle *Dichterliebe* of sixteen songs.

Frauenliebe und leben uses poetry of Adelbert von Chamisso (1781–1838) and is an expression of the extreme emotions of falling in love, marrying, having children, and death. The eight songs are unified by a dramatic narrative, the tonal relationships between the songs, the use of motives, and the repetition of music from the first song in the postlude of the last song.

Like many of his fellow composers, Schumann suffered mightily in his life. He had a complete emotional breakdown in 1854 and attempted suicide by jumping off a bridge into the Rhine River. There were questions about his mental health while he was alive and posthumous study confirms he suffered from deep psychological problems. He also had life-long depression and was a heavy drinker. In spite of these problems, he contributed a great deal to the art song repertoire of the nineteenth century. His songs are very popular and a staple of student's vocal studies and beloved by professional performers.

"Seit ich ihn gesehen" (Since I have seen him) is the first song in Schumann's *Frauenliebe und leben* (A Woman's Love and Life) cycle and serves as the introduction to a loosely organized story about a woman's journey in love and marriage.

Song Title	"Seit ich ihn gesehen" from *Frauenliebe und leben*
Year of Composition	1840
Composer	Robert Schumann
Language	German
Poet	Adelbert von Chamisso
Text	Reflects her awe and joy in seeing the man she loves
Voice	Should bring out emphasis of words like "dream" and "brightness"
Piano	Follows the voice part
Mood	Wonderment
Form	Strophic
Melody	Melody divided into short phrases before opening up to longer, more legato phrases
Harmony	Tonal
Tempo	Larghetto
What to listen for	Schumann starts the piano part with a sparse texture and it becomes more dense as the song progresses, while doubling the movement of the voice. The postlude includes melodic material.

"Im wunderschönen Monat Mai" (in the wonderful month of May) is a song from Schumann's cycle *Dichterliebe*.

Song Title	"Im wunderschönen Monat Mai" from *Dichterliebe*
Year of Composition	1840
Composer	Robert Schumann
Language	German
Poet	Heinrich Heine
Text	Love in Spring
Voice	Longing and urgency
Piano	Use of pedal and arpeggiated movement adds to the mood of romanticism
Mood	Anticipatory
Form	Strophic
Melody	Has a leaning quality
Harmony	Tonal
Tempo	Not too fast
What to listen for	Schumann staggers the melody with the piano part to create an effect of longing and urgency. The postlude brings back music from the introduction to bring the song full circle.

JOHANNES BRAHMS (1833–1897)

Johannes Brahms is known as a romantic classicist—the structure of his songs is classical, but the emotional component is highly romantic. Brahms showed prodigious talents from an early age by studying piano with his father and delving into music training.

Unlike Schumann, melody was always first in Brahms' compositions. Brahms was able to create a sweet lyrical melody as well as a dramatic wide arching tune. He expertly used harmony as an expressive device in song, sophisticated rhythmic ideas including hemiola (two against three), and emphasis of the bass line in the piano. Many of his songs were influenced by folk poetry and style.

"Sapphische Ode" is a strophic song by Brahms that is straightforward in form but contains long phrases that can be challenging for a singer.

Song Title	Sapphische Ode
Year of Composition	1884
Composer	Johannes Brahms
Language	German
Poet	H. Schmidt
Text	Nature and love
Voice	Reflective
Piano	Gently rhythmic
Mood	Sweet and sentimental
Form	Modified strophic
Melody	Bittersweet
Harmony	Tonal with some dissonances firmly rooted in the established tonality
Tempo	Ziemlich langsam (not too slow)
What to listen for	Brahms writes melodic lines that are lyrical but challenging to accomplish in one breath. The singer must make a decision on whether to break up a phrase or move the tempo along more quickly. The form is strophic, but Brahms makes one modification in the second verse.

HUGO WOLF (1860–1903)

Wolf wrote some three hundred songs in three main creative periods. Like many of his contemporaries, Wolf came from a musical family and studied music with his father from an early age. He struggled with poverty and taught piano and violin lessons to make money. In 1884 and for several years, he wrote music criticism for the *Salonblatt*, a fashionable periodical of the time.[11] His critical writing was not always popular with other musicians and the public. In retrospect, it mostly served to only distract him from his own composing. Unfortunately, Hugo Wolf did not have a long life in which to compose. He only lived forty-two years and did not gain mastery of composition until age twenty-eight.[12] In the fourteen years left to him, his songs were written in irregular outbursts, at the rate of one, two, even three a day. These days add up to less than six months and the main creative periods add up to less than eighteen months. On the achievement of this short span, his name and fame rest secure.[13]

Wolf was able to bring other instruments to life in his piano writing. Overall, his stylistic approach is difficult to pin down and changed often, usually to accommodate a poem. Unlike Schubert and Brahms, his songs were not often strophic in form.

His melodies were not lyrical in the typical fashion in that their purpose was to make a pretty vocal line. The melodies sprung forth directly from the poetry and sometimes closely followed speech rhythms. He had an excellent ability to naturally set words and text declamations.

Wolf wrote piano parts that were independent from the vocal line. His genius was in the technique he used to weld the two parts together to create a cohesive texture. He gave the piano an enormous significance. He often used a motivic device (repeated phrase) in the accompaniment.

Wolf had a method of completely absorbing himself in a poem before beginning to write music. He would then spontaneously compose almost fully formed songs. He wrote poems himself and read poems aloud during performances. It is revealing of his personality and strong feeling for poetry that Wolf did not like to set poems that had already been set by other composers. He was known for the way he read poetry. One audience member described it as follows: "Never in my life have I heard such reading. It is impossible to describe it . . . when he spoke the words, they assumed a prodigious truth, they became corporeal things."[14]

Wolf's *Mörike Lieder* consisted of fifty-three songs composed in 1888. Mörike was well regarded as one of Germany's greatest poets, and incredibly, he died without ever hearing his poems set to Wolf's music. The *Spanisches Liederbuch* consist of forty-four songs, German translations of Spanish poetry, and the *Italienisches Liederbuch* are forty-six songs in two volumes (sometimes published in three), 1890 and 1891.

Hugo Wolf was an extremely gifted and troubled man who endured many challenges and still managed to create brilliant songs. He is said to have suffered from violent mood swings related to some mental illness and tried to commit suicide. He lived in an asylum in Vienna the last few years of his life.

He was very close to friend Melanie Kochert who stayed with him throughout his illnesses.

His songs were very ahead of their time in regard to inventiveness and
structure and, unfortunately, the average singer of his day was not interested
in performing his songs. Luckily that is not the case today.

"Verborgenheit" is one of the most musically cohesive songs in German
repertory. The form, harmony, and shape of melodic line all perfectly reflect
the meaning of the text.

Song Title	Verborgenheit
Year of Composition	1888
Composer	Hugo Wolf
Language	German
Poet	Eduard Mörike
Text	Reflective with nature symbolism
Voice	Requires a longing quality within the legato phrasing
Piano	Dotted rhythm in the bass lines serves as a counterpoint to the legato melodic line
Mood	Melancholy
Form	ABA
Melody	Each phrase is related to the next, Wolf makes some specific markings like "with increasing passion and animation"
Harmony	Tonal
Tempo	Moderately and with great feeling (Wolf)
What to listen for	Wolf has created a musical sketch that reflects the melancholy of the poem at hand. The middle section of the song corresponds perfectly with the change in the poem at the return to the

A section and is a repeat of
the original text.

The following is a performance sketch that tries to illustrate what it would
have been like to hear Wolf's music with the composer at the piano.
*It is summer 1896 in Stuttgart, Germany. Hugo Wolf and several singers
are presenting a public Liederabend (song evening) to an audience at 8:00
p.m. The concert includes three soloists and Wolf himself at the piano. The
entire program consists of Wolf songs. The songs are grouped in four and
five with a brief intermission. Soprano Emma Gerok is on stage to sing the
first group of songs. Her second selection is one of Wolf's most popular
pieces,* Verborgenheit. *Wolf has set the romantic poem by Mörike to great
effect.* Verborgenheit, *or seclusion, is about withdrawing into oneself and
asking to be left alone. The piano creates a quiet and contemplative mood
with its almost stealth chordal passages. Hearing the melancholy of the
minor sonorities, it is possible to understand a person's urge to drift away
into himself.*

RICHARD STRAUSS (1864–1949)

Richard Strauss came from a musical and financially comfortable family. He
had comprehensive training in piano, theory, and the classics. Like other
successful composers, he was a child prodigy and began composing early. He
became an accomplished opera composer and conductor.

Strauss wrote about two hundred songs for voice and piano. He was
somewhat conservative in style yet chose contemporary poets and often ones
he knew. Overall, his musical style is mixed; there is an operatic scale to
some songs, and others are more contained and text focused. There is no
question that much of his vocal writing for song was quite similar to his
vocal writing for opera. Many of his songs are demanding for singers and
require an accomplished technique to meet the demands of the composer.

The piano was used more to create texture than as an equal partner with
the voice, obviously a feature of his large-scale composing for opera and
orchestras. He was able to amplify dramatic expression and create mood
quite well with the technique. Strauss was a brilliant musician and actually
sometimes improvised piano parts of his songs on his opera themes during
song performances.[15]

"Schlagende Herzen" is an example of Strauss' ability to take a seeming-
ly innocuous text and create a sophisticated yet entertaining song.

Song Title   Schlagende Herzen

Year of   1895
Composition

Composer	Richard Strauss
Language	German
Poet	Otto Julius Bierbaum
Text	Lighthearted
Voice	Difficulty of melody demands mastery
Piano	Dense texture, highly active and rhythmically sophisticated
Mood	Enchanting
Form	Roughly ABA
Melody	A wide range with chromatic leaps
Harmony	Tonal with rapid movement through dissonances
Tempo	Light, with movement
What to listen for	Strauss has created an explosion of rhythmic movement and sweeping, yet precise, melody. Instead of the piano introducing the voice, the voice begins the song with the piano part quickly joining on the downbeat of the first measure. The voice and piano have an exciting dance and interplay throughout the piece. Listen to the dissonances and rapidly moving harmonies in the piano part that somehow never overwhelm the voice part. The melodic material is highly demanding, but Strauss knows how to just touch the notes above the staff. He uses the nonsense words, "kling, klang," to mimic the heartbeat.

"Morgen!" is a strong contrast to "Schlagende Herzen" in that Strauss uses a more sparse texture to create a dreamy and sensual mood with a recitative-like melodic line.

Song Title	Morgen!
Year of Composition	1894
Composer	Richard Strauss
Language	German
Poet	John Henry Mackay
Text	Highly romantic with themes of the sun and beach
Voice	Requires a kind of stillness while moving breath through sweeping lines
Piano	A long introduction with a romantic, lyrical melody with arpeggiated chords, then continues throughout
Mood	Sensual and drawn-out
Form	Through-composed
Melody	In a nod to opera, recitative-like structure
Harmony	Relished dissonance, shifting tonal center
Tempo	Slow, but not overly slow
What to listen for	Strauss has created a sensual feast for the ear. He brilliantly combines an arpeggiated left hand in the piano with the top note of the right hand in half notes; the result is a push-pull feeling throughout the piece. There is an extended introduction that is used to set up a mood of a brightly shining sun that lingers so much the entrance of the voice is a surprise. Strauss

teases with just a few lyric
phrases that are as
impassioned as they are short
before all motion stops and
the singer creates a spell with
the final two phrases;
"speechless, we shall look
into each other's eyes, and we
will descend the muted
silence of happiness."

Unlike other musicians, Strauss did not leave Germany during Nazi rule. His music and talents were used by the Nazi Party as a propaganda tool.

Other song composers of the nineteenth century included Franz Liszt (1811–1886), Gustav Mahler (1860–1911), Felix Mendelssohn (1809–1847), and Robert Franz (1815–1892).

GERMAN POETRY OF THE NINETEENTH CENTURY

German poetry of the nineteenth century concentrated on allusions and symbolism rather than direct statement and upon the mood and intensity of the individual experience. The poetry addressed themes like death, night, wanderlust, unfulfilled longing, and mystery. Poetry of the late romantic Lied evolved in two major bursts of creativity: the songs of Schubert through Brahms, and the songs of Schumann through Wolf. Three important poets of nineteenth century German poetry were Heinrich Heine, Eduard Mörike, and Richard Dehmel.

HEINRICH HEINE (1797–1856)

Heinrich Heine was an important German poet during the nineteenth century. Heine's poems have been set by more composers than any other poet; there are over 4,000 known musical settings of his poetry. Heine was known for his political satires. He was able to transcend the romantic age and employ both wit and sensuality in his poetry.[16]

His books of poetry were bestsellers but he was not able to live off of his writing. He came from a wealthy family, but was not supported in later years due to a family squabble over money. In addition, Heine was a victim of the Nazi Party when it retroactively stripped him of his German background and listed the writer of his poetry as "unknown."

Eduard Mörike (1804–1875) wrote poems that are distinguished by realistic portraits of life and lend themselves to musical sonority. His ability to write perfect text for a melody is reflected by the fact that his "Das verlassene Mägdlein" was set some fifty times by various composers. Richard Dehmel (1863–1920) came to reject naturalism and his poetry foreshadowed symbolism and expressionism.

As both poetry and music became more complex, the song trend moved gradually away from amateur performers. The ideal fusion of poetry and music is in Wolf, but too difficult for most amateurs, Strauss has operatic vocal lines and orchestrally conceived accompaniments.

THE CROSSOVER COMPOSERS OF THE NINETEENTH AND TWENTIETH CENTURIES

The Second Viennese School included Arnold Schoenberg, Alban Berg, and Anton Webern. Schoenberg was the teacher of Webern and Berg. The three composers are grouped together retrospectively mainly because of the teacher-student relationship and the fact that they are all twentieth-century Austrian composers. They all experimented with polytonality and the 12-tone scale, among other harmonic techniques.

ARNOLD SCHOENBERG (1874–1951)

Schoenberg studied violin and cello and was mostly self-taught as a composer. He was considered the leader of the Second Viennese School. He began developing the 12-tone technique (a composition with twelve tones related only to one another) in 1908, which was the most innovative compositional technique of the time. He was an accomplished teacher who wrote articles on teaching and placed a strict emphasis on classical forms and counterpoint. He taught at the University of Southern California at Los Angeles from 1936–1944 and contributed over one hundred songs to the repertory, mostly before 1914.

His musical style made frequent use of classical forms. His early songs are mostly tonal while later songs incorporate the 12-tone technique. Schoenberg's two best-known works for voice are the cycles *Pierrot Lunaire* (1912) and *Das Buch der hängenden Garten* (1909). In *Pierrot Lunaire*, the principal theme is drawn from commedia dell'arte, and Sprechstimme (speech-singing) is used throughout to great effect.

ALBAN BERG (1885–1935)

Alban Berg is a composer from Vienna who, with Arnold Schoenberg and Anton Webern, makes up the triad of composers to first work with atonality in their published works. Berg learned piano at home and began composing at an early age. He studied composition with Arnold Schoenberg and seemed focused on vocal music from his earliest composing days. Arnold Schoenberg: "Alban Berg is an extraordinarily gifted composer, but the state he was in when he came to me was such that his imagination apparently could not work on anything but Lieder. Even the piano accompaniments to them were songlike."[17] Clearly, Berg's teacher felt that instrumental music deserved his attention as well as works for voice. One of his most successful works was for voice: the opera *Wozzeck* was an artistic and commercial success for Berg and the first full-length atonal opera; it would be followed by *Lulu* years later.

Berg was a prolific writer and contributed over eighty-five songs to the song repertory; only twelve songs were published in his lifetime. His musical style progressed throughout his career and culminated in an individualistic style of atonality and counterpoint as the main forms of expression. His song output includes: *Sieben frühe Lieder* (1905), *Vier Lieder* (1909), and *Altenberg Lieder* (1912).

ANTON WEBERN (1883–1945)

Anton Webern, from Vienna, rounds out the principal composers of the Second Viennese School with Arnold Schoenberg and Alban Berg. Webern was a pupil of Schoenberg from whom he learned the 12-tone method that he applied religiously in his work.[18]

As a boy, Webern studied piano and cello before his formal studies at the University of Vienna. As a composer, his style included use of atonality, clarity of texture, and use of silences. He frequently set the poems of Hildegard Jone.

His songs include: *Sechs Lieder nach Gedichten von George Trakl, Fünf geistliche Lieder* (1921), and *Drei Gesänge.*

KURT WEILL (1900–1950)

Kurt Weill was born in Dessau, Germany, and became an American citizen in 1943. His father was a composer and Chief Kantor at the synagogue in Dessau. He began musical studies at a young age and began composing early. After the Nazi seizure of power in 1933, he fled Germany for Paris and later came to New York to work on Broadway productions like *Street Scene* and *Lost in the Stars*. Weill was a key figure in the development of modern forms of musical theatre. He collaborated with librettist Bertolt Brecht (1898–1956) and their most successful work was *Mahagonny*. He wrote approximately forty songs; half in German.

His musical style included romantic and expressive melodic lines and straightforward phrase structures. In all of his vocal music, there is the clear influence of cabaret and jazz genres.

OTHER COMPOSERS AND POETS OF THE TWENTIETH CENTURY

Additional composers of the twentieth century include Paul Hindemith (1895–1963) and Hans Pfitzner (1869–1949). Germany continued to produce outstanding poets in the twentieth century. They included Rainer Maria Rilke (1875–1926), Hermann Hesse (1877–1962), Franz Werfel (1890–1945), and Erich Kästner (1899–1974).

WELL-KNOWN GERMAN SINGERS AND THEIR SONGS

The following German singers made outstanding contributions to the performance of German Lieder.

DIETRICH FISCHER-DIESKAU (1925–2012)

German baritone Dietrich Fischer-Dieskau is one of the most successful singers of the twentieth century. He earned a stellar reputation as the premier singer of Lieder yet also sang opera roles and oratorio. He is known especially for his performances and recordings of Franz Schubert's cycles *Winterreise* and *Die schöne Müllerin.*

He was born in Berlin and studied briefly at the Berlin Conservatory before starting to take professional singing jobs. Fischer-Dieskau performed opera in Berlin, Munich, Vienna, London, and other cities. He first performed in the United States in 1955 in St. Paul, Minnesota, and, later, at the Town Hall in New York City with pianist Gerald Moore. Fischer-Dieskau and Moore had a long professional partnership that lasted into the early seventies. They undertook the project of recording all of Schubert's songs for the male voice. The recordings that are a result of that project continue to set the standard for German Lieder interpretation. Fischer-Dieskau was one of the first singers of the twentieth century to fully benefit from the phenomenon of recorded music. His recordings helped to popularize song for a much larger audience than before.

Recordings

Schubert: Goethe Lieder, Dietrich Fischer-Dieskau, baritone, Gerald Moore, piano, Deutsche Grammophon, 1999

Schubert Lieder, Dietrich Fischer-Dieskau, baritone, Deutsche Grammophon, 1993
The Art of Dietrich Fischer-Dieskau, Dietrich Fischer-Dieskau, baritone, Deutsche Grammophon, 2012 (Various songs)
Voice of the Century, Dietrich Fischer-Dieskau, baritone, Deutsche Grammophon, 2012 (Songs of Schubert, Schumann, Liszt, Beethoven, Brahms, and others)

CHRISTINE SCHÄFER (1965–)

Christine Schäfer is a German soprano from Frankfurt. She studied in Berlin at the Hochschule der Künste and one of her teachers was Dietrich Fischer-Dieskau. She began her operatic career in Innsbruck and has performed classic and new roles such as the title role in Berg's opera *Lulu.*

Schäfer's work has included innovative projects involving song such as a film project directed by Oliver Hermann featuring the songs of Robert Schumann (*Dichterliebe*) and Arnold Schoenberg (*Pierrot Lunaire*). She has also performed a staged version of Schubert's *Winterreise,* a song cycle usually performed by a male singer. Schäfer's artistic and vocal risks bring a new spotlight to established repertoire that will help to drive audience interest to song.

Recordings

Brahms: The Complete Songs, Volumes One and Two, Christine Schäfer, soprano, Graham Johnson, piano, Hyperion, 2011
Mélodies, Christine Schäfer, soprano, Irwin Gage, piano, Deutsche Grammophon, 2000 (Mélodies of Ernest Chausson and Claude Debussy)
Schoenberg: Pierrot Lunaire, Christine Schäfer, soprano, Deutsche Grammophon, 2012
The Songs of Robert Schumann, Christine Schäfer, soprano, Graham Johnson, piano, Hyperion, 1996
Winterreise, Christine Schäfer, soprano, Erich Schneider, piano, Onyx Classics UK, 2006 (Franz Schubert's song cycle *Winterreise*)

MATTHIAS GOERNE (1967–)

Matthias Goerne is a highly successful German singer of songs, opera, oratorio, and orchestral works. His first opera role was Papageno with the Salzburg Opera in 1997 and since then he has sung opera at many famous venues such as the Royal Opera House, Paris National Opera, and the Metropolitan Opera in New York. In addition to opera, Mr. Goerne regularly appears in recital, often performing Schubert's cycle *Winterreise*, among other song repertoire.

Like other Lieder singers, Mr. Goerne has benefitted by working with great pianists, such as Christoph Eschenbach with whom he has performed live and recorded Lieder. A *New York Times* review of their performance of *Die schöne Müllerin* performed without an intermission in March 2014 at Carnegie Hall comments on the fact that the Hall is a large space to perform an intimate song cycle.[19] It is a testament to Goerne's expressive singing that the performance was critically acclaimed and a success. Goerne is able to fully commit dramatically to whatever text is at hand; "Mr. Goerne inhabited each mini-drama both vocally and physically, sometimes swaying and using his hands demonstratively, his eyes an expressive conduit for each particular emotion."[20] Fully committed, and interesting, song performances will be a large component in the struggle to keep the song recital alive and well into the twenty-first century and beyond.

Recordings

Bach Cantatas, Matthias Goerne, baritone, Decca, 2000
Schubert Erlkönig, Matthias Goerne, baritone, Andreas Haefliger, piano, Harmonia Mundi, 2013 (Franz Schubert's Lieder)
Wanderer's Nachtlied, Matthias Goerne, baritone, Harmonia Mundi, 2014 (Lieder of Franz Schubert)

DIANA DAMRAU (1971–)

Diana Damrau is a soprano from Bavaria. She is known for her operatic performances in the opera houses of Germany and is especially known for her rendition of Mozart's Queen of the Night role from *The Magic Flute.* Damrau is also a frequent interpreter of song literature, with piano and orchestra. She brings a significant intelligence to her singing and is not afraid to modify her voice in order to better express an emotion or word. She has performed her home country's Lieder at many festivals, including in Munich and Salzburg, and in the great performance halls of the world such as Carnegie Hall and La Scala. Her success with song has been evident in its reception from critics and the public. Her recording of Strauss songs with orchestra earned her the "Lieder recording of the year" prize from the German Phono-Akademie's Echo Klassik awards. It is evident that Ms. Damrau takes seriously the German tradition of excellent Lieder singers as she continues the tradition into the twenty-first century.

Recordings

Lieder, Diana Damrau, soprano, Helmut Deutsch, piano, Orfeo, 2008 (Songs of Clara and Robert Schumann, Fanny and Felix Mendelssohn, Brahms, Chopin, and Liszt)
Liszt Lieder, Diana Damrau, soprano, Helmut Deutsch, piano, Erato, 2011
Poesie, Diana Damrau, soprano, Virgin Classics, 2011 (Songs of Richard Strauss with orchestra)

SONG LIST

The following song list includes important songs of the German repertory but is not a comprehensive listing. With Schubert contributing over six hundred songs alone, one list would be a book in itself! Listeners will benefit from studying the songs below for an overview of German Lieder.

J. S. Bach

Bist du bei mir
Mein liebster Jesus is verloren
Nimm mich dir zu eigen hin

Ludwig van Beethoven

Adelaide
An die ferne Geliebte
    Auf dem Hügel sitz ich spähend
    Wo die Berge so blau
    Leichte Seglen in den Höhen
    Diese wolken in den Höhen
    Es kehret der Maien, se blühet die Au
    Nimm sie hin denn, diese Lieder
An die Hoffnung
Sechs geistliche Lieder
Sehnsucht
Wonne der Wehmut

Alban Berg

Altenberg Lieder
Der Wein
    Die Seele des Weines
    Der Wein der Liebenden
    Der sonderbare blick der leichten frauen

Jugendlieder (selections from 46 songs)
Abschied
Am Abend
Augenblicke
Die Nachtigall
Die Näherin
Die Soldatenbraut
Erster Verlust
Ferne Lieder
Furcht
Geliebte Schöne
Grabschrift
Heiliger Himmel
Ich liebe dich!
Ich will die Fluren meiden
Ich und du
Im Morgengrauen
Im Walde
Im Zimmer
Liebe
Liebeslied
Liebesode
Nacht
Nachtgesang
O wär mein Lieb' jen' Röslein Rot
Schattenleben
Scheidelied
Sehnsucht I, II
So regnet es sich langsam ein
Sommertage
Spaziergang
Traum
Über meinen Nächten
Unter der Linde
Vom Ende
Was zucken die braunen Geigen
Wenn Gespenster auferstehen
Wo der Goldregen steht
Sieben frühe Lieder
Nacht
Schilflied
Die Nachtigall
Traumgekrönt

Im Zimmer
Liebesode
Sommertage

Johannes Brahms

Auf dem Kirchhofe
Botschaft
Dein blaues Auge
Der Jäger
Der Schmied
Der Tod, das ist die kühle Nacht
Die Mainacht
Es träumte mir
Feldeinsamkeit
Immer leiser wird mein Schlummer
Meine Liebe ist grün
Nicht mehr zu dir zu gehen
O liebliche Wangen
O wüsst ich doch den Weg
Sapphische Ode
Sonntag
Ständchen
Vier ernst Gesänge
    Denn es gehet dem Menschen wie dem Vieh
    Ich wandte mich und sahe an alle
    O Tod, wie bitter bist du
    Wenn ich mit Menschen
Vergebliches Ständchen
Verrat
Von ewiger Liebe
Wie bist du, meine Königen
Wie Melodien zieht es
Wir Wandelten
Zigeunerlieder

Franz Joseph Haydn

A Pastoral Song
Piercing Eyes
She Never Told Her Love
The Mermaid's Song
The Sailor's Song

Johann Carl Gottfried Loewe

Edward
Erlkönig
Wanderers Nachtlied

Gustav Mahler

Das Knaben Wunderhorn
Der Schildwache Nachtlied
Verlorne müh!
Trost im Unglück
Wer hat dies Liedlein erdacht?
Das irdische Leben
Des Antonius von Padua Fischpredigt
Rheinlegendchen
Lied des Verfolgten im Turm
Wo die schönen Trompeten blasen
Lob des hohen Verstandes
Revelge
Der Tambourgesell
Es sungen drei Engel
Urlicht
Das himmlische Leben
Das Lied von der Erde
Das Trinklied vom Jammer der Erde
Der Einsame im Herbst
Von der Jugend
Von der Schönheit
Der Trunkene im Frühling
Der Abschied
Ich atmet' einen linden Duft'
Ich bin der Welt abhanden gekommen
Kindertotenlieder
Nun will die Sonn' so hell aufgehn
Nun seh' ich wohl, warum so dunkle Flammen
Wenn dein Mütterlein
Oft denk' ich, sie sind nur ausgegangen
In diesem Wetter
Liebst du um Schönheit
Lieder aus Des Knaben Wunderhorn
Rückert Lieder
Wer hat dies Liedlein erdacht

Felix Mendelssohn

Auf Flügeln des Gesanges
Bei der Wiege
Das erste Veilchen
Der Blumenkranz
Herbstlied
Maienlied
Nachtlied
Neue Liebe
Winterlied

Wolfgang Amadeus Mozart

Als Luise die Briefe ihres ungetreuen Liebhabers
Das Veilchen
Der Zauberer
Die Alte
Die kleine Spinnerin
Die Verschweigung
Lied der Freiheit
Sehnsucht nach dem Frühling
Warnung

Arnold Schoenberg

Brettl-Lieder
Das Buch der hängenden Gärten
Gurrelieder
Pierrot Lunaire

C. F. Schubart

Abendlied eines Mädchens
    Abschieds-Lied, bey der Abreise ins Mohrenland
    Am Grabe der Mutter
    An den Mond
    An die Geliebte
    Ballade
    Der Frühlingsabend
    Der Gefangene
    Der Kohlenbrenner
    Die Erscheinung
    Die Forelle

Die Henne
Kaplied
Liebesklage
Lied eines Schwabenmädchens
Luise an Wilhelm
Mädchen Laune
Weihnachtslied der Hirten
Winterlied

Franz Schubert

Abendlied
Adelaide
Am Flusse
Am See
An den Mond
An die Leier
An die Musik
An die Nachtigall
An die Sonne
An Sylvia
Auf dem Wasser zu singen
Aufenthalt
Augenlied
Blumenlied
Das Bild
Das Dörfchen
Geheimes
Das Grab
Der Doppelgänger
Der Einsame
Der Fluß
Der greise Kopf
Der Hirt
Der Jüngling am Bache
Der Knabe in der Wiege
Der Morgenstern
Der Musensohn
Der Rattenfänger
Der Strom
Der Tod und das Mädchen
Der Zwerg
Des Mädchens Klage

Die Allmacht
Die Forelle
DiejJunge Nonne
Die Liebe hat gelogen
Die Mainacht
Die Mondnacht
Die Nacht
Die Nachtigall
Die Spinnerin
Die Schöne Müllerin
    Das Wandern
    Wohin?
    Halt!
    Danksagung an den Bach
    Am Feierabend
    Der Neugierige
    Ungeduld
    Morgengruß
    Des Müllers Blumen
    Tränenregen
    Mein!
    Pause
    Mit dem grunen Lautenbande
    Der Jäger
    Eifersucht und Stolz
    Die liebe Farbe
    Die böse Farbe
    Trockne Blumen
    Der Müller und der Bach
    Des Baches Wiegenlied
Du bist die Ruh
Erlkönig
Frühlingsglaube
Ganymed
Geheimes
Gretchen am Spinnrade
Heidenröslein
Hoffnung
Im Abendrot
Im Frühling
Jägers Abendlied
Jägers Liebslied
Liebe schwärmt auf allen Wegen

Lied der Mignon
Mignon und der Harfner
Mignons Gesang
Mondenschein
Nacht und Träume
Nachtgesang
Nur wer die Sehnsucht kennt
Rastlose Liebe
Romanze
Schlaflied
Sehnsucht
Seligkeit
Ständchen
Versunken
Vor meiner Wiege
Waldesnacht
Wanderers Nachtlied
Wehmut
Wiegenlied
Winterlied
Winterreise
   Gute Nacht
   Die Wetterfahne
   Gefrorene Tränen
   Erstarrung
   Der Lindenbaum
   Wasserflut
   Auf dem Flusse
   Rückblick
   Irrlicht
   Rast
   Frühlingstraum
   Einsamkeit
   Die Post
   Der greise Kopf
   Die Krähe
   Letzte Hoffnung
   Im Dorfe
   Der stürmische Morgen
   Täuschung
   Der Wegweiser
   Das Wirtshaus
   Mut

Die Nebensonnen
Der Leiermann
Zur guten Nacht

Robert Schumann

Aufträge
Aus den hebräischen Gesängen
Belsazar
Dein Angesicht
Dichterliebe
 Im wunderschönen Monat Mai
 Aus meinen Tränen spriessen
 Die Rose, die Lilie, die Taube, die Sonne
 Wenn ich in deine Augen seh'
 Ich will meine Seele tauchen
 Im Rhein, im heiligen Strome
 Ich grolle nicht
 Und wüßten's die Blumen, die kleinen
 Das ist ein Flöten und Geigen
 Hör' ich das Liedchen klingen
 Ein Jüngling liebt ein Mädchen
 Am leuchtenden Sommermorgen
 Ich hab' im Traum geweinet
 Allnächtlich im Traume seh' ich dich
 Aus alten Märchen winkt es
 Die alten, bösen Lieder
Die Kartenlegerin
Erstes Grün
Frauenliebe und leben
 Seit ich ihn gesehen
 Er, der Herrlichste von Allen
 Ich kann's nicht fassen, nicht glauben
 Der Ring an meinem Finger
 Helft mir, ihr schwestern
 Süsser Freund, du blickest
 An meinen Herzen, an meiner Brust
 Nun hast du mir den esten Schmerz getan
Liederkreis
 In der Fremde
 Intermezzo
 Waldegespräch
 Die Stille

Mondnacht
Schöne Fremde
Auf einer Burg
Wehmut
Zwielicht
In Walde
Frühlingsnacht
Die Lotosblume
Die Soldatenbraut
Der Nussbaum
Schöne Wiege
Schneeglöcken
Widmung
Wilhelm Meister Songs
   Ballade des Harfners
   Nur wer die Sehnsucht kennt
   Wer nie sein Brot mit tränen aß
   Heiss mich nicht reden
   Wer sich der Einsamkeit ergibt
   Singet nicht in Trauertönen
   An die Türen will ich schleichen
   So lasst mich scheinen

Richard Strauss

Ach Lieb, ich muss nun scheiden
Allerseelen
All mein Gedanken
Befreit
Breit' über mein Haupt
Brentano Lieder
Cäcilie
Die Nacht
Du meines herzens Krönelein
Freundliche Vision
Ich schwebe
Ich trage meine Minne
Heimkehr
Heimliche Aufforderung
Glückes genug
Kling!
Mein Herz ist stumm
Morgen

Nacht
Nachtgang
Nichts
Ruhe, meine Seele
Schlagende Herzen
Schön sind, doch kalt
Schlechtes Wetter
Seitdem dein Aug'
Ständchen
Stille Tränen
Traum durch die Dämmerung
Vier lezte Lieder
Wie sollten wir geheim sie halten
Wiegenlied
Wozu noch Mädchen
Die Zeitlose
Zueignung

Anton Webern

Acht frühe Lieder
    Aufblick
    Blumengruß
    Bild der Liebe
    Sommerabend
    Heiter
    Der Tod
    Heimgang in der Frühe
Die Freunde
    Wie bin ich froh!
    Des Herzens Purpurvogel
    Stern, ihr silbernen Bienen
Drei Gesänge
    Vorfrühling
    Nachtgebet der Braut
    Fromm
Fünf geistliche Lieder
    Das Kreuz
    Morgenlied
    In Gottes Namen aufstehn
    Mein Weg geht jetzt vorüber
    Fahr hin, O Seel', zu deinem Gott
Sechs Lieder nach Gedichten von Georg Trakl

Kurt Weill

Frauentanz
   Wir haben die winterlange Nacht
   Wo zwei Herzenliebe
   Ach wär mein Lieb ein Brünnlein kalt
   Dieser Stern im Dunkeln
   Eines Maienmorgens schön
   Ich will Trauern lassen stehn
   Ich schlaf, ich wach
Ofrahs Lieder
   In meinem Garten stehn zwei Rosen
   Nichts ist wie Welt mir
   Er sah mir liebend in die Augen
   Denkst du des kühnen Flugs der Nacht
   Nur dir fürwahr
Three Songs
   Song of Sexual Slavery
   Le grand Lustucru
   Surabaya Johnny
Three Walt Whitman Songs
   O Captain! My Captain!
   Beat! Beat! Drums!
   Dirge for Two Veterans

Hugo Wolf

Anakreons Grab
Auch kleine Dinge
Auf ein altes Bild
Auf einer Wanderung
Das Italienisches Liederbuch
Das Spanisches Liederbuch
Das verlassene Mägdlein
Der Feuerreiter
Der Gärtner
Der Rattenfänger
Die ihr schwebet
Die Zigeunerin
Elfenlied
Er ist's
Fussreise
Ganymed

Gebet
Herr, was trägt der Boden hier
Ich hab in Penna
Im Frühling
In dem Schatten meiner Locken
In der Frühe
Mausfallen-Sprüchlein
Mignon
Nachtzauber
Nixe Binsefuss
Nun wandre, Maria
Verborgenheit

Johann Zumsteeg

Kleine Balladen und Lieder
   Ritter Toggenburg
   Ahndung
   Una
   Alles um Liebe
   An Ida
   Liebe
   Nachtgesang
   Schlachtgesang
   Minnelied
   Robert und Käthe
   Rundgesang
   Klagelied
   Sehnsucht
   An die Flasche
   Melancholikon

Chapter Seven

French Mélodie

Early French Song

Throughout the nineteenth century, French song became the height of sophistication of the song genre. The evolution of French song was similar to that of other European countries; the early song forms were strongly related to folk music. Throughout the Renaissance period, singing was taking place both among the common people and in the royal courts. The major song form of the French Renaissance was the "troubadour song," performed by the troubadours and trouvères of southern and northern France, respectively. These men were both musicians and poets, often from the aristocracy, who placed the importance of poetry above all else.

The melodies of troubadour songs were of a small range and could be highly ornamented by the performer. Equally important to the melody was the poetry used in the songs and therefore the development of the troubadour and trouvère songs was largely a literary movement. The themes of these songs were subjects such as courtly love and nature.

It was considered a clever and useful skill to be able to create original poetry and set it to song; therefore, singers were popular and respected for their craft during this time. These roving, performing musicians and poets spoke and wrote in two distinct languages that are different from the modern French we know today. The troubadours of southern France engaged the "langue d'oc" or "Old Provençal" and the trouvères of northern France used the "langue d'oil" or "Old French." The troubadour songs were very popular and peaked during the thirteenth century coinciding with the age of chivalry. There are approximately 264 troubadour melodies, and over 1,400 trouvère surviving melodies. Despite the great number of songs in the repertoire, they are hard to find in print and rarely performed today.

One of the most popular trouvères was Thibaut de Navarre (1201–1253) who was Count of Champagne and, later, King of Navarre. He personified the idea of courtly love as he was reportedly in love with the wife of Louis VIII of France, Blanche of Castile, and wrote many of his songs with her in mind.[1]

The next years brought about the development of ars nova (new art). Ars nova was a musical style of the late Middle Ages (fourteenth century) which was identified in a treatise written by composer Philippe de Vitry. The treatise defined a system for notating music. The motet, a musical piece scored for several individual voices, developed throughout the next two centuries. The motet was scored for two, three, four, or more voices and continued to grow and inspire forms known as ballades and rondeaux.

The sixteenth century brought about an interim phase between polyphonic song (vocal writing for two or more voices) and solo song. Composers began to score their motets, and other polyphonic compositions, with a voice in the top part and instruments, such as the lute, in the lower parts as accompaniment. Before the eighteenth century, the song form was in flux and constantly evolving.

PRE-EIGHTEENTH CENTURY

In the early part of the seventeenth century, the most popular solo song forms were the "air de cour" and the "recit." Their accompaniments were most likely a lute, guitar, and later, a harpsichord. The "air de cour" was subdivided into other forms and types named for the subject matter of their texts. Among the most important of these were the bergerettes and pastourelles (shepherd and shepherdess pieces), the chansons à boire and chansons à danser (drinking and dance songs), and romances, which were a direct continuation of the Medieval troubadour songs. The songs were usually brief and included repetition. The songs most closely resembled the early Italian air and the English lute song. The musical texture of these songs was not ornate. The "recit" was the counterpart of the Italian solo madrigal, and was freer in style than the "air de cour" with more ornamented passages.

In general, French monodic song did not emphasize melody in the same way as Italian song did at that time. It makes sense, then, that the French paid much attention to the text of a poem when composing the melody and were much less interested in text repetition than the Italians. The Italians were highly focused on the melody due to the cross influences of the opera culture flourishing in their country.

In general, during the seventeenth century in France and other parts of Europe, composition for the voice had an emphasis on opera. In fact, vocal writing in seventeenth century France was mostly dominated by the popular operas of Jean-Baptiste Lully, which were considered innovative and exciting. In spite of the domination of opera, further development of the solo song did occur; for example, chamber cantatas (originated in Italy) were popular with composers like Jean-Philippe Rameau, Dominique Clérambault, and Michel de Montéclair.

Unfortunately, there is not much remaining song of the seventeenth century available today. This is possibly due to the lack of music publishing and printing at the time. The decline of the romance, Schubert Lieder, and the impact of romantic poetry all contributed to the development of the mélodie as the most important song form in France.

EIGHTEENTH CENTURY

The eighteenth century in France brought about the "romance" song form. The romance was a direct counterpart to the German "volkstümliches Lied," the descendant of the troubadour song, and the forerunner to the mélodie. The form was basically a couplet form in verse and had a simple musical realization. It did not have elaborate melodies. The text and themes of the romance were usually tragic love stories.

The romance continued to develop throughout the century and eventually split into two types; one in which musical and text expression were the first considerations and one that was Italianate in style and featured melody above all else. The troubadour song and the romance was to French song what folksong was to lieder composers. As the romance continued to develop throughout the century, its traits were somewhat simple, strophic in form, and focused on romantic subjects.

As the century continued, German and Italian influences began to encourage more development of the accompaniment to heighten the expression of performance. From 1815 onward, the romance began to decline and broke into many forms, including the barcarolle, nocturne, and tarantelle. After 1825, the romance was in complete decay and became incidental to the newest form of French song: the mélodie.

NINETEENTH CENTURY

French song came into its own during the nineteenth century. The previous hundreds of years of song evolution developed into a cohesive style and sensibility that was uniquely French: the mélodie. Composers began to fully embrace the trait that would define the next hundred years of song: the art of suggestion. The idea of suggestion in song can be difficult to define. It is woven through every element of song. The Germans had the idea of symbolism in their poetry; one work or phrase meaning something different than what was stated. The nature of French suggestion is more subtle. For example, the texts of songs are often only "suggesting" meaning and are highly interpretive for the listener. The use of rhythm and harmony are not always to be taken at face value but investigated for hidden meaning by the listener.

During the romantic era of the nineteenth century, the mélodie continued to develop from the foundation of the romance to a more free form of song. There was a new vocal declamation that was strongly related to the influence of language on composers as well as an increased expressiveness in the accompaniment.

HECTOR BERLIOZ (1803–1869)

Hector Berlioz was a truly transitional and seminal force in the history of French song. Berlioz was the first composer to call his short vocal pieces "mélodies." His period of composition represented the transition from romance to mélodie. All of the elements of songs of the past several centuries came together and marked a new era in French song through his music. Since Berlioz, "mélodie" has become the generic term for French song. Berlioz' stature and significance in song history is ironic since song is certainly not his best-known genre of composition; he is much better known for his orchestral works and opera. No matter the genre, the music of Berlioz personifies many French artistic ideals such as clarity, elegance, and intense emotion.

Berlioz' cycle of six songs, *Les nuits d'été* (The Summer Nights), was composed in 1841 with poems by Théophile Gautier. The cycle consists of six songs: "Villanelle," "Le spectre de la rose," "Sur les lagunes," "Absence," "Au cimetière," and "L'île inconnue." The melodies have long vocal lines, and vary between very expressive and subtle moods. The texture of the piece is contrapuntal. The songs were first written for voice and piano, then orchestrated over ten years later and are often performed with orchestra today.

Paris, 1843: It is spring in Paris and a few aristocratic music patrons of the city are gathered in a grandiose sitting room after finishing a three-hour dinner. The evening's events are hosted by Mlle. Grimeaux and there are two special guests in attendance. The hostess announces that anyone is welcome to make a musical offering as entertainment for the guests. One young man performs a song by Mozart, another determined patroness plays two Chopin nocturnes, and Mlle. Grimeaux herself sings an aria from Jean-Baptiste Lully's opera Alceste *with one of the special guests at the piano. When she is finished, she announces from the curve of the grand piano, "I would like to ask my friend and guest to play for us. He happens to be the finest musician in France and he is Hector Berlioz." The guests are surprised, excited, and in disbelief that they are in the same room with the man who wrote the* Symphonie fantastique*! Berlioz reaches his hand out to the other special guest that no one seems to know. She is very beautiful and elegant and moves toward the piano with purpose. Taking her hand, Berlioz announces, "The soprano, Marie Recio, and I will perform songs from my new work* Les nuits d'été*. I hope you enjoy." Berlioz begins the opening notes of* "Villanelle" *and the small audience is transported.*

GABRIEL FAURÉ (1845–1924)

The peak of the French mélodie was parallel to the career of Gabriel Fauré. Fauré was a trained organist and taught composition at the Paris Conservatory where he later served as director. As is typical with many composers throughout history, his situation and lifestyle required him to earn a living through multiple forms of employment. He was a professional organist, choirmaster, teacher, and director. Despite the competing demands of his various jobs and family responsibilities, he was the most advanced composer of his generation.

Fauré certainly benefitted from the fact that by the time he wrote his first compositions around 1865, the German Lied was already a firmly established and highly developed genre. As a composer, he was able to draw and learn from composers who had come before him.

His musical style was firmly rooted in classicism yet it continued to evolve and change throughout his career. Unlike more limited composers, Fauré was able to avoid stasis in his compositional style by improving upon his own work. He was an extremely inventive composer. His harmonic and melodic style included the nontraditional use of modes and dissonances which aided in his creation of coloristic effects. The effects anticipated the more impressionistic French song that would come later in the century and into the next. Fauré's compositional inventiveness greatly influenced the teaching of harmony during his lifetime and beyond as young composers were drawn to his new and exciting work. He expanded the idea of what was thought possible in song composition. Because of his influence, he was generally considered the most advanced composer of his generation.

Fauré's basic style reflects a total unified presentation of sophisticated musical elements. No one element is completed separate from the other in his work. The melodic line grows out of the harmony, the harmonic flavor is strongly reflected in the texture of the accompaniment, the accompaniment makes use of arpeggios and repeated chords. Above all else, Fauré emphasizes vocal melody in his songs. The expression of melody is of paramount importance and enhanced by his use of rhythmic patterns that strongly adhere to a poetic structure.

Posthumously, and similarly to many composers, his works are generally thought of in three distinct style periods: early, middle (transitioning between the nineteenth and twentieth centuries), and late (after age sixty). Unfortunately, not all of Fauré's one hundred songs survive today but there is enough work left to give the world an appreciation of his genius and his elegance.

Rêve d'amour is an early song of Fauré's that encapsulates his ability to write graceful melodic lines. His melody flows from one phrase into the next while offering harmonic and rhythmic surprises along the way.

Song Title	Rêve d'amour
Year of Composition	1864
Composer	Gabriel Fauré
Language	French
Poet	Victor Hugo
Text	Highly romantic
Voice	Requires true legato for the sake of lyrical phrasing and the French language
Piano	Charming rising and falling pattern in the left hand that anchors the piece
Mood	Pleasant
Form	Strophic
Melody	Lyrical, mostly lies in the middle and upper middle range
Harmony	Tonal, with some subtle dissonance
Tempo	Lively, moderately fast
What to listen for	The French language is set perfectly in the melody for optimum pronunciation of the French sounds. Fauré is able to seamlessly weave the melody and piano together.

1958 Johannesburg, South Africa: It is September 29th and an audience has gathered to hear baritone Gérard Souzay and pianist Dalton Baldwin perform a song recital for the Johannesburg Musical Society. The program features songs of G. F. Handel, Maurice Ravel, Robert Schumann, and Gabriel Fauré. Mr. Souzay has just sung three songs from the Fauré set: "Après un rêve," "Mai," *and* "Tristesse" *and is about the sing the final song of the set. The last song is* "Toujours" *and the highly romantic text is evocative of a great drama. The concluding verse reads in the program:* "But do not hope *that my soul can uproot its sorrow and douse its flame, as the spring-time can shed its flowers!" Mr. Dalton begins. The piano is rhythmic and has a desperate feel from the start. It has a kind of surging and unfilled mood that is the opposite of contentment. Mr. Souzay begins to sing about leaving the one he loves and how that would be impossible: "you might more easily ask the stars to fall from the sky." The melody is not rushed, but moving forward very quickly in anticipation of an eventual resolution. Mr. Souzay's voice is the epitome of lyrical warmth. He sings with a strength that is always infused with sensitivity to the meaning and emotion of the poem. His French is, of course, flawless and every syllable, nasal vowel, and closed vowel sound is pristine and easily understandable. The vocal line never deviates from true legato and the voice is always sparkling with resonance. By the time Mr. Souzay sings "Comme le printemps de ses fleurs," the song begins to come to a dramatic conclusion as he sings "fleurs" on a double forte dynamic and the piano rolls towards a strong final chord. The room is completely still for at least five full seconds and Souzay and Dalton are frozen in place. The entire audience bursts into loud and sincere applause for almost two full minutes at the conclusion of the Fauré set, knowing that they have never heard a French song sung to perfection before.*

CLAUDE DEBUSSY (1862–1918)

From 1892 to 1902, Claude Debussy perfected impressionism in song. What exactly impressionism is and how it manifests itself in song is a discussion that continues among scholars and music critics. His inventive and original composition style moved away from classicism toward impressionism. He composed about eighty-seven songs in the typical three style periods. Debussy is known for his precise expression of the song form. His style is based on the musical idea of symmetry and parallelism (as opposed to contrapuntal techniques). He changed the idea of what direction a melody should take in song and made it acceptable to truly loosen the forms and traditions from the classical era.

While the melody was of principal importance to Fauré, harmony was the most important element of Debussy's style. He practiced chromaticism as a technique. Chromaticism is a way to use the scale so one octave is divided into twelve equal intervals of semitones. The chromatic scale consists of all twelve notes in an octave on the piano keyboard. He made use of chords for coloristic effect and in parallel motion.

He kept the form of a song open so it would sound somewhat spontaneous. Unresolved dissonances also added to the improvisational quality. His melodic writing often used unequal phrase lengths with a less structured accompaniment. As his style developed, the piano was used less to support the voice and it became its own entity. Like other composers, Debussy often grouped his songs together. His song cycles included: *Ariettes oubliées* (1903), *Cinq poèmes de Baudelaire* (1890), *Trois mélodies* (1891), *Proses lyriques* (1895), and *Chansons de Bilitis* (1897).

His *Chansons de Bilitis* were his first songs to fully incorporate rhythms of speech. Debussy was seriously concerned that the voice yield to the demands of the poetry.

Song Title	Nuit d'étoiles
Year of Composition	1879
Composer	Claude Debussy
Language	French
Poet	Théodore de Banville
Text	Themes of nature and love
Voice	Even phrases and high tessitura
Piano	Debussy utilizes rolled chords in the introduction to create a feeling of night, there is much movement in the right hand throughout
Mood	Romantic
Form	Strophic
Melody	Large range and lyric in nature
Harmony	Some dissonances
Tempo	Allegro
What to listen for	Debussy creates the mood of a night of stars from the first measure by using a technique of softly rolling chords. He is able to weave dissonances effortlessly within the piano part.

JULES MASSENET (1842–1912)

Jules Massenet began studying piano at age ten and eventually became an accomplished pianist. As an adult, he gained a reputation as a composer of opera and had much success in this arena. His operas *Manon*, *Werther*, and *Cendrillon* are still performed today. Massenet is one of the most prolific of all French song composers with approximately 260 compositions. He created a salon ambience with his songs and they were most often performed in the salon environment. Massenet's preferred method of composition was opera and the same interest and care he gave to vocal writing in opera was also applied to his songs. His songs have all the charm and grace expected of French music but over the years have not received as much attention as those by other French composers. It is possible that his operatic works have over-shadowed his other vocal works, like songs and oratorio.

In addition to his great skills as a composer and pianist, Massenet was also known as a caring and judicious teacher and was a popular professor of composition at the Paris Conservatory.

HENRI DUPARC (1848–1933)

Henri Duparc may have only contributed sixteen songs to the French reper-toire but almost all have had significance. His songs are both imaginative and individual in character. Duparc's harmonic texture is based on extensive chromaticism.

He was a perfectionist and practiced self-criticism of his own work. He often revised and polished compositions before letting them be heard. He wrote supple and lyric vocal lines and had a rich harmonic structure. He sought out modest singers to work with and was not fond of vocal exhibition-ism.

ERNEST CHAUSSON (1855–1899)

Chausson came to music rather late after much education in law. He studied composition with Massenet who was impressed by his skills. He was happily married and enjoyed spending time away from Paris in the country where he had a home salon that was very active with artists of the day.

His works in many genres are viewed posthumously in three major peri-ods over which his musical abilities continued to mature. Chausson's songs encompass all the charming traits of French music; perfectly set text that lends itself to true legato, rhythmic interest in the piano that always comple-ments the voice, and a true melding of components that work together to produce a quintessentially French song. "Le charme" is just one example.

Song Title	Le charme
Year of Composition	1879
Composer	Ernest Chausson
Language	French
Poet	Armand Silvestre
Text	Subdued and intellectual

Voice	Requires true legato and perfect phrasing
Piano	Complimentary to voice, not competing
Mood	"Charming"
Form	Roughly ABA
Melody	Middle voice only
Harmony	Tonal
Tempo	Moderate with motion
What to listen for	Chausson has perfected the "charme" of the title in the music. He sets each phrase with an accessible conversational tone, even while sung. The piano part is quite supple and completely responsive to the voice. It is not at all independent. He is confident enough to not insist on a "big finish" at the end, but encapsulates the irony of "your first tear," with a quiet and perfect completion that suggests sensuality.

FRENCH POETRY IN THE NINETEENTH CENTURY

The early French composers were inspired by the poetry of Théophile Gautier, Victor Hugo, and Charles Baudelaire. Paul Verlaine's poetry was the touchstone for mélodie in the nineteenth century.

In general, poetry of different line lengths encouraged an irregularity of melodic line. The poetry of the nineteenth century was more subtle than that of the German Lied.

The Parnassians, 1866–1876, was a group of poets who were reacting against the lyricism and emotionalism of the Romantics. Composers also set poetry by the Parnassian poets, who were inspired by Greek poetry. The group's motto was "art for art's sake." The movement was a reaction to the idea that art should be in service to humanity. The poets were more concerned with the perfection of form than with pure emotion. Poets in the group included Théophile Gautier, Claude de Lisle, Théodore de Banville, and Sully Prudhomme.

Symbolism was a literary movement that only lasted about a dozen years starting in 1885.[2] The movement personified mystery and suggestiveness. It was up to the reader to interpret the meaning. The movement was considered a revolt against descriptive realism. The purpose of symbolist poems was to let the reader delve into his own dreams, sensations, and emotional life. Symbolist poets include Charles Baudelaire, Paul Verlaine, Arthur Rimbaud, and Stéphane Mallarmé.

TWENTIETH CENTURY

The songs of twentieth century France reflected a period of experimentation. The forms and patterns of the past blurred into songs influenced by other genres such as jazz, theatre, and literature.

LES SIX

"Les Six" was the group of French composers Louis Durey, Germaine Tailleferre, Georges Auric, Arthur Honegger, Darius Milhaud, and Francis Poulenc. The group received its name from an article published by Henri Collet in 1920. As a whole, the group emphasized texture and clarity. Their songs demonstrated rhythmic complexity and showed the influence of jazz. The composers shared common goals and they found inspiration for composition in music halls, the circus, jazz clubs, and popular song of the day.

FRANCIS POULENC (1899–1963)

Poulenc was a composer who was clear about who had influenced his career. The dedication to his opera *Dialogues of the Carmelites* reads; "To the memory of my mother who revealed music to me, to Claude Debussy, who inspired me to compose, to Claudio Monteverdi, Giuseppe Verdi, Modest Mussorgsky, who in this work were my models."[3] Poulenc began piano lessons with his mother as a boy.

Poulenc met the man who would be his professional partner for twenty-five years in the spring of 1934. Pierre Bernac was asked to perform at a private party in Salzburg. He says the meeting of Poulenc was predestined. It was a very romantic setting with a piano set up outdoors under a linden tree. Poulenc played the piano and Bernac sang at exactly midnight that evening. Both men were thirty-five years old. Poulenc and Bernac performed in recital together for over twenty years.

Overall, Poulenc's compositional style is both eclectic and highly personal. His personality is especially evident in his piano writing; for example, he made extensive pedal markings to indicate what he expected in performance. As a composer, Poulenc was partial to the poetry of his own time. His vocal writing is varied, but always related to the poem at hand. His melodic writing can be lush and lyrical and also fanciful with patter-like lyrics, also seen in Leonard Bernstein's songs. His songs range from fanciful and patter-like, to tender and lyrical.

Poulenc's song cycle, *La courte paille* (the short straw), is the epitome of how charming French song can be. At only seven minutes in length, the songs perfectly illustrate the child-centric texts while creating musical appeal for adults.

Song Title	"Lune d'avril" (April moon) from *La courte paille*
Year of Composition	1934
Composer	Francis Poulenc
Language	French
Poet	Maurice Carême
Text	Haunting and deceptively dark
Voice	Shifting dynamics throughout
Piano	Sparse mostly
Mood	Haunting
Form	Roughly through-composed
Melody	Sense of stillness, short phrases
Harmony	Quiet dissonances
Tempo	"Very slow and unreal" (composer marking)
What to listen for	The mystery and darkness of the poem is perfectly reflected in the stillness and haunting quality of the piano. Poulenc keeps the piece at a very quiet dynamic until the words, "where there is joy, where there is light, where sunny with primroses . . ." He then brings the dynamic up to a fortissimo for effect. Listen very carefully to the last two measures of the piece. Poulenc made several markings for the pianist, including "pppp."

Spring, 1934, Salzburg: Francis Poulenc was in Salzburg to review several musical productions as a critic for Le Figaro *and also to perform a few concerts. Pierre Bernac was there to study repertoire with Reinhold von Wahrlich.* [4] *There is a story that a wealthy American woman had rented a house in Salzburg through the summer that overlooked the famous Mirabell Gardens. She knew Bernac and asked him if he would sing a few songs at a private concert she was giving during a music festival featuring the works of Debussy. Bernac said "yes" and decided to ask Poulenc, whom he already knew, to accompany him. In one evening of the festival, there was an orches-tral work by Debussy featured at the Mozarteum (conducted by Herbert von Karajan), followed by his ballet "L'Après-midi d'un faune" in the open gardens of Mirabell, and finally, after the audience had climbed over a garden wall on a ladder into the woman's private garden, they encountered a piano under a linden tree. Bernac has described the recital of Debussy mélodies with Poulenc at the piano as "beginning at the stroke of midnight."*[5] *It is difficult to imagine what the audience was thinking at the historical performance. They were most likely not aware they were witnessing the beginning of one of the most enduring musical relationships in the twentieth century.*

REYNALDO HAHN (1874–1947)

Hahn received a Paris Conservatory education and studied with Jules Massenet. He performed for royalty as a young musician, worked in Paris as a music critic and later as director of the Paris Opera starting in 1945. Hahn was an accomplished baritone and often accompanied himself on his own songs in performance. He was a diverse artist, writing opera and songs and also writing as a music critic for journals like *La Presse* and *La Flèche.*[6]

His musical style is marked by graceful lyrical voice writing and uncomplicated harmonic language. He rejected the complexities of Debussy's harmony, preferring a more traditional harmonic language.

Hahn was of Jewish ancestry and was forced to spend part of World War II in hiding from the Nazis. They banned his music during the occupation of France (1940–1944), yet while in hiding, Hahn continued to compose.[7]

DARIUS MILHAUD (1892–1974)

Darius Milhaud is one of the most influential and diverse French composers in history. His influence can be felt in the United States today through the music of his former student, American composer William Bolcom. Milhaud studied at the Paris Conservatory, and like Reynaldo Hahn, was an accomplished baritone.

He was an active member of Les Six and held many of the group's meetings at his home. He was probably the most prolific songwriter of the group with some 265 songs contributed to the genre. Milhaud spent a great deal of time travelling and the influences of the places he travelled and enjoyed influenced his music, including Brazil, and the jazz he heard in London in the 1920s.

Milhaud wrote for many genres, including ballet, theatre, instrumental, orchestras, film, opera, and song. Musically, his songs include his forward-thinking polytonality and complex harmonies yet are always woven with charm, a distinct style, and cohesive form.

As a prominent Jewish musician in 1940 France, Milhaud was negatively identified by the German government and he thought it best to immigrate to the United States. Mills College in Oakland, California, offered him a teaching position. He has been described as a very good teacher who understood the importance of students experimenting with established forms.

Milhaud's group of four songs, *Chansons de Ronsard*, were originally scored for small orchestra and voice and have also been reduced for voice and piano, a common practice. These songs are most appropriate for a soprano with a very high range and are unusual for that reason.

"A une Fontaine" from Milhaud's *Chansons de Ronsard* is the first song of four. The waltz rhythm and stratospheric high notes make for a highly entertaining song about a fountain.

Song Title	"A une Fontaine" from *Chansons de Ronsard* (originally scored for voice and small orchestra)
Year of Composition	1917
Composer	Darius Milhaud
Language	French
Poet	Pierre de Ronsard (sixteenth century)
Text	Traditional couplets, ode to a fountain
Voice	Required to sing in an unusually high tessitura
Piano	Waltz elements with much chordal movement
Mood	Light-hearted
Form	Roughly ABA with coda
Melody	Wide-ranging and often above the staff
Harmony	Dissonant throughout
Tempo	Movement of a waltz
What to listen for	Milhaud creates immediate interest in the prelude by offering the traditional waltz form paired with nontraditional harmonies. The voice part soars above the staff with several unusually high pitches, sustained and quick. The vocal part is very challenging to keep light and graceful. Despite all the dissonance, the waltz comes off as a cohesive piece from beginning to end.

Other noted French song composers include: Maurice Ravel (1875–1937), Jacques Ibert (1890–1962), Henri Sauguet (1901–1989), Olivier Messiaen (1908–1992), Erik Satie (1866–1925), and Albert Roussel (1869–1937).

WELL-KNOWN FRENCH SINGERS AND THEIR SONGS

The following French singers have encompassed the best of song and opera performance and have had distinguished careers.

PIERRE BERNAC (1899–1979)

Pierre Bernac, baritone, enjoyed a fruitful and popular career as the artistic partner of composer Francis Poulenc. He was born in Paris and later studied music in Salzburg. His association with Poulenc began in 1934 and they performed together for his entire career. Bernac was one of the most exceptional singers that ever lived in that Poulenc often composed songs with his voice in mind and for him to sing. Later in life he gained additional status as a teacher of singers. He taught master classes and private students, including Gérard Souzay and Jessye Norman.

Bernac made an indispensible contribution to the study of song with his textbook, *The Interpretation of French Song*, first published in 1978. In addition to Poulenc, the book also discusses the interpretation of songs by Berlioz, Gounod, Duparc, Chausson, Fauré, Debussy, Satie, Ravel, and others.

Recordings

The Essential Pierre Bernac, Pierre Bernac, baritone, Francis Poulenc, piano, Gerald Moore piano, Graham Johnson, piano, Testament, 1999 (Songs of Poulenc, Duparc, and others)
Pierre Bernac Sings Poulenc, Pierre Bernac, baritone, Francis Poulenc, piano, Preiser Records, 2010
Francis Poulenc: The Complete Songs, Pierre Bernac, baritone and other singers, Graham Johnson, piano, Hyperion, 2013

GÉRARD SOUZAY (1918–2004)

Gérard Souzay was one of the most successful professional singers of all time. His great talent, unique and vast repertory, reputation as a professional, and exposure to the general public made him a popular and commercially successful baritone. Souzay came from a musical family and was born in Angers. He started his vocal training as a tenor at the Paris Conservatory and later changed his voice category to baritone. He began appearing in public performances around 1945. Unlike most singers, his opera jobs came after he began performing in oratorio and recital. He quickly became known for his exquisite interpretation of French mélodies and German Lieder and formed a strong working relationship with American pianist Dalton Baldwin. Souzay's devotion to the song genre is obvious in the number of recordings he made in his lifetime: over 750 titles. The recordings include the complete songs of Francis Poulenc and Gabriel Fauré, an incredible achievement for any singer.

Souzay was an intelligent and sensitive performer with a graceful style, superb diction, and excellent musicianship. He commented that he was thinking of emotion only when he sang: "Simply, music means a lot to me and I feel very deeply what I sing."[8]

Recordings

Gérard Souzay, Gérard Souzay, baritone, Jacqueline Bonneau, piano, Testament, 2001 (Songs of Ravel, Debussy, Chausson, and Duparc)
Gérard Souzay, Gérard Souzay, baritone, Jacqueline Bonneau, piano, Polygram Records, 1990 (Songs of Fauré and Chausson)

ROBERTO ALAGNA (1963–)

Roberto Alagna is a very popular operatic tenor known for his original interpretations of classic operatic roles as well as for his controversial marriage to fellow singer soprano Angela Gheorghiu (divorced in 2013). Alagna was born in Paris and was an early winner of the Luciano Pavarotti International Vocal Competition. In the early nineties he performed opera roles in houses all over Europe and in the United States. His performance of Roméo in *Roméo et Juliette* was broadcast in movie theatres all over the world.

Alagna has recently been exploring the songs of Central and South America. He is not afraid to try an unconventional approach as he did with his *Pasión* album and its cabaret approach.

Recordings

Pasión, Roberto Alagna, tenor, Deutsche Grammophon, 2011 (Songs of Central and South America)
Sanctus: Sacred Songs, Roberto Alagna, tenor, EMI Classics, 1997 (Songs of Bach, Gounod, Franck, Fauré, Bizet, and others)
Sicilien, Roberto Alagna, tenor, Deutsche Grammophon, 2008 (Songs of Central and South America)

NATALIE DESSAY (1965–)

Natalie Dessay is a well-known French coloratura soprano from Lyon. She has enjoyed a critically acclaimed career in opera and has performed many roles in controversial and high-profile productions, such as Olympia in the Roman Polanski–directed *Tales of Hoffman* in 1992 at the Opéra Bastille, and Mélisande in the 2009 *Pelléas et Mélissande* at Theatre an der Wien.

Her recordings have proven to be very successful and she signed an exclusive recording contract with EMI Classics/Virgin Classics in 1994. In her performances of song, Ms. Dessay is known to be a very sensitive and emotional performer, and is not afraid to use physicality in performance. Unlike other opera singers, she is likely to perform a song recital in the truest sense, without excerpts from opera or oratorio. Ms. Dessay has said she has been so busy with opera she has not had time for singing much song. [9] With a hiatus from the opera stage set to begin in 2015, hopefully there will be more time for song.

Recordings

Amor, Natalie Dessay, soprano (and other singers), Virgin Classics, 2004 (Songs of Richard Strauss, with orchestra)
Debussy: Claire de Lune, Natalie Dessay, soprano, Philippe Cassard, piano, Virgin Classics, 2011 (Songs of Debussy)

The following list of French songs is not exhaustive but should serve as an overview of the genre.

SONG LIST

Hector Berlioz

Feuilles d'album
  Zaïde
  Les champs
  Chant des chemins de fer
  Prière du matin
  La belle Isabeau
  Le chasseur danois
Fleurs des Landes
  Le matin
  Petit oiseau
  Le trébuchet
  Le jeune pâtre Breton

Le chant des Bretons
Les nuits d'été
  Villanelle
  La spectre de la rose
  Sur les lagunes
  Absence
  Au cimetière
  L'île inconnue

Ernest Chausson

Apaisement
Chanson d'amour
Chanson perpétuelle
Hébé
La fleur des eaux
La mort de l'amour
La nuit
La pluie
L'albatros
Lassitude
L'aveu
Le charme
Le colibri
Le temps des lilas
Les heures
Les morts
Les papillons
Nanny
Nocturne
Printemps triste
Sérénade italienne

Claude Debussy

Apparition
Ariettes Oubliées
  C'est l'extase
  Il pleure dans mon coeur
  L'ombre des arbres
  Chevaux de bois
  Green
  Spleen

Barcarolle
Beau soir
Berceuse
Chansons de Bilitis (selections)
    Chant pastoral
    Les comparaisons
    Les contes
    Chansons
    La Partie d'osselets
    Bilitis
    Le tombeau sans nom
Chanson des brises
Chanson triste
Cinq Poèmes de Baudelaire
    Le balcon
    Harmonie du soir
    Le jet d'eau
    Recueillement
    La mort des amants
Dans le jardin
Fêtes Galantes
    En sourdine
    Fantoches
    Clair de lune
    Les ingénus
    Le faune
    Colloque sentimental
Il dort encore
Le printemps
Les Courtisanes égyptiennes
    L'eau pure du bassin
    La danseuse aux crotales
    Le Souvenir de Mnasidika
    La pluie au matin
    La flûte de Pan
    La chevelure
    Le tombeau des naïades
Les papillons
Nuit d'étoiles
Paysage sentimental
Pierrot
Printemps
Proses Lyriques

Chapter 7

De rêve
De grève
De fleurs
De soir
Romance
Trois Ballades de François Villon
    Ballade de Villon à s'amye
    Ballade que Villon feit à la requeste de sa mere pour prier Nostre-Dame
    Ballade des femmes de Paris

Henri Duparc

Au pays où se fait la guerre
Chanson triste
Élégie
Extase
La vague et la cloche
La vie antérieure
Lamento
Le galop
Le manoir de Rosemonde
L'invitation au voyage
Phidylé
Romance de Mignon
Sérénade florentine
Soupir
Testament

Gabriel Fauré

Après un rêve
Au bord de l'eau
Au cimetière
Aurore
Automne
Barcarolle
Cinq melodies "De Venise"
    Mandoline
    En sourdine
    Green
    À Clymène
    C'est l'extase
Clair de lune

Danseuse
En prière
En sourdine
Fleur jetée
Ici-bas
L'horizon chimérique
    La mer est infinie
    Je me suis embarqué
    Diane, Séléné
    Vaisseaux, nous vous aurons aimés
La bonne chanson
    Une Sainte en son auréole
    Puisque l'aube grandit
    La lune blanche
    J'allais par des chemins perfides
    J'ai presque peur, en vérité
    Avant que tu ne t'en ailles
    Donc, ce sera par un clair jour d'été
    N'est-ce pas?
    L'hiver a cessé
La rose
L'absent
Larmes
L'aube blanche
Le secret
Les roses d'Ispahan
Lydia
Mai
Nell
Nocturne
Notre amour
Prison
Poëme d'un jour
    Rencontre
    Toujours
    Adieu
Rêve d'amour
Soir
Sylvie
Tristesse

Jules Massenet

Chants intimes
  Déclaration
  À Mignonne
  Berceuse
Expressions lyriques
  Dialogue
  Les nuages
  En voyage
  Battements d'ailes
  La dernière lettre de Werther à Charlotte
  Comme autrefois
  Nocturne
  Mélancolie
  Rose de mai
  Feux-follets d'amour
Le poème d'amour
  Je me suis plaint aux tourterelles
  La nuit, sans doute, était trop belle
  Ouvre tes yeux bleus
  Puisqu'elle a pris ma vie et que j'ai pris la sienne
  Pourquoi pleures-tu?
  Oh! Ne finis jamais nuit clémente, nuit divine
Poème d'octobre
  Prélude
  Automne
  Les marronniers
  Qu'importe que l'hiver
  Roses d'octobre
  Pareils à des oiseaux

Darius Milhaud

Chansons bas
La savetier
La marchande d'herbes aromatiques
Le cantonnier
Le marchand d'ail et d'oignons
La femme de l'ouvrier
Le vitrier
Le crieur d'imprimés
La marchande d'habits

Chants populaires Hébraïques
  La séparation
  Le chant du veilleur
  Chant de délivrance
  Berceuse
  Gloire à Dieu
  Chant hassidique
L'amour chanté
  Le vrai amour
  J'aime
  Sonnet
  De sa peine, et des beautés de sa Dame
  Moins je la vois
  Nevermore
  Veillées
  Plusieurs de leurs corps dénués
  Le lai du Chèvrefeuille
Poèmes juifs
  Chant de nourrice
  Chant de Sion
  Chant du laboureur
  Chant de la pitié
  Chant de résignation
  Chant d'amour
  Chant de Forgeron
  Lamentation
Quatre Chansons de Ronsard
  À une fontaine
  À Cupidon
  Tais-toi, babillarde
  Dieu vous gard'

Francis Poulenc

Airs chantés
  Air romantique
  Air champêtre
  Air grave
  Air vif
Banalités
  Chanson d'Orkenise
  Hôtel
  Fagnes de Wallonie

Voyage à Paris
Sanglots
Chansons gaillardes
　La maîtresse volage
　Chanson à boire
　Madrigal
　Invocation aux Parques
　Couplets bachiques
　L'offrande
　La belle jeunesse
　Sérénade
Cinq poèmes de Max Jacob
　Chanson bretonne
　Cimetière
　La petite servante
　Berceuse
　Souric et Mouric
Cinq poèmes de Paul Éluard
　Peut-il se reposer
　Il la prend dans ses bras
　Plume d'eau claire
　Rôdeuse au front de verre
　Amoureuses
Fiançailles pour rire
　La Dame d'André
　Dans l'herbe
　Il vole
　Mon cadavre est doux comme un gant
　Violon
　Fleurs
La courte paille
　Le sommeil
　Quelle aventure!
　La reine de coeur
　Ba, be, bi, bo, bu
　Les Anges musiciens
　Le carafon
　Lune d'avril
Le Bestiaire
　Le dromadaire
　La chèvre du Thibet
　La sauterelle
　Le dauphin

L'écrevisse
Le carpe
Quatre poèmes de Guillaume Apollinaire
L'Anguille
Carte-postale
Avant le cinéma
1904
Tel jour, telle nuit
Bonne journée
Une ruine coquille vide
Le front comme un drapeau perdu
Une roulotte couverte en tuiles
A toutes brides
Une herbe pauvre
Je n'ai envie que de t'aimer
Figure de force brûlante et farouche
Nous avons fait la nuit

Chapter Eight

Songs of the British Isles

The composers of Great Britain, encompassing England, Ireland, Wales, and Scotland, have produced a prodigious amount of song. Despite the relatively small size of the British Isles, its song makes up a substantial portion of the song repertory and has made a significant contribution to music history. It is fascinating to consider the output of composition when one realizes that the entire British Isles are roughly the same size as California!

PRE-EIGHTEENTH CENTURY

Early British songs were known as "lute songs" or "ayres." The songs were conceived for solo voice with lute accompaniment. The lute itself was a wooden and fretted string instrument with a round body in a "half pear" shape.[1] The lute was played with a plucking motion of the fingers on the strings. The lute song's greatest period was from approximately 1597 to 1622, and began with John Dowland's *First Booke of Songes or Ayres*.

Lute songs were the first English songs in which accompaniments were fully composed. The songs were conceived with as much emphasis on the expression of text as the tunes themselves. The lutenists were often associated with the Royal Court and functioned as employees and part of the royal household. Part of the public role of the royals was to endorse and encourage the arts in their home and in the community. It was the expectation of the time that all nobility and royals would keep musicians in their employ to entertain the house, raise the status of the family, and train and tutor their children and ladies. For example, King Henry VIII's court employed approximately seventy to eighty musicians alone. One of his musicians was the famed composer Thomas Tallis. Another musician, Mark Smeaton, had the misfortune to be caught up in a royal scandal involving Anne Boleyn, and was tried, found guilty, and executed by the court.

The upper classes were not the only people who enjoyed lute songs. The lutenists were more integrated into the common classes than with the royals, and the folk poetry and music traditions were strong all over England. Perhaps because the lutenists themselves were mostly of the lower classes, lute songs were easily accessible, enjoyed, and appreciated by the common folk. The quality of the poetry chosen by composers for lute songs was very high; William Shakespeare was often set to music. Each poet-composer wrote his songs with the intention of performing them for an audience. The texts were almost always written from a male perspective because most, if not all, composers were men. The poems focused on love and philosophical musings and could also be self-pitying in nature.

To the modern listener, the harmony of lute songs can sound somewhat "off." This is due to the fact that the available harmonic language at the time of composition was much more limited than in modern times. The harmonic texture will sound different to the modern ear. The rhythms of lute song are based solely on the pace and stresses of the English language. The original lute songs did not include barlines to divide the measures. Modern notation has added barlines to give the songs rhythmic structure. Perhaps lutenists did not divide the measures with barlines in order to aid the flow of the text or because this form of notation was not yet fully established.

Poetry and emotional expression is the most important aspect of lute song performance. The vocal approach to lute song is one of simplicity that serves the text. The songs are not well suited to an operatic production or affect. Modern performances of lute songs are usually with guitar, harpsichord, or piano. The guitar should not be considered an equivalent instrument to the lute as it is completely different in structure and sound. The songs are most ideally performed with the original lute instrument as conceived by the composers. They are best enjoyed in an intimate space or environment so the nuances of the tunes and texts can be fully enjoyed by the audience. There is the risk that the charm of the songs would be lost in a larger space.

JOHN DOWLAND (1563–1626)

John Dowland was considered the premiere English lutenist and song writer of his time. In his lifetime, he enjoyed an international reputation and travelled widely. He spent time at the Danish court in the late-sixteenth century. His songs were published all over Europe; however, he was not appointed as the King's lutenist until 1612 despite having wanted the position for many years. Dowland's career closely paralleled the rise of Queen Elizabeth I, as his *First Booke of Songes or Ayres* was published in 1597.

"Come Again, Sweet Love Doth Now Invite" is one of John Dowland's most well-known songs. Its strophic form, longing text, and gentle ornamentation are all common traits found in lute song.

Song Title	Come Again, Sweet Love Doth Now Invite
Year of Composition	1597
Composer	John Dowland
Language	English
Poet	John Dowland
Text	Typical for the period, song of love
Voice	Mastery of the upper middle voice required
Piano	Modern transcription to the lute part, secondary to the voice, repetitive of the voice
Mood	Romantic and charming, not too deep in thought
Form	Strophic
Melody	Voice part can appear deceptively simple, but requires careful attention paid to the rhythm
Harmony	Tonal
Tempo	Moderate, not too slow or fast
What to listen for	Imagine the piece performed with the original lute accompaniment and how that would have altered the effect of the singing. The melody repeats in each verse and there are challenges for the singer to make the text sound fresh with each repetition.

It is 1597 in London and you are John Dowland. Queen Elizabeth wears the crown and has heard ladies in the court talking about your newly published First Booke of Ayres. As you are dressing one morning, a knock comes on the door. A royal page is standing there and hands you a folded message from one of the Queen's ladies-in-waiting. "Queen Elizabeth requests Mr. John Dowland at court this morning to hear from his First Book of Ayres." You have been to court a few times but never in the presence of the Queen or any other royalty. You put on your best clothes and set out for the castle right away. When you arrive, the same lady-in-waiting explains how to approach the Queen and how not to speak unless addressed directly first. You feel very nervous and excited for the royals to hear your new lute songs. As you enter the Queen's cool private rooms you look downward and when your escort stops walking, you do as well. You hear a commanding, yet warm, voice, "Mr. Dowland, we have heard you can write pretty songs. Will you sing one for us?" You glance upwards slowly, taking in a perfect gold shoe, rich brocade fabric, and finally, the face of the Queen herself which is intelligent, open, and expectant. "Yes, your majesty. I will play a song in your honor," you manage to speak. You don't have much time to consider what song to sing, in fact, it had not even occurred to you until this moment. There is only one song that comes to mind that is suitable for the royal creature before you. You take a breath, strum the lute in your arms, and begin, "Come again, sweet love doth now invite . . ."

After a few moments, you realize the Queen is listening carefully and enjoying the tune and the seductive text, "to see, to hear, to touch, to kiss, to die . . ." With each verse, you vary the dynamics, tempo, and emphasis of certain words to create new interest in the repeated melodic phrases. You keep your lute accompaniment light and free and concentrate on the text. When you finish singing and look at the Queen, she gives you a rare smile and says, "May we have another, Mr. Dowland?"

Thomas Campion (1567–1620) was another successful lutenist living at the same time as John Dowland. He contributed over one hundred songs to the lute song repertory and wrote all of his own poetry. His career as a composer was simultaneous to his career as a physician.

John Danyel (1564–1626) is thought to have been one of the finest lutenists of England but his career has been neglected throughout history. He may have been a royal musician at one time. His music was not readily available in print until it was rediscovered in the twentieth century.

HENRY PURCELL (1659–1695)

Henry Purcell's career represented a major development in the history of British art song. The royal court had been reestablished in 1660 and started the period of Restoration in England. The previous years had been developmental for English music in that the breakdown of the court structure brought about new independence of musicians and the development of English opera and secular choral singing. All of these events contributed to Purcell's career.

Purcell was from a musical family and entered the Chapel Royal at a young age to receive training on string and keyboard instruments, voice, and theory fundamentals. He was a very gifted and versatile musician from a young age. In addition to composing, he held various jobs at court, including teacher, conductor, performer, and several royal titles. In his lifetime, Purcell was influenced by the development of Italian music and in particular Italian opera. Influenced by opera, he integrated the ideas of recitative, text repetition, and the *da capo* (literally "from the head" and musical form of ABA) aria form into his songs. He often used irregular patterns of melody that were both unexpected and fresh. He made the most of rhythm by using dotted phrases and patterns for variety. He understood dance rhythms and used them intrinsically in his work.

Purcell's innovative and broad spectrum of work somewhat overshadowed his contemporary composers; his work was the musical highlight of seventeenth century England. Unfortunately, he died tragically at age thirty-six before he could reach maturity as a composer. Purcell contributed about three hundred songs to the art song repertoire. Many of these songs are for solo voice; some were written for inclusion in plays and others are odes, welcome, and sacred songs. He also contributed to vocal music with his popular operas *Dido and Aeneas* and *The Fairy Queen.*

"Sweeter than Roses" is a song that was used in the staged work *Pausanias* as incidental music. It has many elements of the operatic arias we know today—recitative, a demanding vocal line, and rapidly changing tempi. It is a reminder that early music does not mean easy music.

Song Title	Sweeter than Roses, from *Pausanias*
Year of Composition	1695
Composer	Henry Purcell
Language	English
Poet	Unattributed, possibly Richard Norton
Text	Highly illustrative, often repeated
Voice	Operatic approach, combination of recitative and ornamented melody
Piano	Modern transcription of what would have been the harpsichord and bass viol, more fleshed out bass line
Mood	Almost trance-like then excited energy
Form	Through-composed
Melody	Highly ornamented and demanding
Harmony	Fluid
Tempo	Changing frequently and probably not notated in the original transcriptions, clearly indicated by the melodic writing
What to listen for	Purcell is a master of the technique of "text painting," making a particular word come alive with how it is set musically. Listen to how he brings out words like "cool," "sweeter," and "trembling." The piano part is

there only to enhance the fireworks of the highly
ornamented vocal line. Purcell is able to create an
exciting mood in the last section through use of
rhythm alone.

"Man Is for the Woman Made" is a song from the stage production *The
Mock Marriage*. It is an example of Purcell using a small amount of repeated
musical material to good effect.

Song Title	"Man Is for the Woman Made" from *The Mock Marriage*
Year of Composition	1695
Composer	Henry Purcell
Language	English
Poet	P. A. Motteux
Text	Syllabic and alliterative at times (man, made)
Voice	Requires a light approach, lyrical
Piano	Continuo bass
Mood	Humorous
Form	Verse and refrain
Melody	Repetitive
Harmony	Traditional
Tempo	Moderate
What to listen for	The musical language may at first seem unsophisticated, but the challenge for the performer is how to change the interpretation and nuance of each verse. The music may be repeated, but the intention and emotion should not be. The poet has given us text that is fun, but also an interesting exercise for the singer to imagine what subtext would be most effective.

EIGHTEENTH CENTURY

There were certain popular musical trends in eighteenth century England.
Italian opera had a significant influence on London theatre. The theatre was
an extremely popular activity for the middle and lower classes and they

crowded in large numbers to enjoy the productions of the day. Ballad operas, such as the *Beggar's Opera*, were often performed for the public. In addition, because of the British love of both cultivated and natural gardens, music was often performed outdoors in the gardens of Ranelagh, Vauxhall, and Marley-bone. The songs performed in these environments were the height of charm and grace and often focused on subjects easily tolerated by listeners.

During the eighteenth century, two specific types of song flourished: the art song and the secular cantata. The cantata was basically an extended song that sometimes consisted of a recitative and air or aria, or a multi-movement piece that alternated recitative and aria. The cantata may have had the format of an opera aria, but was performed and interpreted as an extended song. During this century, Scottish and Irish songs were popular all over Great Britain.

G. F. Handel had an enormous influence in England during this time. He often spent time in Italy and wrote Italian opera and cantatas. He continued to write opera for the Royal Academy of Music and eventually devoted his time to oratorio composition that he found to be a more practical way to earn a living than opera.

JOSEPH HAYDN (1732–1809)

Joseph Haydn was an accomplished composer of many genres who also enjoyed writing songs. In 1794, he published a group of songs he called "Canzonettas." These songs were significant as they were the first English songs to have fully written out piano accompaniments that reflected the growing independence of the piano part in song. Haydn was of Austrian birth, but spent three years in England. He had a close friendship with Mrs. John Hunter that had a great influence on his English songs. Mrs. Hunter wrote the lyrics to his canzonettas and Haydn dedicated the pieces to her.

"The Mermaid's Song" is an example of the Canzonettas collaborated on by Haydn and lyricist Anne Hunter.

Song Title	The Mermaid's Song
Year of Composition	1794
Composer	Joseph Haydn
Language	English
Poet	Anne Hunter
Text	Mostly syllabic with occasional short melismatic phrases
Voice	Requires flexibility

Piano	Full texture with a lengthy introduction
Mood	Fantasy-like
Form	Strophic
Melody	The line has much stepwise movement and repeats short phrases
Harmony	Traditional
Tempo	Allegretto, but not rushed
What to listen for	Haydn's long introduction introduces melodic material and rhythms that will be heard throughout the song. Throughout, the piano is deferential to the voice and doubles the melody. The voice does not have much of a rest or even a sustained note to break up the constantly moving melody. Haydn's relentless vocal writing gives the song a vocal and dramatic energy.

NINETEENTH CENTURY

Many British song composers overlap the bridge between the nineteenth and twentieth centuries. (In this chapter, composers will be included in the century of their birth year.) Nineteenth-century England encompassed what was known as the Victorian era. During this century, the drawing room ballad came into being. The idea of the drawing room ballad was very similar to the German "Schubertiad," where art songs were performed for close friends and family in the home. The availability of affordable sheet music encouraged the middle class, as well as the upper classes, to incorporate music and song into their home lives. At this time, most songs performed on the professional stage were not for voice and piano but with orchestral accompaniment; therefore, the accessible art song format was more practical and enjoyable for home use. The ballad became more sentimental and less substantial throughout the century.

1880 was a turning point for British song. Composers like Elgar, Parry, and Stanford helped to improve the English song from the limited drawing room ballad to something more substantial. Edward Elgar (1857–1934) contributed about sixty songs to the repertoire. Hubert Parry (1848–1919) contributed about 150 songs, served as a leader in British music history, was an Oxford professor of music, director of the Royal College of Music, and was knighted by Queen Victoria. Charles Stanford (1852–1924) wrote about 160 songs. He studied in Germany and like Parry was a professor (Cambridge) and taught composition at the Royal College of Music.

Another composer of this time was Arthur Sullivan (1842–1900). Sullivan's primary contribution to vocal writing was operetta. Sullivan and his lyricist partner Gilbert produced what are considered some of the best operettas in music history such as: *The Pirates of Penzance*, *The Mikado*, and *HMS Pinafore*. Sullivan held great promise as a young musician and was expected to be an important classical composer. He found he couldn't earn very much money from classical composition and it was fortuitous that the popularity of the Victorian English theatre coincided with his composing career. He realized there was money to be made in the theatre and paired up with Gilbert.

RALPH VAUGHAN WILLIAMS (1872–1958)

Vaughan Williams was one of the most important figures in English music history. He was a prolific composer who composed for orchestra, opera, ballet, incidental music for plays, and choral works. He also contributed over 150 songs to the repertoire. His song compositions included original music and folk song arrangements.

Vaughan Williams was educated at the Royal College of Music where he studied with Parry and Stanford. He also studied composition in Berlin although his style was quintessentially "English." His style was a strong combination of both the traditional and the impressionist influences of Debussy. His musical style evolved over time and as he matured as a composer, his works became more spare, intense, and dissonant.

Vaughan Williams focused on song in the early part of his career and then moved on to other genres. He never gave song as much attention as he did in the first part of his career. *Songs of Travel* is one of his best-known group of songs. In addition to still being a teaching staple for young singers to this day, it has been recorded by well-known singers such as Bryn Terfel with great success.

Song Title	"The Vagabond" from *Songs of Travel*
Year of Composition	1901–1904
Composer	Ralph Vaughan Williams
Language	English
Poet	Robert Louis Stevenson
Text	Evocative of nature and determined
Voice	Usually sung by the lower male voice
Piano	Vaughan Williams uses a very steady staccato chord progression throughout the piece to bring the Vagabond's walking clearly to mind

Mood	Jovial yet colored with sadness
Form	AABA
Melody	Lyrical and romantic interspersed with rhythmic variation
Harmony	The harmony is inextricably linked to the rhythmic structure
Tempo	Moderately fast, like a march
What to listen for	The first song of the cycle is the beginning of the journey for the Vagabond. His walking and wandering is fully realized by the left hand of the piano in a clear walking pattern. Vaughan Williams imposes a sweeping and mostly lyric melodic line over the sharp rhythms of the piano for a clear contrast. "Or let autumn fall on me. . . ." marks the first major shift in the poem and the strict pianistic march lets up for the first time as the piano becomes as lyrical as the voice. The return of "winter" brings the return of the march rhythm and toward the end of the piece, the walker's steps slow, and finally cease.
Song Title	"Whither Must I Wander?" from *Songs of Travel*
Year of Composition	1904
Composer	Ralph Vaughan Williams
Language	English
Poet	Robert Louis Stevenson
Text	Retrospective and inward focused
Voice	Long phrases and a wide range require good vocal technique
Piano	Traditional accompaniment that doubles the voice
Mood	Sentimental and sad
Form	Strophic
Melody	The shape and contour of the melody is very wide and varied; step-wise motion and leaps work together to form a cohesive phrase
Harmony	Traditional
Tempo	Slow and tranquil

What to listen for   Vaughan Williams has written a new song in the British folk style. The elements of folk music are present; repeated melody, piano doubling the voice, and traditional harmony. There are distinctive characteristics as well: ritardandos at the ends of phrases to make the most of a held pitch, "colla voce" or "with the voice" in the piano markings, rhythmic variation in the piano, and use of the upper register of the piano at "spring shall come again." All the elements conspire to create a song that is as original as it is traditional.

ROGER QUILTER (1877–1953)

Roger Quilter studied composition at the Hoch Conservatory in Frankfurt and was a member of the "Frankfurt Group" of composers along with Percy Grainger, Cyril Scott, Balfour Gardiner, and Norman O'Neill. The group was named because they all studied with the Russian composer Iwan Knorr.

Quilter contributed about 112 songs to the British repertory. His songs come across as very elegant and effortless and do not reflect the fact that composition did not come easily to Quilter. The elegance of his style is due to the combination of fresh vocal writing, easily changing rhythms, and buoyant piano writing. Quilter used a tonal harmonic center and strove for a natural declamation of text. Unlike some composers, his song style changed very little over time. He preferred to set well-known poets.

Quilter was a talented pianist and featured the salon style song in his repertoire. He was a favorite of aristocratic culture and society. Because of his reputation and popularity, many well-known performers of the day included his songs on their recital programs and therefore propagated his success. Unlike the majority of song composers, Quilter came from a wealthy family and never had to worry about earning a living; he was a financially generous man who gave money to friends in need and founded the Musicians' Benevolent Fund.

JOHN IRELAND (1879–1962)

John Ireland lost his parents at an early age and the realities of that fact were said to greatly color his musical works. He studied piano at the Royal College of Music and gradually became more invested in composition. He earned a living in church music as an organist and choirmaster and later taught at the Royal College of Music. Ireland composed string quartets, chamber music, piano sonatas, music for orchestra, choral works, and song.

He had the ability to infuse both the piano and the voice with the emotion of the poem he set. His most well-known songs include "Sea Fever," "The Vagabond," and "The Bells of San Marie."

GEORGE BUTTERWORTH (1885–1916)

George Butterworth was an English composer who showed musical ability from an early age. He studied at Oxford and later at the Royal College of Music. He became acquainted with fellow composers Cecil Sharp and Ralph Vaughan Williams at Oxford. His very short life was ended by warfare in 1916 before he was able to mature as a composer. He leaves behind a small repertory of folk arrangements and original songs that at times epitomize the charm of the English countryside. His most well-known songs are *Six Songs from a Shropshire Lad* with poetry by A. E. Housman.

PETER WARLOCK (1894–1930)

Peter Warlock was an unusual British composer in that he was not formally educated in music. He studied at Eton and became obsessed with the music of Delius. The two men developed a life-long friendship. Warlock wrote over one hundred songs that included a wide variety of styles. He was able to combine traditional harmony with chromaticism and free declamation.

He was known for brilliant piano writing and had a strong sensitivity to texts and a strong appreciation of English poetry. Unfortunately, he suffered from mental problems and committed suicide. A resurgence of interest in his music contributed to the founding of the Peter Warlock Society in 1963.

Other composers of the nineteenth century were: Frederick Delius (1862–1934), Arthur Somervell (1863–1937), Cyril Scott (1879–1970), Herbert Howells (1892–1983), Frank Bridge (1879–1941), and Ivor Gurney (1890–1937).

TWENTIETH CENTURY

The twentieth century was a newly productive era of music in Great Britain. Composers emphasized the importance of vocal music and song composition flourished in this environment. Twentieth-century song was a culmination of the two hundred previous years of compositions and English, Irish, Scottish, and Welsh folk traditions.

BENJAMIN BRITTEN (1913–1976)

Benjamin Britten is arguably the most important composer of the twentieth century. He certainly single-handedly revitalized British vocal music and created an impressive and influential body of work. Britten was adept at music from an early age and began composing as a child. Like many of his composer contemporaries, he studied piano and viola in his youth. He attended the Royal College of Music and he studied composition with John Ireland. Britten shared his life with his partner Peter Pears and was continuously at odds with the political and social structure of England. He felt isolated in the repressive society during that time in England. Eventually, in 1939 he and Peter Pears migrated to America but returned home in 1942.

Britten partnered with W. H. Auden on several projects to great success. Auden had a special passion for opera and its sense of melodrama. He worked with Britten on films, opera, symphonies, plays, radio broadcasts, and songs.

Britten's song style reveals a simultaneous combination of tonic and dominant harmony and an expansive treatment of melody. He often used a melismatic approach in his melodies that was both innovative and exciting.

His use of piano accompaniments was innovative in that he built short melodic motives that were used contrapuntally. Britten expanded what was previously thought possible in the harmonic language. He was able to combine tonic and dominant harmony and integrate it with chromaticism.

"The Trees They Grow So High" is one example of Britten's extensive folk song settings. It is taken from his *Folk Song Arrangements, Volume 1, British Isles.* "The Last Rose of Summer" is another folk song arrangement from a different volume, *Volume 4, Moore's Irish Melodies*, that aptly expresses angst with an Irish color.

Song Title	The Trees They Grow So High
Year of Composition	1943
Composer	Arranged by Benjamin Britten
Language	English
Poet	Somerset Folk Song
Text	Intertwining of love and nature themes
Voice	The length of the song and the repetition of the melodic material require a strong sense of drama and storytelling to keep the listener's interest
Piano	Britten employs an extremely unique technique in the piano; he starts the piano part in the right hand with

one pitch per measure and gradually builds up texture; after a turning point in the text, he begins to take away layers in the piano part until the singer is alone, just like at the beginning of the song

Mood	Somewhat maudlin
Form	Strophic
Melody	Relentless with virtually no rest for the singer, lyrical and often syllabic
Harmony	Traditional at first, then increasing dissonance
Tempo	Marked "simply, with movement"
What to listen for	The song is titled a "folk song," but the demands on the singer are substantial. Britten has built in no rest for the singer, and a seemingly simple piano part becomes quite complex toward the middle of the song. There is an abrupt change in the piano, dynamic, and melody at the point the singer sings of her lover's death; it makes for a very dramatic shift.

Song Title	The Last Rose of Summer
Year of Composition	1960
Composer	Arranged by Benjamin Britten
Language	English
Poet	Thomas Moore
Text	The rose symbolizing solitude and death
Voice	Britten takes a simple folk melody and embellishes it to great effect
Piano	Rolled chords accent the dotted rhythms of the melody, towards the end of the piece the piano becomes more active and quite relentless before resuming the rolled pattern
Mood	Sentimental
Form	Strophic
Melody	Highly embellished, rhythmically complex, marked "freely"
Harmony	Mostly traditional
Tempo	Free, should move with the voice

What to listen for	It is interesting to identify the core of the original melody within Britten's ornamentation. He includes pianistic flourishes throughout that serve to accentuate the text. The third verse brings about a large shift in the piano part as the texture thickens significantly. Britten paints the idea of bleakness at the end in the piano and with dynamic markings as the voice sings: "bleak world alone."

"Let the Florid Music Praise!" is the first song from Britten's group *On This Island*. It is highly ornamented in both the voice and piano and is operatic in nature.

Song Title	"Let the Florid Music Praise!" from *On This Island*
Year of Composition	1937
Composer	Benjamin Britten
Language	English
Poet	W. H. Auden
Text	Grand poetry
Voice	High level of difficulty
Piano	Personifies the idea of florid, operatic in its pace and structure
Mood	Stately and joyous
Form	Through-composed
Melody	Extremely ornate, rhythmic, melismatic, and syllabic
Harmony	Shifting tonality
Tempo	Maestoso, non troppo presto (majestic, but not too much) and con bravura (with boldness) and poco più grazioso e rubato (little by little graceful with freedom)
What to listen for	Britten has written a stunning vocal line that is operatic in nature. The voice has long melismatic phrases on the word "shine" that are as challenging technically as any vocal work. Britten uses dynamic changes and tempo shifts to introduce new sections of the poem and change the mood and dramatic intent. The final section of the piece includes a chromatic

downward motion on the word "break" that is as sad
as the intent of the word itself.

GERALD FINZI (1901–1956) AND WILLIAM WALTON (1902–1983)

Finzi wrote over seventy songs and is known for accompaniments that are
subtly contrapuntal. His songs were well conceived and had a strongly integrated texture of voice and piano. He favored the poetry of Thomas Hardy
and over fifty of his songs were set to Hardy's texts. While he never met
Hardy, both men shared an agnostic worldview, and this could have influenced Finzi to favor his songs. Finzi loved words and would hear the vocal
melody when he read poems.

William Walton (1902–1983) contributed twenty-six songs to the genre.
He studied piano, violin, and sang in choir during his youth. He is known for
his innovative and impressionistic technique and was influenced by jazz in
his compositional style.

MICHAEL DEWAR HEAD (1900–1976)

Head contributed approximately one hundred songs to the British song repertory and was an accomplished pianist and singer. "The Ships of Arcady" is
one of his most well-known songs.

He studied composition with Frederick Corder at the Royal Academy of
Music and later returned there to teach for many years. Head's musical style
was conservative and traditional and influenced by Gerald Finzi.[2] Head practiced a unique style of performance; he simultaneously performed his songs
as both singer and pianist. While some composers like Schubert, Schumann,
Milhaud, and Barber utilized this unique performance method in private
homes, they did not perform in public. Head used the method in public and
had a great deal of success with it. An American contemporary of Head, John
Jacob Niles, also accompanied himself when performing in public, usually
with a guitar and sometimes piano.

BRITISH SINGERS AND THEIR SONGS

The following singers have enjoyed successful careers and have each included song in their performance repertory.

PETER PEARS (1910–1986)

Peter Pears is a British tenor whose career was closely tied to the composer Benjamin Britten. He attended Keble College, Oxford, and the Royal Academy of Music. Pears met Benjamin Britten through friends and they soon became close. Britten composed many works with Pears' voice in mind such as the *Seven Sonnets of Michelangelo* (1940), *Serenade for Tenor, Horn and Strings* (1943), the opera *Peter Grimes* (1945), *War Requiem* (1962), and many more. Pears has often been criticized for utilizing his relationship with Britten to further his own career but in truth, he was an accomplished and capable singer and performer on his own merits. Even after Britten died, Pears still performed in concert for several more years. Pears and Britten made many recordings together that are considered the ultimate authority on Britten's musical style.

Recordings

A Treasury of English Song, Peter Pears, tenor, Benjamin Britten, piano, Decca, 1964 (Songs of Britten, Delius, Warlock, Ireland, Butterworth, and others)
Britten, Peter Pears, tenor, Benjamin Britten, piano, Polygram Records, 1991
English Song, Peter Pears, tenor, Benjamin Britten, piano, Heritage Records, [1960] 2012
Peter Pears Anniversary Tribute, Peter Pears, tenor, Decca, 2010 (Six disc set of various songs)
Winterreise, Peter Pears, tenor, Benjamin Britten, piano, Decca, 2000 (Franz Schubert's song cycle)

ROSALIND PLOWRIGHT (1949–)

Rosalind Plowright is a British mezzo-soprano. She studied at the Royal Northern College of Music, where Jane Eaglen later studied, and began her opera career in 1975 with the Glyndebourne Opera. She only made her Metropolitan Opera debut in 2003 in *Jenufa.* Like American soprano Audra McDonald, Ms. Plowright has appeared on television and in musical theater. After many years of performing song in concerts and at international music festivals, Ms. Plowright's first recording was released in 2014. The record includes the songs of Stradella, Brahms, Tchaikovsky, Falla, Weill, Quilter, Britten, and others. She has said that the art of the song recital can give an audience a close insight into who a singer is; she hand-picked all the music on her first album because it has meant something to her during her career.

Recording

La Belle Dame Sans Merci, Rosalind Plowright, mezzo-soprano, Philip Mountford, piano, www.rosalindplowright.com, Roméo Records, 2014 (Songs of Stradella, Brahms, Tchaikovsky, Falla, Weill, Britten, and others)

JANE EAGLEN (1960–)

Jane Eaglen is a dramatic soprano from Lincoln, England. She studied at the Royal Northern College of Music in England before beginning her opera career in 1984 with the English National Opera. She has performed many roles such as Isolde in *Tristan und Isolde* and Donna Anna in *Don Giovanni.* She is known for her interpretations of Wagner's *Wesendonck Lieder* and Strauss' *Four Last Songs* with orchestra. Ms. Eaglen has branched out from classical music and gained international recognition for her recording of the film soundtrack *Sense and Sensibility* with original music by Scottish composer Patrick Doyle. Ms. Eaglen is committed to working with young singers and is currently on the faculty of the New England Conservatory in Boston, Massachusetts.

Ms. Eaglen possesses a glorious and unusual voice; a large and supple instrument that is never too dark and always colorful. She has performed with the best musicians in the world. When she decided to present a song recital in 2000, she probably did not realize how vulnerable she was making herself to criticism. Once a singer is closely associated with certain opera roles, it can become difficult for audiences to accept any variation from that theme. For Ms. Eaglen's opera fans, a song recital might seem the equivalent to Herbert von Karajan giving a viola recital. So it is all the more impressive that she was willing to take the stage in a song recital. The *New York Times* criticized her voice, diction, and interpretations. The critic claimed that her "vocal imperfections were magnified in the 1,000 seat Alice Tully Hall," her English diction was "careless," and that there was "insufficient stylistic variety between the Schubert group and four Bellini ariettas."[3] The critic concluded: "The response of the audience, which packed the place, had been surprisingly restrained. But the ovations erupted after Ms. Eaglen's first Wagner encore, an ardent account of "Dich, teure Halle" from *Tannhauser* that nearly took the roof off this hallowed hall . . . the message seemed to be: 'This is what I really do.' She's right." From the title of the review "From Full-Voiced Opera to Subtleties of Art Songs" to the concluding remarks, it almost seems that Ms. Eaglen's abilities were pigeon-holed before she sang the first note of the recital. Audiences and critics alike will only benefit from varied interpretations of song. An artist like Jane Eaglen surely deserves the opportunity to perform song in New York or anywhere else.

Recordings

Jane Eaglen, Jane Eaglen, soprano, SME, Sony Classical, 2000 (Berg's *Seven Early Songs,* Wagner's *Wesendonck Lieder,* and Strauss' *Four Last Songs*)
Sense and Sensibility, Original Motion Picture Soundtrack, Featuring Jane Eaglen, 1995 (Original songs of Patrick Doyle)

BRYN TERFEL (1965–)

Bryn Terfel is a bass-baritone from Wales known for his interpretations of Mozart and Wagner opera roles, concert performances, and song recordings. He studied at the Guildhall School of Music and Drama in London and began singing in European and American opera houses in the early 1990s. Mr. Terfel is interested in classical and popular song and has worked on projects outside the realm of classical music. He has performed musical theatre (concert version of *Sweeney Todd*) and recorded songs by Lerner and Loewe and Rodgers and Hammerstein. His voice has both the power and force to sing Wagner with full orchestra but also the subtlety and flexibility to sing British folk songs. In live performance, he has been described as: "a big voice, capable of hall-filling power but also gentleness and subtlety, and a poet's affinity for words and their underlying worlds of color and emotion."[4] Terfel has continued performing song throughout his career and even in recent years when he is taking on bigger Wagnerian roles. He is an artist who understands that telling stories in song is closely related to telling stories in opera. John von Rhein has written: "With a big, mellifluous voice that's the aural equivalent of polished oak, a formidable stage presence, a deep musicality and a rare communicative gift that reaches out to each listener, the man clearly enjoys telling stories through song."[5]

Recordings

Silent Noon, Bryn Terfel, bass-baritone, Malcolm Martineau, piano, Deutsche Grammophon, 2005 (Songs of Ralph Vaughan Williams and Roger Quilter)
Simple Gifts, Bryn Terfel, bass-baritone, Universal Music Group, 2005 (Various songs in English and Latin, religious theme)
The Vagabond, Bryn Terfel, bass-baritone, Deutsche Grammophon, 1995 (Songs of Vaughan Williams, Butterworth, Finzi, and Ireland)

SONG LIST

Benjamin Britten

A Charm of Lullabies
    A Cradle Song
    The Highland Balou
    Sephestia's Lullaby
    A Charm
    The Nurse's Song
Cabaret Songs
    Tell Me the Truth About Love
    Funeral Blues
    Johnny
    Calypso
Fish in the Unruffled Lakes
    To lie flat on the back
    Night covers up the rigid land
    The sun shines down
    Fish in the unruffled lakes
    What's in your mind?
    Underneath the abject willow
Five Flower Songs
    To daffodils
    The succession of the four sweet months
    Marsh flowers
    The evening primrose
    The Ballad of Green Broom
Folk Songs
    Bird Scarer's song
    Bonny at morn
    Lord! I married me a wife
    She's like the swallow
On This Island
    Let the florid music praise!
    Now the leaves are falling fast
    Seascape
    Nocturne
    As it is, plenty
Seven Sonnets of Michaelangelo
Winter Words
    At day-close in November
    Midnight on the Great Western

Wagtail and Baby
The little old table
The choirmaster's burial
Proud songsters
At the railway station, upway
Before life and after

George Butterworth

Bredon Hill
    Bredon Hill
    O Fair Enough are Sky and Plain
    When the Lad for Longing Sighs
    On the Idle Hill of Summer
    With Rue My Heart is Laden
Folk Songs
    Yonder Stands a Lovely Creature
    A Blacksmith Courted Me
    Sowing the Seeds of Love
    A Lawyer He Went Out
    Come My Own One
    The Cuckoo
    A Brisk Young Sailor Courted Me
    Seventeen Come Sunday
    Roving in the Dew
    The True Lover's Farewell
    Tarry Trousers
Love Blows as the Wind Blows
    In the Year That's Come and Gone, Love, His Flying Feather
    Life in Her Creaking Shoes
    Fill a Glass with Golden Wine
    On the Way to Kew
Six Songs from a Shropshire Lad
    Loveliest of Trees
    When I Was One-and-Twenty
    Look Not in My Eyes
    Think No More, Lad
    The Lads in Their Hundreds
    Is My Team Ploughing

Thomas Campion

Awake, awake, thou heavy sprite

Be thou then my Beauty named
Beauty is but a painted hell
Beauty, since you so much desire
Breake now my heart and dye
Come, O come, my life's delight
Could my heart more tongues imploy
Fair, if you expect admiring
Fire, fire, fire
Fire that must flame
Followe thy faire sunne
Follow your saint
Harke all you ladies
I care not for these Ladies
I must complain
Oft have I sigh'd
Most sweet and pleasing are thy ways
Now winter nights enlarge
It fell on a summer's day
Shall I come, sweet love?
Sing a song of joy
There is a garden in her face
Thou art not fair
Tune thy Musicke to thy hart
What is a day, what is a yeere?
When Laura smiles
When thou must home

John Dowland

A shepherd in a shade
Behold a wonder here
By a fountain where I lay
Clear or cloudy
Come again, sweet love doth now invite
Dear, if you change
Disdain me still
Farewell unkind
Fine knacks for ladies
Flow not so fast, ye fountains
Go crystal tears
I saw my lady weep
In darkness let me dwell
It was a time when silly bees

Love those beams
My heart and tongue were twins
Shall I sue?
Sweet, stay awhile
Tell me, true love
The lowest trees have tops
Time stands still
To plead my faith
Weep you no more, sad fountains
Were every thought an eye
White as lilies was her face

Gerald Finzi

A Young Man's Exhortation
 A Young Man's Exhortation
 Budmouth Dears
 Ditty
 Her Temple
 The Comet at Yell'ham
 Shortening Days
 The Sigh
 Former Beauties
 Transformations
 The Dance Continued
Earth and Air and Rain
 Summer Schemes
 When I Set for Lyonnesse
 Waiting Both
 The Phantom
 So I Have Fared
 Rollicum-rorum
 To Lizbie Browne
 The Clock of the Years
 In a Churchyard
 Proud Songsters
Let Us Garlands Bring
 Come Away, Come Away, Death
 Who is Silvia?
 Fear No More the Heat O' the Sun
 O Mistress Mine
 It Was a Lover and His Lass

Joseph Haydn

A Pastoral Song
Content
Despair
Fidelity
O Tuneful Voice
Piercing Eyes
Pleasing Pain
Recollection
Sailor's Song
She Never Told Her Love
Sympathy
The Mermaid's Song
The Spirit's Song
The Wanderer

Michael Dewar Head

A Blackbird Singing
Beloved
Five Songs
    Green rain
    The King of China's daughter
    Fallen veils
    The singer
    The blunder
Nine Cornish Songs
    Mystic Melody
    My Young Man's a Cornishman
    Mary, Mary Magdalene
    As I went home zig-zag
    Gyllyngdune
    The Burial
    The Lark
    Kynance
    Porthleven
Nocturne
Six Sea Songs
    A sea burthen
    Limehouse Reach
    Back to Hilo
    A dog's life

Lavender Pond
Sweethearts and Wives
Songs of Reminiscence
    A Christmas childhood
    Memory of my father
    If Ever You Go to Dublin Town
    My Room
    The Rowley Mile
    Plough Horses
    September Morning
The Ships of Arcady

Henry Purcell

Ah! How sweet it is to love
Come if you dare
Fairest Isle
I'll Sail Upon the Dog-Star
I Sighed and Owned my Love
No, resistance is but vain
Nymphs and Shepherds
Oh! How you protest
Prepare, Prepare, New Guests Draw Near
Shepherd, leave decoying
Sweeter than Roses
Tell me no more
The Danger is Over
There's Nothing So Fatal as Woman
Though You Make No Return
To Arms, Heroick Prince
What power art thou

Roger Quilter

Five English Love Lyrics
    There be none of Beauty's daughters
    Morning song
    Go, lovely rose
    O, the month of May
    The time of roses
Five Jacobean Lyrics
    The Jealous lover
    Why so pale and wan?

I dare not ask a kiss
To Althea, from prison
The constant lover
Five Lyrics of Robert Herrick
Cupid
A dirge
Morning song
To Electra
To violets
Five Shakespeare Songs
Fear no more the heat o' the sun
Under the greenwood tree
It was a lover and his lass
Take, o take those lips away
Hey, ho, the wind and the rain
Four Child Songs
A good child
The lamplighter
Where go the boats?
Foreign children
Four Shakespeare Songs
Who is Silvia?
When daffodils begin to peer
How should I your true love know
Sigh no more, ladies

Ralph Vaughan Williams

A Sea Symphony
Song for all seas, all ships
On the beach at night alone
Scherzo—The Waves
O vast Rondure, swimming in space
O we can wait no longer
Passage to more than India!
Along the Field
Along the field
We'll to the Woods no more
The half-moon westers low
In the morning, in the morning
The sigh that heaves the grasses
Good-bye
Fancy's knell

With rue my heart is laden
Five Mystical Songs
    Easter
    I got me flowers
    Love bade me welcome
    The call
    Antiphon
Four Poems by Fredegond Shove
    Motion and Stillness
    Four Nights
    The New Ghost
    The Water Mill
Four Last Songs
    Procris
    Tired
    Hands, eyes, and heart
    Menelaus
On Wenlock Edge
    On Wenlock Edge
    From far, from eve and morning
    Is my team ploughing
    Oh, when I was in love with you
    Bredon Hill
    Clun
Pilgrim's Progress
    Watchful's Song
    The Song of the Pilgrims
    The Pilgrim's Psalm
    The Songs of the Leaves of Life and the Water of Life
    The Song of Vanity Fair
    The Woodcutter's Song
    The Bird's Song
Songs of Travel
    The vagabond
    Let Beauty awake
    The Roadside Fire
    Youth and Love
    In dreams
    The infinite shining heavens
    Whither must I wander?
    Bright is the ring of words
    I have trod the upward and the downward slope
Ten Blake Songs

Infant Joy
A poison tree
The piper
London
The lamb
The shepherd
Ah! Sun-flower! Weary of time
Cruelty has a human heart
The divine image
Eternity
The House of Life
Lovesight
Silent noon
Loves' minstrels
Heart's haven
Death-in-Love
Love's last gift
Three Poems by Walt Whitman
Nocturne
A clear midnight
Joy, shipmate, joy
Three Songs from Shakespeare
Take, o take
When icicles hang by the wall
Orpheus with his Lute

William Walton

A Song for the Lord Mayor's Table
The Lord Mayor's Table
Glide Gently
Wapping Old Stairs
Holy Thursday
The Contrast
Rhyme
Bank Holiday
By the Lake
Country Dance
Four in the Morning
Hornpipe
I Gave Her Cakes and I Gave Her Ale
King Herod and the Cock
My Love in Her Attire

Polka
Popular Song
Rose Castles
Small Talk
Springing Jack
The Twelve
The White Owl
Three Songs
    Daphne
    Through Gilded Trellises
    Old Sir Faulk
To Couple is a Custom
Tritons

Chapter Nine

American Song: Part One

Early America

The earliest Americans were pilgrims and Puritans who brought from Europe memorized psalm-tunes and praise songs to the New World. These forms of song predated the hymn and were sung Psalms meant to praise God. The colonists also brought with them the tradition of English ballads known as "broadside ballads" that were secular in nature.[1] The *Bay Psalm Book* was the foundation of musical composition in the United States. It was printed at Harvard College in 1640 and was the first publication of the colonies. It included psalms from the Bible written in a measured and rhythmic way for singing. Early American culture was not without intellectual pursuits, including music, and the establishment of Harvard College was a milestone of intellectual life for the colonists.

One of the first commentators on the seventeenth-century American musical scene was the Reverend Thomas Symmes. He was responsible for the start of the celebrated New England "singing war" of the 1720s. He felt musical literacy had disappeared from the population at large and wrote a treatise called *The Reasonableness of Regular Singing* (Boston, 1720). It was basically a spirited argument in favor of learning how to read music. The beginning of American musical education started with a small pamphlet by Reverend John Tufts one hundred years after the *Mayflower* landed. *An Introduction to the Singing of Psalm-Tunes* was published in Boston in 1726. Most singing took place at meeting houses or a "place to church" and was religious in nature.

Both of these publications would indicate that music and singing were valued at the inception of the United States. Secular music in Puritan New England is more difficult to chronicle than psalmody as most of the music printed was closely tied with religion and ministers. During the Colonial period, the term "ballad" was used for any kind of secular traditional or popular song. The term ballad came with the settlers from England. In early settlements, most gentlemen and ladies of the upper class studied music in their own homes as a social grace. Ladies generally performed music only for their families, friends, and guests, similar to the European tradition.

Right alongside the Puritans were the first African slaves who arrived in Jamestown in 1619. Before strict slave codes were enacted, they were allowed to maintain some of their music culture. [2] The traits of their music laid the foundation for the American spiritual we know today. Various African tribal traditions, including call and response, found their way into the American style of Christian worship from the very beginning of the settled New World.

It should be noted that the settlers of the New World encroached upon the deeply rooted and valuable culture of the Native American that was already established. The Western world has largely ignored the music of America's original people and, unfortunately, this overview of song in America does not include the history of that music.

There is evidence of Native American music dating to the seventh century but musicologists did not begin to avidly study the culture's music until the late nineteenth century. It is probably not surprising, given what we know of Indian music and ceremony today, that Native Americans had a strong singing tradition. To learn more about the traditions of Native American music, contact the National Museum of the American Indian, part of the Smithsonian Institution in Washington, D.C., for the best resources available. One resource is the book *Creation's Journey: Native American Music* available at the National Museum of the American Indian.

EIGHTEENTH CENTURY

America's first composers were self-taught and viewed music as a functional activity of everyday life. Due to the extremely harsh and unpredictable conditions of the New World, people worked all the time and music was integrated into everyday activities. There was simply not time to set aside solely for the purpose of enjoying music with the exception of a quiet evening at home.

Tunesmiths, the earliest American composers, were located primarily in New England and collected their music into compilations called "tune-books." These collections were then used to teach others the rudiments of music in singing schools. Tune-books became very popular in the late eighteenth century. A typical tune was four parts, with the tenor part serving as the "air" or melody. An example of an early tune-book is the well-known *Federal American Songs*.

The Moravian religious tradition first appeared in America in 1735 and came from a European tradition dating to the mid-fifteenth century. Moravian music features the influence of German composers and their song repertory is largely unexplored. Moravian composers included Jeremiah Denecke, Johannes Herbst, and Johann Friedrich Peter.

By the mid-eighteenth century, Protestant churches began using hymns in worship instead of the sung Psalms. Later in the century, public concerts and performances by military bands became popular. Church music continued to develop with the appearance of the organ in Boston in 1770.

Late-eighteenth-century New England composers included: Francis Hopkinson, James Lyon, William Billings, Jacob French, and Samuel Holyoke. These men were tradesmen; music composition was something they did in addition to their full-time jobs. They wrote psalms, hymns, anthems, and rounds for the singing-schools. Early American composers were influenced by the music they heard all around them such as: Anglo-Celtic folk music, American hymnody, African tunes, and British secular music.

As the eighteenth century progressed, music printing increased and copies of songs were circulated and sung by all classes of people. Poetry was slow to develop because of the Puritan influence; the poetic element did not spur song growth in the United States as it did in Germany. The development of theatre in many urban locales encouraged song development both in and outside the theatre.

THE AMERICAN SPIRITUAL

When a Dutch vessel transported African natives to Jamestown in 1619, it was the beginning of the African slave trade to the American Colonies. From *The Book of American Negro Spirituals*: "These people came from various localities in Africa. They did not all speak the same language. Here they were, suddenly cut off from the moorings of their native culture, scattered without regard to their old tribal relations, having to adjust themselves to a completely alien civilization, having to learn a strange language, and, moreover, held under an increasingly harsh system of slavery, yet it was from these people this mass of noble music sprang; this music which is America's only folk music and, up to this time, the finest distinctive artistic contribution she has to offer the world."[3] It was from this circumstance that the African people made a significant contribution to American folk song.

One can reasonably argue that the spiritual is the original American art song. The concept of the spiritual does not fit the definition of an art song (a song composed for voice and piano); however, the spiritual has been cultivated over time and continues to be arranged and updated by song composers for voice and piano. The spiritual represents much more than music; it is a culmination of expression of a people away from home, in pain, acclimating to a new culture, and trying to survive. It represents influences of African music and dance, European hymn tunes, and national folk music. The tunes of spirituals have been arranged into choral works and have been woven into the orchestral works of many composers, but it is hard to deny the power of a single voice relating the melody and text of a spiritual.

The birth of the spiritual in America is a story of triumph over the most adverse of conditions. From the book *Slave Songs of the United States* first published in 1867: "The voices of the colored people have a peculiar quality that nothing can imitate, and the intonations and delicate variations of even one singer cannot be reproduced on paper."[4]

American spirituals have been sung by countless famous singers of every nationality in the finest performance halls in the world. Slaves were the original performers of spirituals as songs of praise, instruction, and history. The performance of spirituals and the opportunities for the African American singers who sing them has an ugly American history. One of the most well-known circumstances occurred in 1939 when the Daughters of the American Revolution (DAR) refused international opera star Marian Anderson the opportunity to sing in a concert at Constitution Hall. The act caused First Lady Eleanor Roosevelt to resign from the organization and arrange for Ms. Anderson to perform on the steps of the Lincoln Memorial. Over 75,000 people came to hear her sing that day.[5] Over forty years later, soprano Leontyne Price opened the DAR convention with a concert honoring Marian Anderson at Constitution Hall.[6]

THE SONGS

There are some questions as to the method of composition of the Negro spiritual. Are these songs the result of talented individuals? Did the songs come about from the spontaneous singing and chanting of workers in the fields? Did the slaves create songs while working or during their leisure time in the evening? Was all of the melodic material original? Some scholars have theorized that individuals created the verses, and the refrains, or calls, happened in a more spontaneous manner. It is very difficult to answer these questions definitively; however, there can be no doubt that these songs were passed from generation to generation by oral tradition and repetition, like early hymns and white folksongs.

The musical structure of a spiritual is usually in strophic form or as verse and refrain (call and response form). The text is often repeated multiple times and is religious in nature. The rhythmic patterns can be straightforward or polyrhythmic (more than one rhythm at a time).

"Give me Jesus" is an example of a serious reflective spiritual. It can be sung very well by singers at every skill level. When in the hands of a consummate performer, it can be stunning.

Song Title	Give Me Jesus
Year of Composition	1942 (published)
Composer	Arranged by Hall Johnson
Language	English
Poet	Traditional, unattributed
Text	Religious, triumphant
Voice	Can be sung by a variety of skill sets and ages, but will benefit from a mature perspective. The singer must be emotionally invested in the text
Piano	Supportive role, hymn-like
Mood	Depends on the skill of the singer, text allows itself to be infused with a variety of emotions
Form	Strophic
Melody	Lyrical with rhythmic passages
Harmony	Major key and traditional
Tempo	Must not be too slow
What to listen for	The defiance of the lyrics is striking. Listen for how the singer handles the repetitiveness of the text. Is there variation in mood and emotion? Hall perfectly serves the text with an understated, yet effective, piano part.

"I Couldn't Hear Nobody Pray" is a piercing lament that speaks plainly to the desperation and pain of someone feeling very alone.

Song Title	I Couldn't Hear Nobody Pray
Year of Composition	1949 (published)
Composer	Arranged by Hall Johnson
Language	English
Poet	Traditional, unattributed

Text	Reflective and somewhat self-pitying
Voice	Very rhythmic but not rushed
Piano	Supportive role but complementary of the voice
Mood	Contained desperation
Form	Strophic
Melody	Tuneful and lyric
Harmony	Traditional
Tempo	Steady and rhythmic
What to listen for	Listen for how the singer handles the call and response "Oh, Lord" throughout the piece. Hall doubles the voice in the piano and inserts the occasional dissonant pitch for additional interest. Does the singer alter the interpretation while repeating melodic material?

THE SINGING

Slaves did not always sing for enjoyment but sometimes they certainly did. On the plantations, overseers required slaves to sing in order to keep track of their location while working. Slaves sang during their regular daily routines, in religious ceremonies, at home, at dances, and to communicate coded messages to each other.

When performing spirituals today, it is useful for singers to keep in mind that spirituals were often used to accompany a repetitive task and had a practical use. Everything the slaves did had a practical use; they did not have the luxury of musical style for style's sake, although their songs had a great deal of style.

THE TEXTS

The texts of spirituals may seem simplistic or repetitive at first glance. It is true, there can be a great deal of text repetition; however, there is usually a subtext to every lyric, a code, or a message that is not at first apparent.

The words of spirituals usually fall into three categories, all of them religious; the Old Testament and Moses, the New Testament and Jesus, and a personal story usually relating to heaven or God. There are certain words and ideas that had a specific meaning to slaves. For example; "King Jesus" referred to the son of God, but it also meant a friend who knew the struggles of the slaves and a caretaker of those in trouble. "Heaven" was not only a place in the sky, but a land where freedom was possible.

It is sometimes difficult to decipher dialect spellings of certain words in spirituals. After reading the texts a few times, words will repeat and are easier to understand. A few examples: "Huddy-do?" (How do you do?), "Bro'" (brother), "Studdy" (steady), "Titty" (mother or oldest sister), "Enty" (ain't he?), "Day-clean" (daybreak), "Chu" (this or that there), "One" (alone), "Meet" (find), "Gwine" (going).

PERFORMANCE

In 1892, composer Antonin Dvořák became the artistic director and professor of composition at the National Conservatory of Music in New York. It was at the conservatory that he came to know and teach African American composer Harry T. Burleigh, who published the first American spiritual, *Deep River*, in 1917. Through their interaction, Dvořák was introduced to spiritual melodies and was inspired to use several of these melodies in his symphonic work, the *"New World Symphony."* It was Dvořák's belief that "America's Negro folk music could serve as a nationalistic school of music in the United States."

It is truly ironic that the horrors of slavery produced some of the most poignantly beautiful tunes that rival the most striking German Lied or French mélodie. The fact that these melodies and texts have survived and thrived to this day is a testament to their inherent qualities of grace, simplicity, and the earnestness of heart of their creators.

NINETEENTH CENTURY

The development of song in nineteenth-century America is complex and closely tied to social and cultural issues. Minstrelsy was principally a commercial venture that came about at a time when the United States lacked a definable national culture.[7] It was most certainly a direct result of slave culture. The minstrel show was a type of popular theater that included singing as entertainment. The actors and singers were in blackface disguise and sang many types of popular songs as well as music from Europe. Apparently, there was more to this type of "entertainment" than ridiculing African Americans. Minstrelsy critiqued white culture and mimicked European culture.[8] For more information about American minstrelsy, please contact the University of South Florida, Tampa, library for information on their comprehensive exhibit, "The History of Minstrelsy: From 'Jump Jim Crow' to 'The Jazz Singer.'"

The genre of the blues is shrouded in mystery but is definitely an important part of the development of American song. It is impossible to say when it was created or whom the first person was to play the style. What we do know is toward the end of the nineteenth century various casual musical forms were evolving at the same time and blues was performed in out-of-the-way joints and bars throughout the South. The musical form of blues is marked by a harmonic progression that is mostly unchanging. At the heart of the genre is the fact the music is infused by a state of mind. It is emotional pain and sadness that gives the blues its bite. The unabashed expression of grief is sometimes tinged with humor, but is always from a place of truth. Its influence is felt in American song composer's works to the present day.[9]

Another genre that came of age in the nineteenth century and has contributed to American song is gospel. The roots of gospel are as entrenched in America as our forefathers. The form is a combination of African influences, eighteenth-century European hymns, and early Christian traditions. The form blossomed after the Civil War and with the formation of the Fisk Jubilee Singers of Fisk University in Nashville, Tennessee. The group was performing music no white American had ever heard all over the country and in Europe. They were hugely successful, well paid, and the first people to commercialize gospel.[10]

STEPHEN C. FOSTER (1826–1864)

Stephen Foster was born in Pittsburgh to a family that valued musical education. He attended private academies and was self-taught on many instruments including flute, clarinet, violin, and guitar. Foster was influenced by minstrel shows even though he only visited the South briefly and did not have first-hand knowledge of minstrelsy. He was able to produce songs of authenticity despite his lack of knowledge. Foster was industrious in promoting his compositions. He gave copies of songs to anyone who might perform them including professional and amateur singers. With the large success of his minstrel song "Oh! Susanna," he became the first American to earn a living composing songs. Eventually, he matured away from minstrel songs and into the parlor ballad. He was able to conjure a uniquely American perspective with songs like "Beautiful Dreamer," "Gentle Annie," and "Hard Times Come Again No More." Despite his successes, he was not able to achieve financial stability.

Foster was ahead of his time when it came to the issue of racial tolerance. He wrote a song called "Nelly Was a Lady" in 1849 that described African Americans in a respectful manner (unfortunately, this was unusual). He dropped the dialect in his minstrel lyrics halfway through his career and did not allow caricatures of black individuals to appear on his score covers like other composers of the day.

Foster's work is the first body of American song. Because his work is integrated into the culture of minstrelsy, there has often been controversy surrounding his name and music. As musicologists and historians learn more about minstrelsy and its subcultures, perceptions of Foster's music have shifted. The American culture at the time Foster lived may be worth learning more about in order to draw individual conclusions. Foster's genius was his ability to transform himself and keep true to his own perspective of music for all people.

"Gentle Annie" is the type of sentimental ballad with which Foster was most comfortable. His gift for melody and melancholy sweetness is evident in this song.

Song Title	Gentle Annie
Year of Composition	1856
Composer	Stephen C. Foster
Language	English
Poet	Stephen C. Foster
Text	Melancholy
Voice	Folk-like approach
Piano	Broken chords alternated with blocks of chords
Mood	Sentimental and sweet
Form	Verses
Melody	Some wide leaps, enough variety to provide interest
Harmony	Traditional
Tempo	Not too fast, but moving
What to listen for	Foster moves somewhat suddenly in the piano part at the start of the refrain, indicating a sense of urgency. In the interweaving of images of nature with the memory of "Annie," Foster's gift for melody is clear.

"Beautiful Dreamer" is probably Foster's most well-known song. It was not published until after his death and has been featured in many television shows and films as well as recorded by artists from every genre of music.

Song Title	Beautiful Dreamer

Year of Composition	1864
Composer	Stephen C. Foster
Language	English
Poet	Stephen C. Foster
Text	Romantic
Voice	Straightforward and lyrical
Piano	Broken chords alternated with a rhythmic chordal structure
Mood	Sentimental
Form	AAB
Melody	Wide intervallic leaps
Harmony	Traditional
Tempo	Moderate
What to listen for	Foster creates a lyrical and tuneful melody that aptly expresses the romantic text. The broken chords support the voice so the text is amplified. The last line of the piece allows the voice to break the rhythmic structure and take some time with the last words.

AMY C. BEACH (1867–1944)

Amy C. Beach was an American composer and pianist and one of the first well-known female composers of any music including art song. She displayed prodigious musical talent from a very early age and took piano lessons from her mother. She later studied piano professionally in Boston. After she married, she turned to composition rather than performance and was able to teach herself theory and composition techniques to further her composing career.

Beach was known to be a prolific and disciplined composer who was very apt at promoting her own compositions. She was a generous colleague to other women composers and active in establishing associations and societies devoted to promoting composers. Her works have been studied and revived by students, historians, and musicologists throughout the twentieth century.

CHARLES IVES (1874–1954)

Ives was born in Danbury, Connecticut, and the culture of New England was an important influence on his work. Ives studied composition with Horatio Parker at Yale University. He worked in insurance as a career and also composed songs and other works. His music was not published until 1922 and was not immediately accepted by the music community due to its experimental nature. By changing traditional chord progressions and integrating American tunes in his music, Ives established a style of experimental composition.[11] His vocal lines were stylized and often used declamation approximate of speech, known in Europe as sprechstimme (speech singing). Ives used atonal harmonic language including chord blocks and was ahead of his time in this regard. In 1922, he printed a collection titled *114 Songs*. The *Charles Ives Society* was founded in 1973 and continues to promote the man and his work today.

CHARLES GRIFFES (1884–1920)

Charles Griffes studied piano at Elmira College in New York and later went to Berlin in 1903 expecting to prepare for a career as a concert pianist. While there, he studied composition with Engelbert Humperdinck. Griffes was harmonically conservative and his songs show the influence of Brahms and Strauss. He had sensitivity to the text and mood when setting a poem as well as a gift for melody.

HALL JOHNSON (1888–1970)

Hall Johnson was an American composer and conductor educated at the University of Pennsylvania. He played the violin and viola before becoming interested in choral music. He started the famous Hall Johnson Choir in 1925 that was very successful and appeared internationally and in film.[12] In addition to his compositions for film, he also wrote Broadway productions, music for theatre, the cantata *Son of Man*, choral music, songs, and many arrangements of music of all genres.

For many, Johnson's contribution to the American spiritual is his most important work. His arrangements of traditional spirituals set the standard for all arrangers, composers, and singers who followed him. His spiritual arrangements are never heavy-handed, are always a perfect frame for the existing melodies and texts, lyrical and poignant.

FLORENCE PRICE (1888–1953)

Florence Price was one of the first women composers to gain recognition in America. She learned music from her mother before studying composition at the New England Conservatory in Boston. She was an accomplished composer who received national attention for her symphonic works, songs, and spiritual arrangements. Her arrangements were very popular with singers and touted by fellow female musicians such as Marian Anderson and Leontyne Price.

As one of the very few women composers of the first half of the twentieth century, Price makes a significant contribution to American song with her eerily contained "Night."

Song Title	Night
Year of Composition	1946
Composer	Florence B. Price
Language	English
Poet	Louise C. Wallace
Text	Mysterious and infused with imagery
Voice	Lyrical and sustained
Piano	Broken chords in a sinuous and even rhythm
Mood	Haunting
Form	Through-composed
Melody	Hangs in the upper register, some accidentals
Harmony	Traditional with chromaticism
Tempo	Andante
What to listen for	Price has created a song that is as atmospheric as it is mysterious. The melody begins in the low range and climbs slowly in the first phrase to E flat. The largest melodic leap is a 7th on the word "turns" and concurs with a shift in harmony. Price offsets the last phrase of the poem "the wearied day" with complete silence in the piano before finishing the piece with the original piano pattern slowing to a stop.

JOHN JACOB NILES (1892–1980)

John Jacob Niles was born into a musical family in Louisville, Kentucky. He learned how to read music at an early age and fell in love with folk songs. He remains the American expert on music of the Appalachian Mountain region. Niles was a travelling salesman and repairman for the Burroughs Adding Machine Company. His district was in eastern Kentucky. He went deep into the mountains and hills looking for folk music.

He served in the First World War and later attended the Cincinnati Conservatory of Music. Niles made lutes and dulcimers and accompanied himself on them in concert. He transcribed folk tunes, made arrangements to existing folk tunes, and wrote original songs. His performance style and vocal stylings were unique. He had a freedom of interpretation and often used his falsetto register.

The University of Kentucky at Lexington houses the John Jacob Niles Center for American Music. The comprehensive exhibit includes papers, writings, song collections, sound recordings, films, and even furniture built by Niles. It is an excellent resource for anyone interested in first-hand sources about the composer.

"The Carol of the Birds" was written by Niles for his young son in 1941. It is essentially a holiday carol. Its sentimentality is balanced by the gentle swing of the 6/8 time signature and Niles' surprising octave leaps interspersed throughout.

Song Title	The Carol of the Birds
Year of Composition	1941
Composer	John Jacob Niles
Language	English
Poet	John Jacob Niles
Text	Religious, Christmas text
Voice	Lyrical, folk-like
Piano	Mostly doubles the voice, the right hand occasionally above the staff helps create an interesting texture
Mood	Sweet
Form	Strophic
Melody	Graceful with undulating rhythm
Harmony	Traditional
Tempo	"In graceful, pastoral style"

What to listen for	The piece is clearly influenced by folk music with the strophic form and piano doubling the voice. Niles expands the expectation of a simple folk melody by including octave leaps, rhythmic variation, and fermatas at the end of phrases. His device of two sixteenth notes on the upbeats of most phrases helps to propel the melody forward. The repeated "curoo, curoo, curoo" of the birds is charming and provides a bridge between verses.

The Gambling Songs were commissioned by the baritone John Charles Thomas. They have been sung in performance and on recordings by George London, Thomas Stewart, Leonard Warren, and Thomas Hampson.

Song Title	"Gambler's Song of the Big Sandy River" from *The Gambler's Songs*
Year of Composition	Mid-1940s
Composer	John Jacob Niles
Language	English
Poet	John Jacob Niles
Text	Light-hearted and jovial
Voice	Rhythmic and jaunty
Piano	Sweeping and rhythmic chord progressions, full use of keyboard and chromatic riffs
Mood	Energetic
Form	Strophic
Melody	Syllabic and requiring showmanship
Harmony	Traditional
Tempo	"In graceful, pastoral style"
What to listen for	One of Niles' few quick-tempo songs marked "rapidly"; the piece is entertaining and fun. The singer expresses his carefree attitude with "high, high, high, high" in between each verse and teases the listener with his tales of gambling and chasing girls. After several relentless verses, there is a slowing down on "when turn of chance and kiss of lips are added up to profit," then a return to the original tempo.

DOUGLAS MOORE (1893–1969)

Douglas Moore came from a family that was one of the first to inhabit Long Island, New York. His mother exposed him to music at an early age and taught him about opera. Like Charles Ives, he studied composition with Horatio Parker at Yale University, although much later. After serving in World War I, he joined the music faculty at Columbia University in 1926 and remained in that position for many years. In 1951, he won the Pulitzer Prize for his opera, *Giants in the Earth*, but his opera *The Ballad of Baby Doe* is his most well-known and frequently performed work.

His musical style was influenced by hymns, reels, fiddle tunes, ballads, and opera. In his songs, the vocal line is the most important and there is a clear sense of drama.

WILLIAM GRANT STILL (1895–1978)

William Grant Still was born in Mississippi. Like many composers, he studied the violin in his youth. He graduated from Wilberforce College and had intended to study medicine before committing to a music career. He wrote arrangements for nationally known entertainers such as W. C. Handy and Sophie Tucker.

Mr. Still has many singular credits and milestones to his name. He is the first African American to have his own symphony performed, to conduct an all-white radio orchestra, to conduct a major symphony orchestra in the United States, and to have an opera performed by a major house.

He had a conservative musical style, yet incorporated many different idioms such as jazz, folk song, and the music of Spain and India. His songs have an operatic grandness to them yet still embody warmth and accessibility.

Still's understanding of how to write effectively for the voice is evident in his song, "Grief."

Song Title	Grief
Year of Composition	1953
Composer	William Grant Still
Language	English
Poet	Leroy V. Brant
Text	Repetitive

Voice	Marked "freely" by the composer, repetitive note patterns are challenging for the singer; they appear simple, but are not easy to sing or interpret
Piano	Rolling chords at the beginning and end with a flurry and thickening of the texture in the middle of the piece
Mood	Dire
Form	Through-composed
Melody	Phrases have many repeated notes with occasional leaps upward
Harmony	Tonal with dissonances
Tempo	Free, and "colla voce" (with the voice)
What to listen for	Still contains the grief of emotional expression with even vocal phrases and rolled chords before opening up the piano in the next section to a much more dense texture and marking it "fervently." He uses the text to great effect as it becomes more desperate each time it is repeated.

JOHN DUKE (1899–1984)

John Duke is one of the most important American composers of the twentieth century. He was a prolific composer who contributed some 265 songs to the genre of art song. As a composer, he is best known for his songs that were composed between 1920 and his death in 1984. He was also an accomplished pianist and taught piano at Smith College from 1923 until 1960. He was interested in new works and artists as evidenced by his involvement with the Seagle Music Colony and Yaddo Summer Music Colony, both in New York State. His contributions as a composer were recognized by the American Society of Composers, Authors, and Publishers (ASCAP) for twenty-two consecutive years with their Standard Award. After his retirement from Smith College, he composed 126 of his 265 catalogued songs.

Musically, John Duke's songs are very satisfying. The melodies are lyric and singable and never too complex. The harmonies are tonally conceived, unlike some other twentieth-century composers! Duke uses a wide-ranging list of poets and texts of high quality and provides a careful integration of words into the overall fabric of the musical texture.[13] Seventy-five percent of his songs are set to texts of American poets. His compositions continue to influence modern American song composers such as Ricky Ian Gordon and Richard Faith.

The John Duke Papers collection is housed at Smith College in the College Archives in Northampton, Massachusetts. The scores of Duke's compositions make up the most important part of the papers in this collection. There are copies of all of Duke's 265 catalogued songs including the song he was composing at the time of his death. [14]

"Loveliest of Trees" is a vocally accessible song with sophisticated lyrics by A. E. Housman. It is certainly one of Duke's most well-known pieces and was composed early in his career.

Song Title	Loveliest of Trees
Year of Composition	1928
Composer	John Duke
Language	English
Poet	A. E. Housman, from *A Shropshire Lad*
Text	Sentimental
Voice	Accessible for the young singer, but subject matter lends itself to a more mature person
Piano	Appealing motivic device that paints a picture of Spring
Mood	Light at first, then serious and melancholy
Form	Roughly ABA
Melody	Medium range
Harmony	Interesting shift from a flat to sharp key at the beginning of the B section makes for an instantly darkening feel
Tempo	Intended to be graceful above all else
What to listen for	The song begins as a typical spring ode, then quickly shifts to a dark key and regret over the loss of youth. Housman has written the most charming poem about denial. It is interesting how Duke keeps the charm of the piano writing in the sharp key intact by maintaining the rhythmic structure from the beginning. There is a melancholy and deep emotional feeling to Housman's juxtaposition of the "cherry tree" full in bloom, and later "hung with snow."

Duke's "Bells in the Rain" is a dance between the piano and voice. By using the upper register of the piano, Duke creates an atmosphere that is evocative of the title of the song.

Song Title	Bells in the Rain
Year of Composition	1948
Composer	John Duke
Language	English
Poet	Elinor Wylie
Text	Sleep as it relates to nature
Voice	The range is in the upper voice
Piano	The right hand of above-the-staff sixteenth note patterns reflects the fall of rain
Mood	Lightness
Form	Roughly ABA, with a coda
Melody	Requires vocal lightness and great intervallic leaps
Harmony	Dissonances within a tonal center
Tempo	Steady and not too fast
What to listen for	The right-hand piano part is unyielding until the last few measures of the piece. It is evocative of the bells or rain. Duke marks the beginning of the piece as "quietly, with bell-like evenness." The words "tenderly" and "peace" are marked with a piano dynamic marking.

Other key composers born in the nineteenth century include: Charles A. Tindley (1856–1933), Virgil Thomson (1896–1989), Charles Loeffler (1861–1935), Harry Thacker Burleigh (1866–1949), Roy Harris (1898–1979), Edward Boatner (1898–1981), Ernst Bacon (1898–1990), John Alden Carpenter (1876–1951), and Edward MacDowell (1860–1908).

Chapter Ten

American Song: Part Two

Twentieth Century

The twentieth-century American art song differs greatly from its counterparts in European culture. The twentieth-century songs of France, Germany, Italy, and Great Britain represent the culmination of four hundred years of developing musical styles and language. The American art song of the twentieth century is the cultivation of fewer years and reflects a less diverse and shifting culture that draws upon many sources for inspiration. To further complicate matters, several American composers went to Europe to study with established and well-known European composers and brought their influence and musical sensibilities to their compositional style.

America has a rich musical tradition of its own that includes jazz, spirituals, musical theater, blues, the Appalachian tradition, hymn-tunes, minstrel music, and folk music. The combination of European tradition and our own musical genres has resulted in an eclectic and entertaining repertoire of song.

AARON COPLAND (1900–1990)

Aaron Copland was born in New York and studied in Paris with Nadia Boulanger. He worked as a teacher, music critic and commentator, pianist, conductor, and composer. He was very involved in foundations, music associations, and international academies. His role was one of a champion of new American music.

"The Dodger" is an example of a traditional tune given a spirited and fresh update by Copland. Using a rhythmically vivid approach in the piano part and specific markings in the voice, he is able to bring to life this old campaign tune.

Song Title	"The Dodger" from *Old American Songs*, Set One
Year of Composition	1950
Composer	Arranged by Aaron Copland
Language	English
Poet	Traditional
Text	Humorous commentary
Voice	A substantial voice can elevate the text, requires a singer who can relate to humor
Piano	Effective and jaunty with a brilliant use of rhythm
Mood	Playful
Form	Verse and refrain
Melody	Largely in the middle range, syllabic with occasional held note
Harmony	Traditional
Tempo	Marked "heavy, not too fast," by the composer
What to listen for	The lyrics about the "candidate" supposedly relate to the real candidates of the Cleveland-Blaine campaign. The song is furious and free, but there is a message in the text that is serious-minded. Copland epitomizes Americana with lively rhythm and well-set text. The style is similar to campground songs of the early nineteenth century. Listen for Copland's use of the fermata (stop) toward the end of each verse.

New York City: It is January 28, 1951, and you are sitting in New York City's Town Hall. The lights are warm and glowing and there is a shiny black grand piano on stage. It is the night of the American premiere of Aaron Copland's Old American Songs. *There is a great deal of excitement in the air as the composer himself will be playing the piano. The singer will be William Warfield, American bass-baritone and one of the most intriguing people of the year. It is generally known that he will be recreating the role of "Joe" in the new MGM version of* Showboat *which comes out this year. The lights dim and the audience reflexively applauds. Mr. Warfield walks out and Mr. Copland follows behind him. The bass-baritone cuts an impressive figure and is appropriately imposing on the stage. In his tuxedo, he could be about to sing*

any operatic aria in the repertoire. Mr. Copland begins to play "The Boatman's Dance." *He strikes a dramatic chord and Mr. Warfield's unbelievable
voice fills the hall,* "Hi, ho the boatman row. . . . rollin' down the river, the
Ohio." *The voice is as vibrant as a voice can be and the singer is in complete
command, stunning the audience with the size and grace of his instrument.
All of a sudden, the tempo changes and suddenly Mr. Warfield is totally in a
different light, having as much fun as a person can have onstage. The tempo
picks up and it is amazing to hear how he can fit all the words into the
melodic shape. It is inspiring to hear an American tune sung to perfection
and you are just grateful to have been a part of the experience.*

SAMUEL BARBER (1910–1981)

Samuel Barber had a diverse career as an American composer and his music
made an indelible impression on American culture. For example, in the
1960s he was commissioned to write three pieces to be premiered at the
opening of Lincoln Center in New York City. His opera, *Antony and Cleopatra* (1966), was the piece debuted at the Metropolitan Opera that year, star-
ring Leontyne Price, one of Barber's favorite collaborators.

The second movement from his String Quartet, Opus 11, the Adagio,
grew into the *Adagio for Strings*, which is one of the most famous classical
pieces of all time. It was featured in the motion picture *Platoon* in 1986 and
performed at many high-profile public occasions such as the funerals of
Albert Einstein and Princess Grace of Monaco.

Barber was born in Pennsylvania. His aunt was an opera singer and must
have had a great influence on his love for the voice. He began studying music
very early and at age fourteen he began formal studies at the Curtis Institute
of Music. It was at Curtis where met fellow composer Gian Carlo Menotti
with whom he formed a close friendship. He also studied in Rome and was
awarded the Prix de Rome in 1935.

Barber's musical style can be described as neoromantic. His songs contain lyrical melodies that demonstrate his innate understanding of the voice.
He often uses counterpoint throughout the texture of a song. Barber is similar
to Hugo Wolf in the way he fully embraces the meaning of a poem prior to
composing so that the musical component is as vivid in meaning as the text.
Barber did not compose much after 1966.

"Sure on this Shining Night" is an early composition of Barber's and one
of his most-loved songs. It is an excellent example of his ability to perfectly
integrate text and musical language while creating a cohesive mood.

Song Title	Sure on this Shining Night
Year of Composition	1938

Composer	Samuel Barber
Language	English
Poet	James Agee, from *Permit Me Voyage*
Text	Images of nature, sky, and night
Voice	Can be sung successfully by singers of all ages
Piano	Use of constant pedal in the left hand enforces the quiet mood
Mood	Dreamy and quiet, musical portrait of night
Form	ABA
Melody	Medium high, B section hangs at the top of the staff
Harmony	Key change is very subtle at the start of the B section
Tempo	Not fast, but must not drag too slowly
What to listen for	The right hand in the piano repeats portions of the melody, almost in a delayed round format. The B section of melody presents a challenge to the singer with the combination of a high tessitura and demanding dynamics, requiring loud and soft singing within just a few measures. Barber resolves the final cadence in a charming and subtle manner.

Barber's *Hermit Songs* is one of the most fascinating song cycles ever written. The texts were written by monks in the twelfth century and each song is a unique musical experience. "The Crucifixion" is an example of Barber's ability to successfully set religious text.

Song Title	"The Crucifixion" from *The Hermit Songs*
Year of Composition	1953
Composer	Samuel Barber
Language	English
Poet	The Speckled Book, twelfth century
Text	Haunting and tragic
Voice	Lyrical, requires independence from the piano
Piano	Sparse at times and dense at others
Mood	Desolate
Form	Through-composed

Melody	Emphatic and tender when needed
Harmony	Some dissonant chromatic harmonies
Tempo	Moderate
What to listen for	There is a principal motive in the right hand of the piano that repeats throughout the piece. The only fermata (stop) in the piece is on the word "swan" to emphasize the subject of the text. Barber has created a terrifying mood with the subtle and motivic interaction between the voice and the piano.

PAUL BOWLES (1910–1999)

Paul Bowles was an American composer who travelled frequently for musical inspiration and was fascinated with Morocco, where he ultimately made his permanent home. He began composing at a very early age. He received his first commission with the help of Virgil Thomson and collaborated often with the writer Tennessee Williams. He wrote music criticism for the publication *Modern Music* and was on the staff of the *New York Herald Tribune*. He also wrote commissions for Broadway. After 1949, there were not many new compositions. Bowles' music displays the influence of French music as well as American jazz and folk music.

MARGARET BONDS (1913–1972)

Margaret Bonds is one of the few female composers recognized from the early twentieth century. Like many of her composer colleagues, she first studied piano at home with her mother. She attended and graduated Northwestern University and the Juilliard School, where she studied composition. Throughout her career, she worked as a professional pianist in addition to composing. She focused on vocal composition, including songs, spirituals, and theatre.

The utterly original "Dream Variation," with Langston Hughes' brilliant poetry, is as fresh and shocking today as it ever was. Musically its boldness matches the poetry and is defiant in its beauty.

Song Title	"Dream Variation," from *Three Dream Portraits*
Year of Composition	1959 (Published)
Composer	Margaret Bonds
Language	English

Poet	Langston Hughes
Text	Defiant and joyful
Voice	Sweeping and light approach required
Piano	Great use of dissonance, moves with the voice and independent and active during interludes
Mood	Joyful and inspirational
Form	Strophic with a coda
Melody	Dissonant leaps, much movement throughout the middle range
Harmony	Surprisingly dissonant
Tempo	Marked "andante—tranquillo," in contrast to the text
What to listen for	Hughes' brilliant poem lends itself well to Bonds' sweeping vocal lines and inventive piano. There is a clear contrast between the "dancing" and "resting" phrases of the song as the mood distinctly shifts. The last phrase is marked "espressivo" and should be approached by the singer as "tenderly" as possible.

LEONARD BERNSTEIN (1918–1990)

Leonard Bernstein is the very rare classical musician who has permeated popular culture. He is probably known by most people from his *Young People's Concerts* television specials broadcast in the 1960s that brought classical music to the masses. He also wrote a famous musical called *West Side Story*. His name even found its way into a popular R.E.M song, "It's the End of the World as We Know It (And I Feel Fine)" in 1987. Bernstein was a brilliant composer who wrote for the Broadway stage, symphonies, religious works, choral works, chamber music, film, ballet, and much more. He was an astonishing and beloved conductor of the world's greatest orchestras and a person who sincerely cared about teaching and education.

He started piano at age ten when his family bought a modest piano for their home. He enjoyed a prestigious education at the Boston Latin School, Harvard University, and the Curtis Institute, where he studied piano, orchestration, and conducting. He gained employment with the New York Philharmonic Orchestra at one of the best periods for classical music in America.

His music is diverse and varied and encompasses the melting pot of American influences. One of his unique compositional traits is that he is able to bridge classical and popular music through song. He incorporates interesting treatments of rhythm and melody into his song style. Many of his texts are set in rapid speech-like patter; Poulenc may have been an influence.

Many people do not know what to make of Bernstein's *I Hate Music* cycle. The important point to know is that, while the songs are written from a child's perspective, for adults, Bernstein meant for them to be performed as a child would, fully believing every word.

Song Title	"I Hate Music!" from *I Hate Music: A Cycle of Five Kid Songs for Soprano*
Year of Composition	1943
Composer	Leonard Bernstein
Language	English
Poet	Leonard Bernstein
Text	Witty and funny
Voice	Requires a light touch but great skill
Piano	Chordal, sweeping groups of three
Mood	Adult with juvenile lyrics
Form	Roughly ABA
Melody	A wide range with chromatic leaps
Harmony	Dissonances
Tempo	Sustained, then faster, then back to first tempo
What to listen for	Mr. Bernstein has a specific notation in the score that stresses the importance of the singer not trying to be childlike. He says, "coyness is to be assiduously avoided." He wants to let the music and text communicate the child-like feel. These are not songs for children. Listen to the demands of the vocal lines and how they contrast with the words of a little girl. These songs are significant in the way that the composer has enough courage to write songs that are fun and silly.

NED ROREM (1923–)

Ned Rorem is considered by many to be America's most accomplished song composer and the ultimate champion of American song. In addition to song composition, he has made significant contributions to music criticism and brought art song to the forefront of culture through his writing. His works include *The Paris Diary* (1966), *Music From Inside Out* (1967), *Paul's Blues* (1984), and *Knowing When to Stop: A Memoir* (1994).

He was raised as a Quaker and began piano study at age seven. He was a composition major at Northwestern University, then at the Curtis Institute, and later at the Juilliard School and Tanglewood Music Center under Aaron Copland. In between educational bursts, he quit formal study and moved to New York City where he worked for composer Virgil Thomson as a copyist.

He spent time in France, particularly Paris, and the country was a huge influence on his compositional style and outlook. Rorem's style is a combination of new classical and baroque elements and full of wit and American frankness. He regularly used imitative passages between the voice and piano.

His piano writing frequently made use of independent left and right hands that complemented the melody. He usually began a song with a basic tonality and moved into different keys, and a third or closing section returned to the basic tonality. Rorem enjoyed working with singers and even coached them singing his songs in venues such as the Aspen Music Festival and the Juilliard School.

What is striking about "See How They Love Me" is the warmth and sensuousness Rorem infuses in the melody and piano. He also impresses by using very traditional European influences in the piece but manages to produce a song with uniquely American sensibilities.

Song Title	See How They Love Me
Year of Composition	1956
Composer	Ned Rorem
Language	1956
Poet	Howard Moss
Text	A sincere question of love's rebuke
Voice	Legato important to balance with the syllabic text
Piano	Warm and expressive, right hand is often higher than voice part
Mood	Could be angry or contemplative, depending on the singer's approach
Form	Roughly through-composed with a short repeat of the opening phrase at the end
Melody	Somewhat demanding, with an unusually high tessitura toward the end

Harmony	No key signature indicates movement through tonalities, free use of dissonance
Tempo	Marked "quietly"
What to listen for	Rorem is able to combine dissonant harmony with an overall warmth and charm. There is an internal counterpoint within the piano part that adds weight to the sometimes sparse texture. The sudden dramatic shift at the end; "yet you rebuke me, O love, love I only pursue," resolves quietly back to "see how they love me," in an unexpected and surprising shift.

DOMINICK ARGENTO (1927–)

Dominick Argento was born in Pennsylvania in 1927. He did not have the typical education of a young musician who immersed himself in musical study from a young age, rather, he taught himself music theory and piano. Later, his formal studies took place at the Peabody Conservatory in Baltimore, Maryland, at the Eastman School of Music in Rochester, New York, and in Italy. He later joined the faculty as a theory professor at the University of Minnesota.

His musical style is considered traditional but also individualistic. The songwriting is very lyrical and he often sacrifices the melodic material to clearly declaim the text. In his eclectic vocal writing, he is able to blend the lyrical with a conversational style harkening back to opera recitative or sprechstimme. His piano writing provides balance to the vocal line and reiterates parts of the melody. He engages in changing tempos, meters, and complete rhythmic patterns. Argento won the Pulitzer Prize for his song cycle *From the Diary of Virginia Woolf* in 1975.

RICHARD HUNDLEY (1931–)

Richard Hundley was raised in Kentucky. He began piano study at age eight. He attended the Cincinnati College-Conservatory of Music and studied composition in New York City. His musical style is in the bel canto lyrical style, with vocal writing in the comfortable middle range, a mostly light piano texture, and use of tonal harmony.

Song Title	"Come Ready and See Me" from the collection of *Eight Songs*
Year of Composition	1971

Composer	Richard Hundley
Language	English
Poet	James Purdy
Text	Sincere and touching, with a touch of desperation
Voice	Set well for singers, some phrases are challenging for breath control
Piano	A modern update of the bel canto style of arpeggiated chords, blocked chords double the voice to emphasize triplet in the melody, "under the bluest sky"
Mood	Highly romantic
Form	Basically repeats melodic material twice with an extended coda
Melody	Lyrical and tuneful, requires balance of passion and dynamic control
Harmony	Set in unusual G flat
Tempo	Requested by the composer, "simply and legato"
What to listen for	This song has often been classified, or written off, as more suitable as a pop or Broadway song. It is interesting to consider why an appealing, romantic, and enjoyable song could not belong in the art song genre. Notice the melancholy feel of the words combined with the hopefulness and optimism of the piano.

LEE HOIBY (1926–2011)

Lee Hoiby came from a family of amateur musicians. He was a piano major at the University of Wisconsin and received a graduate degree from Mills College where he studied composition with Darius Milhaud. He cites Mozart, Strauss, Puccini, Barber, and Menotti as influences. He contributed over fifty songs to the genre. In addition to song, Hoiby also composed operas, especially in the short form of monologues and one-acts. Hoiby has a special affinity for melody and a strong sense of the dramatic.

Song Title	"The Serpent" from *Songs for Leontyne*
Year of Composition	1979
Composer	Lee Hoiby

Language	English
Poet	Theodore Roethke
Text	Humorous and entertaining
Voice	Operatic demands
Piano	Complex rhythms and rapidly shifting meter
Mood	Playful
Form	Through-composed
Melody	Wide range, includes vocal effects to communicate the text
Harmony	Mostly tonal, some accidentals
Tempo	Allegro giocoso
What to listen for	Hoiby's song was written for Leontyne Price and is a joyful romp about the life of a snake that considers himself a singer. The melody is wide-ranging and its energy does not slow. The voice is sometimes doubled with the piano, often soaring in lyrical phrases over complex rhythms in the piano, or in a rhythmic counterpoint with the piano part. Hoiby's sense of drama in this piece is unparalleled.

WILLIAM BOLCOM (1938–)

William Bolcom is a successful American composer who performs regularly. He is trained as a pianist and studied composition with Darius Milhaud at Mills College, and also the Paris Conservatory. He was a long-time faculty member at the University of Michigan's School of Music from 1973 to 2008.

Bolcom won the Pulitzer Prize in 1988 for his *12 New Etudes for Piano.* He has also been recognized with a Grammy Award for his settings of William Blake's *Songs of Innocence and of Experience* on the Naxos label.[1] He is especially known for his original opera *A View from the Bridge.*

Mr. Bolcom has done much to perpetuate the genre of song. He has made a substantial contribution to the American songbook. His songs include: *Cabaret Songs* (1977–1985), *Ancient Cabaret* (2001), the cycle *Briefly It Enters* (1996), *From the Diary of Sally Hemings* (2000), the cycle *I Will Breathe a Mountain* (1990), and the ever popular *Lime Jell-O Marshmallow Cottage Cheese Surprise* (1975). Mr. Bolcom is often joined in performance by his wife, mezzo-soprano Joan Morris. Together, they have performed all over the world and made twenty-four recordings. As a working and performing song composer and teacher at a major university, Mr. Bolcom has built upon the songbook of the twentieth century and used his position and talents to take America into the twenty-first century of song.

Song Title	"Amor" from *Cabaret Songs* (Volumes 1 and 2)
Year of Composition	1978
Composer	William Bolcom
Language	English
Poet	Arnold Weinstein
Text	Humorous and entertaining
Voice	Requires a sophisticated approach, cannot be "oversung"
Piano	Mr. Bolcom provides plenty of guidance with his markings in the score, the rhythmic structure is clear, clearly influenced by jazz
Mood	Seductive and sly
Form	Basically through-composed with some repeated material
Melody	Rhythmic and syllabic, use of lower register
Harmony	Tonal with dissonances for effect
Tempo	"Light, rhythmic; Pachanga tempo" (Cuban)
What to listen for	"Amor" is a highly entertaining song that achieves perfect symmetry between the text and the music. Bolcom had a clear vision of how to express Weinstein's fun and engaging poem with this piece. There is a tribute to jazz scat toward the middle of the song. The highly rhythmic and precise piano part interplays with the melody throughout almost as if the two parts are passing a ball back and forth to each other. The singer can use humor and storytelling to enrich a performance, but if the singer follows Bolcom's lead, the song sings itself.

LIBBY LARSEN (1950–)

Libby Larsen is one of the most successful female composers of all time. She is known for her prodigious portfolio of work that includes many genres of music including: theatre music, opera, instrumental music, music for band, choral works, music for voice and instruments, and song. Ms. Larsen attended the University of Minnesota where she studied composition with Dominick Argento.[2] Unlike other American composers such as William Bolcom and John Duke, Larsen has not affiliated herself with an academic institution. She has enjoyed many successes including a Grammy Award (1994) for *The Art of Arleen Augér*, which included her song cycle *Sonnets from the Portuguese*. Her contribution to American song includes *Love After 1950* (2000), *Margaret Songs* (1996), and her most well-known composition, *Cowboy Songs* (1979).

JOHN MUSTO (1954–)

John Musto is an American working composer and performer who has an affinity for vocal writing and is known for his operas. Mr. Musto studied piano performance at the Manhattan School of Music. He is an active recording artist and performer in addition to his composition work. His recent operas are *Volpone* (Wolf Trap Opera premiere, 2004), *Later the Same Evening* (University of Maryland, National Gallery of Art premieres, 2007), *Bastianello* (New York Festival of Song premiere, 2008), and *The Inspector* (Wolf Trap Opera premiere, 2011). The Wolf Trap recording of *Volpone* was nominated for a Grammy Award in 2010.[3] These works make Mr. Musto one of the most active American opera composers of the decade.

Musto frequently performs in concert with his wife, soprano Amy Burton. His songs include "Recuerdo," "Shadow of the Blues," and "The Brief Light." Peter G. Davis of *Musical America*: "Musto's many songs are treasures of the American repertory."

RICKY IAN GORDON (1956–)

Ricky Ian Gordon is an American composer from New York. He studied piano and composition at Carnegie Mellon University and began writing vocal music soon after for artists as diverse as Dawn Upshaw, Judy Collins, Kristin Chenoweth, and Betty Buckley. He has had much success with song and opera, including the productions *The Grapes of Wrath* and *Twenty-Seven*, both commissioned works. His songbooks have become part of the teaching repertory and are often performed by students as well as professionals.

JAKE HEGGIE (1961–)

Jake Heggie is an American song composer who has contributed over 250 songs to the repertory and has had a high-profile and public career as a composer of opera, orchestral, choral, and chamber music. One of his most popular works is the opera *Dead Man Walking* (libretto by Terrence McNally) which premiered at the San Francisco Opera in 2000. The opera is based on the book of the same name by Sister Helen Prejean which was also the focus of the 1995 film *Dead Man Walking*.

He began his musical education on the piano at an early age and later attended the University of California, Los Angeles. Mr. Heggie has a great appreciation for writers and has featured poems of American poets Emily Dickinson and Maya Angelou. He has had many public successes and opportunities to work with some of the most accomplished singers in the world. For example, in 2014 he fulfilled a commission for the Ravinia Festival in honor of Dame Kiri Te Kanawa's seventieth birthday. He performed his cycle of songs *Newer Every Day: Songs for Kiri* with Dame Te Kanawa in August 2014.

Other accomplished twentieth century composers include; John W. Work (1901–1967), Undine Smith Moore (1904–1989), Theodore Chanler (1902–1961), Paul Nordoff (1909–1977), Norman Dello Joio (1913–2008), Irving Fine (1914–1962), David Diamond (1915–2005), Vincent Persichetti (1915–1987), Milton Babbitt (1916–2011), George Rochberg (1918–2005), Jack Beeson (1921–2010), Seymour Barab (1921–), Betty Jackson King (1928–1994), David Del Tredici (1937–), John Corigliano (1938–), and Thomas Pasatieri (1945–).

AMERICAN MUSICAL THEATRE SONGS

American musical theatre is an institution that reflects the diversity of the United States. There has always been and continues to be original song within the musical theatre show. Musical theater and solo vocal music share many qualities, characteristics, and trends. There are some musical theater songs that closely resemble opera; a song called "Art is Calling for Me" from the *Enchantress* (1911) is much like an opera aria with its high showy notes, various dynamic and tempo markings, and illustrative text. Gilbert and Sullivan's late nineteenth-century operettas such as *The Pirates of Penzance* and *The Mikado* cross over the genres of opera, operetta, and musical theater and incorporate traits of all three. Gilbert and Sullivan's shows are performed in major opera houses and companies and on Broadway. *Porgy and Bess* is an American opera that is often mistaken for a musical and performed as such; Gershwin intended for the piece to be performed as an opera the same as Puccini's works. Musical theatre songs that are sung well use many of the same vocal techniques as art song. Songs from musicals such as Kurt Weill's *One Touch of Venus,* Bernstein's *Candide*, Boublil and Schönberg's *Les Miserables*, and Andrew Lloyd Webber's *Phantom of the Opera* and *Evita* all require a strong classical vocal technique to sing well. Current and recent American musicals such as *Wicked*, *Grey Gardens*, *Memphis*, and *Light in the Piazza*, continue to produce songs that are a valuable contribution to American musical theatre.

THE FUTURE OF SONG

The current state of art song composition is very different today than it was in the nineteenth and first half of the twentieth centuries. In fact, it is almost a revival of the lifestyles of the early lutenists in England, troubadours in France, and Puritans in the United States.

Musicians who are composing today are most likely writing songs in addition to teaching full time or holding down other full-time professions. It is a necessary practicality to have some kind of structure in which to do creative work; many modern composers work within a university or college or professional society. In these established structures they are able to network with other musicians, find eager young singers to perform and record their works, and venture out toward opportunities for publication and advertising, as is convenient.

Today's climate for composers is extremely competitive, challenging, and limited. Music education continues to trend downward and there are fewer opportunities to work in music or the performing arts. Digital music has brought about a huge shift in how music is bought and shared and has changed both the music publishing landscape and opportunities for composers.

There are positive trends as well. Organizations such as the American Composers Forum (ACF) support and encourage new song composition with the "Art Songs for the 21st Century" competition. In addition to monetary awards, the competition performances offer composers an excellent opportunity for their songs to be heard by an influential and diverse audience.

American composers John Musto, Ricky Ian Gordon, and Jake Heggie use the forum of websites to connect themselves to the rest of the world. For example, on Musto's website, it is possible to listen to his songs, watch live performances, see what work he has been doing, review a list of his compositions and discography, order and purchase music, and contact him directly.

Current American song composers include: André Previn (known in popular culture as the stepfather of Woody Allen's wife Soon-Yi), John Corigliano, Judith Zaimont, Libby Larsen, John Musto, Lori Laitman, Ricky Ian Gordon, William Bolcom, Judith Cloud, and Jake Heggie, among others.

The New York Festival of Song (NYFOS) is dedicated to "the presentation of vocal music and the creation of unusual performance opportunities for singers. The mission of the NYFOS is to recreate the song recital through the development of programming that is both unique and diverse in language, culture, and theme."[4] NYFOS has set the standard for themed recitals such as: *Lyrics by Shakespeare, Scenes from Childhood, New American Works, The Russian Masters, Great American Songwriting Teams, Birthday Bash for Francis Poulenc*, and *A Modern Person's Guide to Hooking Up and Breaking Up*. Its founders are Steven Blier and Michael Barrett.

Other organizations like the Art Song Project, Florestan Recital Project, the African American Art Song Alliance, the Ravinia Stean's Music Institute, the Aspen Music Festival, the Vancouver International Song Festival, the Vocal Arts Society in Washington, D.C., Songfest, the Marilyn Horne Legacy at the Weill Institute at Carnegie Hall, and the newly formed Song Source Festival in Minneapolis, MN, all work to provide opportunities for the art song to evolve.

AMERICAN SINGERS AND THEIR SONGS

American singers are known for their ability to sing well in several languages, for their acting skills, and for their professionalism. American singers are comprehensively trained in conservatories, universities, and colleges and have the option to obtain a liberal arts education while working on a music degree if they choose.

HAROLYN BLACKWELL (1955–)

Harolyn Blackwell is an American soprano from Washington, D.C. She has performed all over the world in opera, oratorio, musical theatre, and song recital. Ms. Blackwell began studying music in elementary school and has said that her high school choral director encouraged her to pursue music as a career. She received two degrees in music from Catholic University in Washington, D.C. She is a graduate of the Lyric Opera of Chicago young artist program and a winner of the Metropolitan Opera National Council Auditions. Ms. Blackwell has performed many opera roles including Zerlina in *Don Giovanni* and Gilda in *Rigoletto*. She recorded the role of Clara in *Porgy and Bess* and the recording won a Grammy Award. She has sung on Broadway in Bernstein's *Candide* and performed at the White House for President George W. and Laura Bush.

Ms. Blackwell has championed the songs of American composers consistently throughout her career. An early association with Leonard Bernstein on a *West Side Story* revival sparked an interest in performing and recording his works. In later years, she has debuted and recorded songs of more recent composers such as Ricky Ian Gordon's *Genius Child*.

Recordings

Blackwell Sings Bernstein: A Simple Song, Harolyn Blackwell, soprano, RCA Victor, 1996
Strange Hurt, Harolyn Blackwell, soprano, Masterworks Broadway, 1994 (Songs of Ricky Ian Gordon, including the cycle *Genius Child*)

THOMAS HAMPSON (1955–)

Thomas Hampson is a highly successful American baritone. He has enjoyed a wide-ranging career including many opera roles, recitals, recordings, and concerts with orchestra.

He is from the state of Washington and achieved many important milestones very early in his career. He was noticed by San Francisco Opera at an audition and completed the Merola Opera Program. Around the same time, he was a winner in the Metropolitan Opera National Council Auditions. He then won a contract with an opera house in Düsseldorf, Germany where he began his opera career in earnest. Unlike some opera singers, Hampson began seeking out opportunities to perform song early in his career. He ended up performing at several high-profile occasions such as the Bernstein-conducted Vienna Philharmonic performances of Mahler's *Kindertotenlieder, Rückert Lieder,* and *Lieder einses fahrenden Gesellen,* and the opening of the 1991 New York Philharmonic season on live television by singing Aaron Copland's *Old American Songs.*

Hampson has a great interest in song and founded the Hampsong Foundation in 2003. He has made great efforts to bring song to a wide audience through projects like the "Song of America" radio series co-produced with the WFMT Radio Network of Chicago. The program presents different hour-long programs that explore the history of American culture through song.[5] The program also included a national tour of song recital performances across the United States. Another one of his projects is in collaboration with the Library of Congress and is called the "Song of America" project.[6] His other projects include research delving into the lives of American composers, an examination and recording of Schubert's *Winterreise,* an in-depth study of Schumann's first song cycle originally titled *Lieder und Gesänge aus dem "Lyrischen Intermezzo"* and later known as *Dichterliebe,* and a study of the poet Walt Whitman.

Recordings

American Dreamer: Songs of Stephen Foster, Thomas Hampson, baritone, Angel Records, 1992

American Songs—Aaron Copland, Thomas Hampson, baritone, Dawn Up-
shaw, soprano, Teldec, 1994 (Copland's *Old American Songs* and *Eight
Poems of Emily Dickinson*)
Des Knaben Wunderhorn, Thomas Hampson, baritone, Geoffrey Parsons,
piano, Warner Classics, 2014 (Songs of Mahler, Brahms, Mendelssohn,
Strauss, Schoenberg, and others)
Lieder, Thomas Hampson, baritone, Armen Guzelimian, piano, Warner Clas-
sics, 1991 (Songs of Ives, MacDowell, and Griffes)
Rossini and Meyerbeer, Thomas Hampson, baritone, Geoffrey Parsons, pia-
no, EMI Classics, 1992
Song of America: Music from the Library of Congress, Thomas Hampson,
baritone, Angel Records, 2005 (Songs of Griffes, Foster, Bernstein, Weill,
Burleigh, and others)
To the Soul: Thomas Hampson Sings the Poetry of Walt Whitman, Thomas
Hampson, baritone, Craig Rutenberg, piano, EMI Classics, 1997 (Songs of
Rorem, Bernstein, Busby, Ives, Bacon, Vaughan Williams, and others)

DAWN UPSHAW (1960–)

Dawn Upshaw is an American soprano from Tennessee. She was trained at
Illinois Wesleyan University, Manhattan School of Music, and the Aspen
Music School. She had early success as a winner of the Naumburg Competition. She has been a regular on the roster of the Metropolitan Opera and has
performed many roles there and in other opera houses. She is known for her
commitment to modern repertory, her intelligence, and her outstanding musicianship.

Ms. Upshaw has a special interest in song study and performance and in
premiering works by new composers, including works written for her. She
has introduced new techniques in song performance such as in a recent
performance at the Brooklyn Academy of Music: "Upshaw turned her back
to the audience and leaned over the uncovered strings of a grand piano . . .
steadying herself on the instrument's frame with her hands, she bent over
deeply and began to sing . . . echoes floated up from the instrument and
hovered about her like an iridescent aura."[7] This performance was of George
Crumb's *Ancient Voices of Children*, a famous vocal work with many nontraditional instruments that was first recorded in 1971 by Upshaw's teacher Jan
DeGaetani. Upshaw is the rare singer who is truly interested in bringing new
works to life. She has said that she feels "more alive when working with
composers on new pieces than when I'm doing anything out of the canon . . .
the interaction with my colleagues became much more fun and exciting than
whether I was going to sing again at the Vienna Staatsoper."[8] She continues

to take risks musically and choose projects that she cares for deeply. Many of her song recordings have set the standard for song interpretation.

Recordings

Forgotten Songs, Dawn Upshaw, soprano, James Levine, piano, Sony Classical, 1997 (Songs of Claude Debussy)
Goethe Lieder, Dawn Upshaw, soprano, Richard Goode, piano, Nonesuch, 1993 (Lieder with poems by Goethe)
I Wish it So, Dawn Upshaw, soprano, Nonesuch, 2008 (Songs of Marc Blitzstein, Bernstein, Sondheim, and Weill)
Songs of the Auvergne, Conducted by Kent Nagano, Dawn Upshaw, soprano, Erato, 1994 (Songs from *Chants d'Auvergne* by Joseph Canteloube)
Voices of Light, Dawn Upshaw, soprano, Gilbert Kalish, piano, Nonesuch, 2014 (Songs of Messiaen, Debussy, Golijov, and Fauré)

AUDRA MCDONALD (1970–)

Audra McDonald has had a career that is as successful as it is rare. She has performed in concert, on Broadway, and on television. As of 2014, she is the Tony Awards' most recognized artist with six awards.

Ms. McDonald is from California and completed her music degree at the Juilliard School. Her Broadway career began at Lincoln Center Theatre in *Carousel* and her opera career at the Houston Grand Opera. She has many television credits included *Having Our Say: The Delaney Sisters' First 100 Years; Annie; Law and Order: Special Victims Unit; Wit; Private Practice;* and the *The Sound of Music.* Her film credits include *The Object of My Affection* and *She Got Problems.* Her work on national television, high profile performances in various genres, and Broadway career have given Ms. McDonald a recognizability that few artists who sing classical music obtain.

Despite her diverse musical interests, she has maintained her instrument extremely well. Carnegie Hall commissioned a song cycle for her called *The Seven Deadly Sins: A Song Cycle* that she performed in 2004.

Recordings

Carousel, Broadway Revival Cast Recording, Angel Records, 1994
How Glory Goes, Audra McDonald, soprano, Conducted by Eric Stern, Nonesuch, 2000 (Various musical theatre songs, including Harold Arlen)
Lady Day at Emerson's Bar and Grill, Original Broadway Cast Recording, P. S. Classics, 2014
Porgy and Bess, New Broadway Cast, P. S. Classics, 2012

Ragtime: The Musical, Original Broadway Cast, RCA Victor Broadway, 1996

The following list of songs by American composers is not comprehensive but provides an overview of the material available.

SONG LIST

Dominick Argento

Six Elizabethan Songs
  Spring
  Sleep
  Winter
  Dirge
  Diaphenia
  Hymn
From the Diary of Virginia Woolf
  The Diary
  Anxiety
  Fancy
  Hardy's Funeral
  Rome
  War
  Parents
  Last Entry
Letters from Composers
  Frederic Chopin to a Friend
  W. A. Mozart to His Father
  Franz Schubert to a Friend
  J. S. Bach to the Town Council
  Claude Debussy to a Friend
  Giacomo Puccini to a Friend
  Robert Schumann to His Fiancée
Songs About Spring
  who knows if the moon's a balloon
  Spring is like a perhaps hand
  in Just-Spring
  in Spring comes
  when faces called flowers float out of the ground

Samuel Barber

Despite and Still
  A Last Song
  My Lizard
  In the Wilderness
  Solitary Hotel
  Despite and Still
Hermit Songs
  At Saint Patrick's Purgatory
  Church Bell at Night
  Saint Ita's Vision
  The Heavenly Banquet
  The Crucifixion
  Sea-snatch
  Promiscuity
  The Monk and His Cat
  The Praises of God
  The Desire for Hermitage
Mélodies passagères
  Puisque tout passé
  Un cygne
  Tombeau dans un parc
  Le clocher chante
  Départ
Three Songs
  Now Have I Fed and Eaten Up the Rose
  A Green Lowland of Pianos
  O Boundless, Boundless Evening

Amy Beach

A Light That Overflows
A Prelude
A Song of Liberty
Across the World
An Old Love-Story
April Dreams
Autumn Song
Canzonetta
Chanson d'amour
Dark is the Night
Dusk

In June
Ecstasy
Empress of Night
Evening Song
Fairy Lullaby
Fire and Flame
Forget-Me-Not
Forgotten
I Know Not How to Find the Spring
May Flowers
My Love Come Through the Fields
My Star
O Sweet Content
Prayer of a Tired Child
Sea Song
Separation
Scottish Cradle Song
Silent Love
Song in the Hills
Sweetheart, Sigh No More
The Blackbird
The Canticle of the Sun
The Children's Thanks
The Clover
The Moonpath
The Night Sea
The Rainy Day
The Singer
The Western Wind
Though I Take the Wings of Morning
Time Has Wings and Swiftly Flies
Twilight
When Mama Sings
Who Has Seen the Wind?
With Granny
With Violets
Within Thy Heart

Leonard Bernstein

I Hate Music!: A Cycle of Five Kid Songs
    My Name is Barbara
    Jupiter Has Seven Moons

I Hate Music!
A Big Indian and a Little Indian
I'm a Person Too
La Bonne Cuisine
 Plum Pudding
 Queues de Boeuf
 Tavouk Gueunksis
 Civet à Toute Vitesse
Two Love Songs
 Extinguish My Eyes
 When My Soul Touches Yours

William Bolcom

Ancient Cabaret
 On a Statue of a Runner
 Unlucky Eutichus
 An Encaustic Painting
 Timomarchus's Picture of Medea
 In Rome
 Praxiteles' Aphrodite
Briefly It Enters
 Who
 The Clearing
 Otherwise
 February
 Thinking of Flowers
 Twilight: After Haying
 Man Eating
 The Sick Wife
 Peonies at Dusk
 Briefly It Enters
 Briefly Speaks
Cabaret Songs (Volumes 1 and 2)
 Over the Piano
 Fur (Murray the Furrier)
 He Tipped the Waiter
 Waitin
 Song of Black Max
 Amor
 Places to Live
 Toothbrush Time
 Surprise!

The Actor
Oh, Close the Curtain, George
Cabaret Songs (Volumes 3 and 4)
    The Total Stranger in the Garden
    Love in the Thirties
    Thius, King of Orf
    Miracle Song
    Satisfaction
    Radical Sally
    Angels are the Highest Form of Virtue
    Poet Pal of Mine
    Can't Sleep
    At the Last Lousy Moments of Love
    Lady Love
    Blue
Canciones de Lorca
    Balanza
    La casada infiel
    Alba
    Danza da lua en Santiago
    Arboles
    Soneto de la dulce queja
    El poeta llega a la Habana
From the Diary of Sally Hemings
    I Will Breathe a Mountain
Laura Sonnets
    Lime Jell-O Marshmallow Cottage Cheese Surprise
    Mary
    Minicabs
    Old Addresses
    Rhyme
    September 1, 1939
Songs of Innocence and of Experience
Songs to Dance
    Sonnet 29
    The Digital Wonder Watch
    The Last Days of Mankind
    Tillinghast Duo
    Vaslav's Song
    Villanelle

Margaret Bonds

Dry Bones
He's Got the Whole World in His Hands
Lord I Just Can't Keep From Crying
Stopping by Woods on a Snowy Evening
The Negro Speaks of Rivers
The Pasture
Three Dream Portraits
    Minstrel Man
    Dream Variation
    I, Too

Paul Bowles

A Little Closer Please
Blue Mountain Ballads
    Heavenly Grass
    Lonesome Man
    Cabin
    Sugar in the Cane
David
Her Head on the Pillow
In the Platinum Forest
Letter to Freddy
Lullaby
Night Without Sleep
On a Quiet Conscience
Secret Words: A Suite of Six Songs
    Once a Lady Was Here
    In the Woods
    April Fool Baby
    Farther from the Heart
    My Sister's Hand in Mine
    Secret Words
Sleeping Song
Song for My Sister
The Piper
They Cannot Stop Death

Aaron Copland

A Summer Vacation
Alone

An Immorality
Dirge in Woods
Night
Old American Songs, First Set
    The Boatman's Dance
    The Dodger
    Long Time Ago
    Simple Gifts
    I Bought Me a Cat
Old American Songs, Second Set
    The Little Horses
    Zion's Walls
    The Golden Willow Tree
    At the River
    Ching-a-Ring Chaw
Twelve Poems of Emily Dickinson
    Nature, the Gentlest Mother
    There Came the Wind Like a Bugle
    Why do They Shut Me Out of Heaven?
    The World Feels Dusty
    Heart, We Will Forget Him
    Dear March, Come In!
    Sleep is Supposed to Be
    When They Come Back
    I Felt a Funeral in My Brain
    I've Heard an Organ Talk Sometimes
    Going to Heaven!
    The Chariot
Pastorale
The House on the Hill

John Duke

A Piper
April Elegy
Bells in the Rain
Dirge
Evening
Five Lewis Carroll Poems
    The Lobster Quadrille
    Jabberwocky
    The little Crocodile
    The Mock Turtle's song

The Duchess' Lullaby
Four Poems by Emily Dickinson
    New feet within my garden go
    The rose did caper on her cheek
    Have you got a brook in your little heart
    I taste a liquor never brewed
From the Sea, Five Songs for Soprano
    All beauty calls you to me
    Listen, I love you
    I am so weak a thing
    O my love
    All things in all the world
Go, Lovely Rose
Good Morning! A Cycle of Six Songs for High Voice
    Good morning!
    Walking in the rain
    Those great clouds there
    Water that falls and runs away
    Listen to us, the leaves say
    Merry-go-round
Jabberwocky
Just-Spring
I Can't Be Talkin' of Love
i carry your heart
I Ride the Great Black Horses
Little Elegy
Luke Havergal
One Red Rose
Remembrance
Silver
Songs Out of Sorrow
    Spirit's house
    Mastery
    Lessons
    In a burying ground
    Wood song
    Refuge
The Bird
The Grunchin' Witch
The Heart of a Rose
The Mountains are Dancing
The Old King
The Shoreless Sea

The White Dress
There Will be Stars
Velvet Shoes
White in the Moon
Wild Swans
Woman, if You Were Dead

Stephen Foster

Beautiful Dreamer
Better times are coming
Come where my love lies dreaming
De Camptown Races
Gentle Annie
Hard times, come again no more
Jeanie with the Light Brown Hair
My Old Kentucky Home
My wife is a most knowing woman
Nelly Bly
Nelly was a lady
Oh! Susanna
Old Black Joe
Some folks
Summer longing
The song of all songs
The Swanee River
Thou art the queen of my song
Was my brother in the battle?

Ricky Ian Gordon

A horse with wings
and flowers pick themselves . . .
Autumn Valentine Suite
Blessing the Boats
Can You Look Me in the Eyes?
Five Americans
Fury
Genius Child
    Winter moon
    Genius child
    Kid in the park
    To be somebody

Troubled woman
Strange hurt
Prayer
Border line
My people
Joy
Green Sneakers
Heartbeats
Heaven
Home of the Brave
I Never Knew
I understand you coyotes
I Was Thinking of You
Is it Morning?
Late Afternoon
Night Flight to San Francisco
Open All Night
Orpheus and Euridice
Poem
Sweet Song
The Red Dress
Three floors
Through Mortal Waters
Too Few the Mornings Be
Virginia Woolf
What the Living Do
Will there really be a morning?

Charles Griffes

A Feast of Lanterns
An den Wind
An Old Song Re-Sung
By A Lonely Forest Pathway
Des Müden Abendlied
Elfe
Evening Song
Frühe
In a Myrtle Shade
In the Harem
Le jardin
Le réveillon
Nachtlied

Night on Ways Unknown Has Fallen
Phantoms
Pierrot
Si mes vers avaient des ailes
Song of the Dagger
Symphony in yellow
The First Snowfall
The Half-Ring Moon
The Lament of Ian the Proud
The Old Temple Among the Mountains
The Rose of the Night
The War-Song of the Vikings
The Water-Lily
Two Birds Flew into the Sunset Glow
We'll to the Woods and Gather May
Winternacht
Wo ich bin, mich rings umdunkeit

Jake Heggie

A Question of Light
    The Light of Coincidences
    Eccentric Flint
    Yellow Flowers in a Vase
Camille Claudel: Into the Fire
Encountertenor
    Countertenor's Conundrum
    The trouble with trebles in trousers . . . (Pitch can be a bitch!)
    A Gift to Share
Farewell, Auschwitz, from Out of Darkness
For a Look or a Touch, from Out of Darkness
Friendly Persuasions: Homage to Poulenc
    Wanda Landowska
    Pierre Bernac
    Raymond Linossier
    Paul Éluard
Grow Old Along with Me!
Here/After Song Collections
Here and Gone
    The Farms of Home
    In Praise of Songs that Die
    Stars
    The Factory Window Song

In the Morning
Because I Liked You Better
The Half-Moon Westers Low
How Well I Knew the Light
Ample Make This Bed
The Sun Kept Setting
Natural Selection
Creation
Animal Passion
Alas! Alack!
Indian Summer—Blue
Connection
Newer Every Day: Songs for Kiri
Silence
I'm Nobody! Who are You?
Of Gods and Cats
In the beginning . . .
Once upon a universe
Of Laughter and Farewell
By the Spring, At Sunset
Under the Blessing of Your Psyche Wings
Passing By
Motherwit
Grounded
Hummingbird—for Tess
Mother in the Mirror
Facing Forward
Songs and Sonnets to Ophelia
Ophelia's Song
Women Have Loved Before
Not in a Silver Casket
Spring
Songs to the Moon
Prologue: Once More—To Gloriana
Euclid
The Haughty Snail-King
What the Rattlesnake Said
The Moon's the North Wind's
Statuesque
Henry Moore: Reclining Figure of Elmwood
Pablo Picasso: Head of a Woman, 1932
Hapshetsut: The Divine Potter
Alberto Giacommetti: Standing Woman

Winged Victory: We're Through
The Breaking Waves
  Advent
  Darkness
  Music
  Return
The Starry Night
  The Starry Night
  Celestial Locomotion
  Go Thy Great Way
Thoughts Unspoken
  A learning experience over coffee . . .
  You enter my thoughts
  To speak of love
  Unspoken thoughts at bedtime

Lee Hoiby

Four Dickinson Songs
  A Letter
  How the Waters Closed
  Wild Nights
  There Came the Wind Like a Bugle
I Was There
  Beginning My Studies
  I Was There
  A Clear Midnight
  O Captain! My Captain!
  Joy, Shipmate, Joy!
Night Songs
  Night
  Pierrot
  Angélique
  The Shroud
Rain Forest
  Giant Toad
  Strayed Crab
  Giant Snail
  Sandpiper
Songs for Leontyne
  The Doe
  Evening
  Autumn

Winter Song
In the Wand of the Wind
The Serpent
Southern Voices
  Butterflies
  Lullaby
  Bells for John Whiteside's Daughter
  Berenice Sadie Brown
The Life of the Bee
  Millennium Approaches
  The Spirit of the Hive
  The Queen
  The Sting
  The Swarm
Three Ages of Woman
  Manners
  Filling Station
  Insomnia
Three Women
  Miss Alma Calls
  Lady of the Harbor
  The Waltz
Two Songs of Innocence
  The Shepherd
  The Lamb

Richard Hundley

Arise My Love
Astronomers
Ballad on Queen Anne's Death
Come Ready and See Me
Epitaph of a Young Girl
Epitaph on a Wife
Evening Hours
For Your Delight
I Do
Isaac Greentree
Maiden Snow
Moonlight's Watermelon
My Master Hath a Garden
O My Darling Troubles Heaven with her Loveliness
screw spring

seashore girls
Softly the Summer
Some Sheep are Loving
Spring
Straightway Beauty on Me Waits
Strings in the Earth and Air
Sweet River
Sweet Suffolk Owl
Waterbird
When Children are Playing Alone on the Green
When Orpheus Played
Will There Really Be a Morning

Charles Ives

A Night Song
A Scotch Lullaby
A Sea Dirge
Abide With Me
An Old Flame
Because of You
December
Die Lotosblume
Dreams
Du alte Mutter
Evening
Far From My Heav'nly Home
Feldeinsamkeit
General William Booth Enters Into Heaven
God Bless and Keep Thee
Her Gown Was of Vermilion Silk
His Exaltation
I Knew and Loved a Maid
I Travelled Among Unknown Men
Immortality
In April-Tide
In Flanders Fields
In the Mornin'
Maple Leaves
Minnelied
My Lou Jennine
No More
Omens and Oracles

Peaks
Pictures
Resolution
Rock of Ages
Slugging a Vampire
Soliloquy
Songs My Mother Taught Me
The Ending Year
The Greatest Man
The Indians
The Light that is Felt
The New River
The One Way
The Side Show
The Waiting Soul
The White Gulls
There is a Certain Garden
Those Evening Bells
The World's Highway
To Edith
Two Little Flowers
Widmung
Yellow Leaves
Five Street Songs
    Old Home Day
    In the Alley
    A Son of Gambolier
    Down East
    The Circus Band

Libby Larsen

Chanting to Paradise
Cowboy Songs
    I. Bucking Bronco
    II. Lift Me Into Heaven Slowly
    III. Billy the Kid
Late in the Day
Love After 1950
Lullay of the Nativity
Margaret Songs: Three Songs of Willa Cather
    I. Bright Rails
    II. So Little There

III. Beneath the Hawthorne Tree
Me (text by Brenda Ueland)
    I. Why I Write This Book
    II. Childhood
    III. Adolescence
    IV. Greenwich Village
    V. Marriage . . . Divorce
    VI. Work
    VII. Art (Life is Love . . .)
    VIII. The Present
My Antonia
    I. Landscape—From the Train
    II. Antonia
    III. Landscape II—Winter
    IV. The Hired Girls
    V. Landscape III—Prairie Spring
    VI. Antonia in the Field . . .
    VII. Landscape IV—Sunset
My Candle Burns
Songs from Letters
    I. So Like Your Father's (1880)
    II. He Never Misses (1880)
    III. A Man Can Love Two Women (1880)
    IV. A Working Woman (1882–1893)
    V. All I Have (1902)
Take
The Apple's Song
The Magdalene
Try Me, Good King: Last Words of the Wives of Henry VIII
    I. Katherine of Aragon
    II. Anne Boleyn
    III. Jane Seymour
    IV. Anne of Cleves
    V. Katherine Howard
When I am an Old Woman

Douglas Moore

Dedication
Simon Legree
The Ballad of William Sycamore
The Cupboard
The Mysterious Cat

Three Sonnets of John Donne Set to Music
   Batter My Heart
   Thou Hast Made Me
   Death Be Not Proud
Under the Greenwood Tree

Undine Smith Moore

Watch and Pray
Love Let the Wind Cry . . . How I Adore Thee
I Am In Doubt
Is There Anyone Here That Loves My Jesus
Come Down Angels

John Musto

Canzonettas
   Western Wind
   All Night by the Rose
   The Silver Swan
Dove Sta Amore
   Maybe
   Sea Chest
   The Hangman At Home
   How Many Little Children Sleep
   Dove Sta Amore
Enough Rope
   Social Note
   Résumé
   The Sea
Flamenco
I stop writing the poem
I want
Lament
Love is a place
Nude at the Piano
Old Photograph
Passacaglia
Penelope
   Prologue
   Penelope's Lament
   Weaving Song
   Epithalamium

The Suitors
Odyssey
Penelope's Song
Quiet Songs
    maggie and milly and molly and may
    Intermezzo
    Quiet Song
    Christmas Carol (To Jesus on His Birthday)
    Palm Sunday: Naples
    Lullaby
Recuerdo
    Echo
    Recuerdo
    Last Song
San José Symphony Reception
Sarah's Song
Scottish Songs
    Spell of the Bridge
    Atheist Lighting a Candle in Albi Cathedral
    Flowers
    Not That It's Loneliness
    Langsyne, When Life Was Bonnie
    Driven Home
Shadow of the Blues
    Silhouette
    Litany
    Island
    Could Be
The Brief Light
    When you danced
    Song
    The Voices
    The Brief Light
    The Summons
    I have drifted
Triolet
Two by Frost
    Nothing Gold Can Stay
    The Rose Family
Viva Sweet Love
    as is the sea marvelous
    Rome: In the Café
    You came as a thought

Crystal Palace Market
Sweet Spring
Witness
Words to Be Spoken

John Jacob Niles

Folk Songs
I'm in the Notion Now
I wonder as I wander
Jack O'Diamonds
Jesus, Jesus, rest your head
Lulle Lullay
O Waly, O Waly
Sing We the Virgin Mary
The Carol of the Birds
The Cuckoo
The Frog in the Spring
The Seven Joys of Mary
The Turtle Dove
You Got to Cross that Lonesome Valley
Original Songs
Black is the color of my true love's hair
Evening
Go 'way from my window
Little Black Star
My lover is a farmer lad
Ribbon Bow
Sweet Little Boy Jesus
The Black Dress
The Carol of the Birds
The Flower of Jesse
The Gambler's Songs
The Rovin' Gambler (based on preexisting material)
The Gambler's Lament
The Gambler's Wife
Gambler, don't you lose your place
Gambler's Song of the Big Sandy River
The Lass from the Low Countree
The Lotus Bloom
The Robin and the Thorn
The Wild Rider
Unused I am to lovers

What Songs Were Sung
When I get up into Heaven

Florence Price

Dreamin' Town
Feet o' Jesus
Go down, Moses
My dream
My little soul's goin' to shine
My soul's been anchored in the Lord
Night
Songs to the dark virgin
Trouble done come my way
What's the use?

William Grant Still

And They Lynched Him on a Tree
From the Hearts of Women
    Little Mother
    Midtide
    Coquette
    Bereft
Grief
Plain Chant for America
Songs of Separation
    Idolatry
    Poème
    Parted
    If You Should Go
    A Black Pierrot
The Breath of a Rose
Wailing Woman
Winter's Approach

Appendix A

Recommended Recordings

ITALIAN SONG RECORDINGS

Amore: Romantic Italian Love Songs
Luciano Pavarotti, tenor
Decca, 1992
(Compilation of Italian songs and arias)

Cecilia Bartoli: An Italian Songbook
Cecilia Bartoli, mezzo-soprano
London Decca, 1997
(Songs of Rossini, Bellini, and Donizetti)

Composer as Pianist: Alfredo Casella and Ottorino Respighi
Pierian, 2005
(Songs of Respighi and traditional Italian songs)

Dmitri Hvorostovsky: Arie Antiche
Dmitri Hvorostovsky, baritone
Polygram Classics, 1998
(Various 18th century Italian songs)

Farinelli: Il Castrato
Film Soundtrack
Auvidis Travelling, 1995

Early Italian Songs and Mozart Arias
Ezio Pinza, tenor
Pearl, 1993

(Songs of Monteverdi, Scarlatti, Cavalli, Mozart, and others)

Enrico Caruso: The Complete Recordings
Enrico Caruso, tenor
Naxos, 2004

Enrico Caruso in Song
Enrico Caruso, tenor
Nimbus, 1990
(Various traditional Italian songs)
Farinelli

If You Love Me: 18th Century Italian Songs
Cecilia Bartoli, mezzo-soprano
London Decca, 1992
(Various 18th century Italian songs)

In Song
Enrico Caruso, tenor
RCA, 1965
(Compilation of Italian songs)

Italian Songs
Enrico Caruso, tenor
RCA, 2002
(Various Italian songs)

Live in Italy
Cecilia Bartoli, mezzo-soprano
Decca, 1998
(Bellini, Caccini, Rossini, Mozart, and others)

Neapolitan Songs and Romances
Enrico Caruso, tenor
Butterfly Italy, 2013
(Traditional Neapolitan songs)

O Sole Mio: Favourite Neapolitan Songs
Luciano Pavarotti, tenor
London Decca, 1983
(Traditional Neapolitan Songs)

O Holy Night
Luciano Pavarotti, tenor
Decca, 1990
(Italian and Latin songs with a religious theme)

Renata Tebaldi: The New York Farewell Recital 1976

Renata Tebaldi, soprano
Video Artists International, 1976
(Italian songs by various composers)

Rossini and Meyerbeer
Thomas Hampson, baritone
Geoffrey Parsons, piano
EMI Classics, 1992
(Songs of Rossini and Meyerbeer)

Sicilia Bella
Marcello Giordani, tenor
Video Artists International, 2002

Sumi Jo: La Promessa, Italian Songs
Sumi Jo, soprano
Alliance, 1998
(Songs of Tosti, Caldara, Donaudy, Gluck, and others)

The Last Castrato: Complete Vatican Recordings
Alessandro Moreschi, castrato
Pearl, 1902 and 1904

Volare: Popular Italian Songs
Luciano Pavarotti, tenor
Decca, 1990
(Various Italian songs)

GERMAN SONG RECORDINGS

Bach Cantatas
Matthias Goerne, baritone
Decca, 2000
(Cantatas by J. S. Bach)

Brahms: The Complete Songs, Volumes One and Two
Christine Schäfer, soprano
Graham Johnson, piano
Hyperion, 2011
(Songs of Johannes Brahms)

Das Lied von der Erde
Dietrich Fischer-Dieskau, baritone
Fritz Wunderlich, tenor
Deutsche Grammophon, 2011

(Songs of Gustav Mahler)

Des Knaben Wunderhorn
Thomas Hampson, baritone
Geoffrey Parsons, piano
Warner Classics, 2014
(Songs of Mahler, Brahms, Mendelssohn, Strauss, Schoenberg, and others)

Goethe Lieder
Dawn Upshaw, soprano
Richard Goode, piano
Nonesuch, 2008
(Lieder with poems by Goethe)

Jane Eaglen
Jane Eaglen, soprano
SME (Sony Music Entertainment), 2000
(Berg's *Seven Early Songs*, Wagner's *Wesendonck Lieder*, and Strauss' *Four Last Songs*)

Lieder
Thomas Hampson, baritone
Armen Guzelimian, piano
Warner Classics, 2014
(Songs of Ives, MacDowell, and Griffes)

Lieder
Diana Damrau, soprano
Helmut Deutsch, piano
Orfeo, 2008
(Songs of Clara and Robert Schumann, Fanny and Felix Mendelssohn, Brahms, and Liszt)

Liszt Lieder
Diana Damrau, soprano
Helmut Deutsch, piano
Erato, 2011
(Songs of Franz Liszt)

Poesie
Diana Damrau, soprano
Virgin Classics, 2011
(Songs of Richard Strauss with orchestra)

Schoenberg: Pierrot Lunaire
Christine Schäfer, soprano

Deutsche Grammophon, 1998
(Arnold Schoenberg's song cycle *Pierrot Luna*ire)

Schubert: Die schöne Müllerin
Fritz Wunderlich, tenor
Hubert Giesen, pianist
Deutsche Grammophon, 1996
(Franz Schubert's song cycle *Die schöne Müllerin*)

Schubert Erlkönig
Matthias Goerne, baritone
Andreas Haefliger, piano
Harmonia Mundi, 2013
(Franz Schubert's Lieder)

Schubert: Goethe-Lieder
Dietrich Fischer-Dieskau, baritone
Gerald Moore, piano
Deutsche Grammophon, 1999
(Franz Schubert's Lieder with poetry by Goethe)

Schubert Lieder
Dietrich Fischer-Dieskau, baritone
Deutsche Grammophon, 2010
(Song cycles of Franz Schubert)

Schubert: Winterreise
Peter Pears, tenor
Benjamin Britten, piano
Polygram Records, 2000
(Franz Schubert's song cycle *Winterreise*)

Schubert: Winterreise
Christine Schäfer, soprano
Eric Schneider, piano
Onyx Classics UK, 2006
(Franz Schubert's song cycle *Winterreise*)

Schuman: Dichterliebe
Fritz Wunderlich, tenor
Hubert Giesen, pianist
Deutsche Grammophon, 1997
(Robert Schumann's song cycle *Dichterliebe*)

The Art of Dietrich Fischer-Dieskau
Dietrich Fischer-Dieskau, baritone
Deutsche Grammophon, 2005

(Various songs)

The Songs of Robert Schumann
Christine Schäfer, soprano
Graham Johnson, piano
Hyperion, 1996
(Songs of Robert Schumann)

Ute Lemper Sings Weill
Ute Lemper, singer
Decca, 1988
(Songs of Kurt Weill)

Voice of the Century
Dietrich Fischer-Dieskau, baritone
Deutsche Grammophon, 2014
(Songs of Schubert, Schumann, Liszt, Beethoven, Brahms, and others)

Wanderer's Nachtlied
Matthias Goerne, baritone
Harmonia Mundi, 2014
(Lieder of Franz Schubert)

FRENCH SONG RECORDINGS

Amor
Natalie Dessay, soprano (and other singers)
Virgin Classics, 2010
(Songs of Richard Strauss, with orchestra)

Debussy: Mélodies
Gerard Souzay, baritone
Deutsche Grammophon, 2008
(Songs of Debussy)

Debussy: Mélodies
François Le Roux, baritone
Noël Lee, piano
Le Chant de Monde, 2000
(Songs of Debussy)

Debussy: Claire de Lune
Natalie Dessay, soprano
Philippe Cassard, piano
Virgin Classics, 2012

(Songs of Debussy)

Forgotten Songs
Dawn Upshaw, soprano
James Levine, piano
Sony Classical, 1997
(Songs of Claude Debussy)

Francis Poulenc: The Complete Songs
Pierre Bernac, baritone and other singers
Graham Johnson, piano
Hyperion, 1977
(Songs of Francis Poulenc)

Gérard Souzay
Gérard Souzay, baritone
Jacqueline Bonneau, piano
Polygram Records, 1990
(Songs of Fauré and Chausson)

Mélodies
Christine Schäfer, soprano
Irwin Gage, piano
Deutsche Grammophon, 2000
(Mélodies of Ernest Chausson and Claude Debussy)

Pierre Bernac Sings Poulenc
Pierre Bernac, baritone
Francis Poulenc, piano
Preiser Records, 2010
(Songs of Francis Poulenc)

Sanctus: Sacred Songs
Roberto Alagna, tenor
EMI Classics, 1997
(Songs of Bach, Gounod, Franck, Fauré, Bizet, and others)

Songs of the Auvergne
Conducted by Kent Nagano
Dawn Upshaw, soprano
Erato, 1994
(Songs from *Chants d'Auvergne* by Joseph Canteloube)

The Essential Pierre Bernac
Pierre Bernac, baritone
Francis Poulenc, piano
Gerald Moore, piano

Graham Johnson, piano
Testament, 1999
(Songs of Poulenc, Duparc, and others)

BRITISH SONG RECORDINGS

A Treasury of English Song
Peter Pears, tenor
Benjamin Britten, piano
Decca, 2011
(Songs of Britten, Delius, Warlock, Ireland, Butterworth, and others)

Britten
Peter Pears, tenor
Benjamin Britten, piano
Polygram Records, 1991
(Music of Benjamin Britten)

Bryn Terfel: The Vagabond
Bryn Terfel, bass-baritone
Deutsche Grammophon, 1995
(Songs of Ralph Vaughan Williams)

English Song
Peter Pears, tenor
Benjamin Britten, piano
Heritage Records, 2012
(British songs)

Folk Songs
Anne Sofie von Otter, mezzo-soprano
Bengt Forsberg, piano
Deutsche Grammophon, 2000
(Songs by Benjamin Britten and Percy Grainger)

Peter Pears Anniversary Tribute
Peter Pears, tenor
Decca, 2010
(Six disc set of Britten songs and songs by others)

Scarborough Fair: Songs from the British Isles
Bryn Terfel, bass-baritone
Deutsche Grammophon, 2009
(Traditional songs of the British Isles)

Sense and Sensibility
Original Motion Picture Soundtrack, 1995
Featuring Jane Eaglen
(Original songs of Patrick Doyle)

Silent Noon
Bryn Terfel, bass-baritone
Malcolm Martineau, piano
Deutsche Grammophon, 2005
(Songs of Ralph Vaughan Williams and Roger Quilter)

Simple Gifts
Bryn Terfel, bass-baritone
Universal Music Group, 2005
(Various songs in English and Latin, religious theme)

The Vagabond
Bryn Terfel, bass-baritone
Deutsche Grammophon, 1995
(Songs of Vaughan Williams, Butterworth, Finzi, and Ireland)

AMERICAN SONG RECORDINGS

A Horse with Wings
Ricky Ian Gordon, voice and piano
BGR (Blue Griffin Records), 2010
(Songs of Ricky Ian Gordon)

After the Ball
Joan Morris, mezzo-soprano
William Bolcom, composer and pianist
Elektra Nonesuch, 1974
(Turn-of-the-century American songs)

All My Heart
Deborah Voigt, soprano
Angel Records/EMI Classics, 2005
(Songs of Ives, Bernstein, Amy Beach)

American Anthem
Nathan Gunn, baritone
EMI Classics, 1999
(Bolcom Cabaret Songs)

American Dreamer: Songs of Stephen Foster

Thomas Hampson, baritone
EMI Classics, 1992
(Songs of Stephen Foster)

American Folk and Gambling Songs
John Jacob Niles
Camden, 1956
(Songs of J. J. Niles and traditional songs)

American Songs
Thomas Hampson, baritone
Dawn Upshaw, soprano
Teldec, 1994
(Copland's *Old American Songs* and *Eight Poems of Emily Dickinson*)

An Evening with John Jacob Niles: The Tradition Years
John Jacob Niles
Empire Musicwerks, 2006
(Songs of J. J. Niles and traditional folk songs)

Blackwell Sings Bernstein: A Simple Song
Harolyn Blackwell, soprano
RCA Victor, 1996
(Songs of Leonard Bernstein)

Carousel
Broadway Revival Cast Recording
Angel Records, 1994

Connection: Three Song Cycles
Regina Zona, soprano
Kathleen Tagg, piano
Naxos, 2014
(Songs of Jake Heggie)

Daniel Okulitch: The New American Art Song
Daniel Okulitch, bass-baritone
GPR Records, 2011
(Song compilation, including songs of Jake Heggie)

Flesh and Stone: The Songs of Jake Heggie
Various singers
Americus Records, 2007
(Songs of Jake Heggie)

From the Diary of Sally Hemings
Alyson Cambridge, soprano
Lydia Brown, piano

White Pine Records, 2010
(Song cycle of William Bolcom)

Grand Larsen-y: Vocal Music of Libby Larsen
Terry Rhodes, soprano
Ellen Williams, mezzo-soprano
Benton Hess, piano
Albany Records, 2004
(Songs of Libby Larsen including *Margaret Songs, Songs from Letters,*
and others)

How Glory Goes
Audra McDonald, soprano
Conducted by Eric Stern
Nonesuch, 2001
(Various musical theatre songs, includes Harold Arlen)

I Wish it So
Dawn Upshaw, soprano
Nonesuch, 2008
(Songs of Marc Blitzstein, Bernstein, Sondheim, and Weill)

Kathleen Battle: Honey and Rue
Kathleen Battle, soprano
Deutsche Grammophon, 1995
(Song cycle *Honey and Rue* by André Previn)

Lady Day at Emerson's Bar and Grill
Original Broadway Cast Recording
P. S. Classics, 2014

Licorice Stick
Kathleen Roland, soprano
Katarina Strom-Harg, piano
Other performers
(Includes *Songs from Letters: Calamity Jane to her Daughter Janey*)
Independently produced, 2002

Once I Was: Songs of Ricky Ian Gordon
Stacey Tappan, soprano
Ricky Ian Gordon, piano
BGR (Blue Griffin Records), 2012
(Songs of Ricky Ian Gordon)

Open House: Song Cycle by William Bolcom and Robert Beaser
Paul Sperry, tenor
Innova, 2012

(Songs by Bolcom and Beaser)

Passing By: Songs by Jake Heggie
Various Singers
Jake Heggie, piano
Avie, 2010
(Songs of Jake Heggie)

Porgy and Bess
New Broadway Cast
P. S. Classics, 2012

Rappahannock County
Mark Walters, baritone
Various singers
Ricky Ian Gordon, piano
Naxos, 2013
(Songs of Ricky Ian Gordon)

Ragtime: The Musical
Original Broadway Cast
RCA Victor Broadway, 1998

Song of America: Music from the Library of Congress
Thomas Hampson, baritone
Angel Records, 2005
(Songs of Griffes, Foster, Bernstein, Weill, Burleigh, and others)

Songs of Innocence and of Experience
Various Singers
William Bolcom, composer
Naxos/American Classics, 2004
(Songs of William Bolcom)

Songs of Her Self
Liria Duo
Emily Murdock, soprano
Sara Parkinson, piano
Independently produced, 2013
(Songs of Libby Larsen)

Spirituals: Jessye Norman
Jessye Norman, soprano
Phillips, 1979
(Traditional spirituals)

Strange Hurt
Harolyn Blackwell, soprano

Masterworks Broadway, 2010
(Songs of Ricky Ian Gordon, including the cycle *Genius Child*)

Surprise
Measha Brueggergosman, soprano
William Bolcom, composer and pianist
Deutsche Grammophon, 2007
(Bolcom Cabaret Songs)

The Essential Leontyne Price: Spirituals, Hymns, and Sacred Songs
Leontyne Price, soprano
RCA, 1997

To the Soul: Thomas Hampson Sings the Poetry of Walt Whitman
Thomas Hampson, baritone
Craig Rutenberg, piano
EMI Classics, 1997
(Songs of Rorem, Bernstein, Busby, Ives, Bacon, Vaughan Williams, and
   others)

Thomas Hampson: An Old Song Re-Sung
Thomas Hampson, baritone
EMI, 1991
(Various folk and original songs)

Under the bluest sky: Songs of Richard Hundley
David Parks, tenor
Read Gainsford, piano
Produced by Steven Stucky
CD Baby, 2007
(Songs of Richard Hundley)

Voices of Light
Dawn Upshaw, soprano
Gilbert Kalish, piano
Nonesuch, 2014
(Songs of Messiaen, Debussy, Golijov, and Fauré)

William Bolcom and Arnold Weinstein: Cabaret Songs
Joan Morris, mezzo-soprano
William Bolcom, piano
Centaur, 2004
(Bolcom *Cabaret Songs*)

Woman Spirit
Ann Tedards, soprano
Marva Duerksen, piano

MSR Classics, 2010
(Libby Larsen's *Sonnets from the Portuguese*, *My Antonia*, *Margaret Songs*, and *Try Me, Good King: Last Words of the Wives of Henry VIII*)

Appendix B

List of Composers by Country of Birth

Note: This is not a comprehensive list.

ITALY

Franco Alfano
Vincenzo Bellini
Giovanni Bononcini
Giulio Caccini
Antonio Caldara
Giacomo Carissimi
Alfredo Casella
Mario Castelnuovo-Tedesco
Francesco Cavalli
Marc Antonio Cesti
Luigi Dallapiccola
Stefano Donaudy
Gaetano Donizetti
Francesco Durante
Claudio Monteverdi
Giovanni Paisiello
Giovanni Pergolesi
Goffredo Petrassi
Giacomo Puccini
Ottorino Respighi

Gioacchino Rossini
Alessandro Scarlatti
Barbara Strozzi
Paolo Tosti
Giuseppe Verdi
Riccardo Zandonai

GERMANY AND AUSTRIA

C. P. E. Bach
J. S. Bach
Ludwig van Beethoven
Alban Berg
Johannes Brahms
Peter Cornelius
Robert Franz
G. F. Handel
Joseph Haydn
Franz Liszt
Johann C. G. Loewe
Gustav Mahler
Felix Mendelssohn
Wolfgang Amadeus Mozart
Hans Pfitzner
Max Reger
Arnold Schoenberg
Franz Schubert
Clara Schumann
Robert Schumann
Louis Spohr
Richard Strauss
Anton Webern
Kurt Weill
Hugo Wolf
Carl Zelter
Johann Zumsteeg

FRANCE

Hector Berlioz
Joseph Canteloube
Claude Debussy
Henri Duparc
Gabriel Fauré
César Franck
Charles Gounod
Reynaldo Hahn
Arthur Honegger
Jacques Ibert
Jules Massenet
Darius Milhaud
Francis Poulenc
Maurice Ravel
Camille Saint-Saëns
Erik Satie

GREAT BRITAIN

Thomas Arne
Benjamin Britten
George Butterworth
William Byrd
Thomas Campion
Peter Maxwell Davies
Frederick Delius
John Dowland
Patrick Doyle
Edward Elgar
Gerald Finzi
Ivor Gurney
Michael Head
John Ireland
Hubert Parry
Henry Purcell
Roger Quilter
John Rutter
Cyril Scott
Charles Stanford

Ralph Vaughan Williams
William Walton
Peter Warlock

UNITED STATES

Dominick Argento
Ernst Bacon
Samuel Barber
Amy Cheney Beach
Leonard Bernstein
Marc Blitzstein
William Bolcom
Margaret Bonds
Paul Bowles
Harry T. Burleigh
John Cage
John Alden Carpenter
Theodore Chanler
Ernest Charles
Aaron Copland
George Crumb
David Diamond
John Duke
Vernon Duke
Richard Faith
Stephen Foster
Ricky Ian Gordon
Charles T. Griffes
Richard Hageman
Jake Heggie
Lee Hoiby
Richard Hundley
Charles Ives
Erich W. Korngold
Lori Laitman
Libby Larsen
Charles Martin Loeffler
Edward MacDowell
Douglas Moore
Undine Smith Moore

John Musto
John Jacob Niles
André Previn
Florence Price
Ned Rorem
William Grant Still
Virgil Thomson
Judith Lang Zaimont

Glossary

air de cour: French secular song of the early seventeenth century
allegro mosso: "more quickly"
andante: "at a walking pace"
andante cantabile: "song like"
andante quasi adagio: "like walking slowly"
aperture: opening between the lips
arietta: early Italian song form; not related to the operatic aria today
arpeggiated: a chord that is played one note at a time
art song: a song written for voice and piano
atonal: music not within a key signature
ayre: an early sixteenth-century English song form
ballad: early German song form perfected by J. R. Zumsteeg
ballad opera: popular musical theatre of the early eighteenth century, for example, John Gay's *The Beggar's Opera*
bass: a male voice category that is lower than the tenor voice
bass-baritone: a male vocal category higher than the bass and lower than the tenor
bel canto: "beautiful singing"; term used to describe the vocal writing of nineteenth-century opera composers like Vincenzo Bellini
bergerette: early French song form
Biedermeier: German term used to describe a European period (early to mid-nineteenth century) that includes the aesthetics of literature, furniture design, architecture, and music
binary: two parts
blues: a twentieth-century American genre of music that was created by African Americans and has had a great influence on many forms of secular music; a song with a fixed harmonic progression and sincere expression of emotion and feeling
Broadside ballads: in England, a popular song printed on a one-sided large sheet of paper
broken chords: a chord played one note at a time instead of all notes together; arpeggiated chords
bronchi: branches of cartilage that carry air from the trachea to the lungs
cantata: a work for one or more voices and instruments
canzonettas: song form; classification used by Joseph Haydn for his English songs
castrati: male opera singers who were castrated in order to perform opera roles that required a high voice and church music; boys who developed their falsetto register from an early age during the seventeenth and eighteenth centuries
chamber music: music written for two, three, four, or more instruments, but not a full orchestra

265

chanson à boire: French drinking song
chanson à danser: French dancing song
choral singing: group singing; a group of singers traditionally made up of sopranos, altos, tenors, and basses
chord progressions: changing harmony within a chordal structure
chromatic: music based on an octave of twelve semitones
chromaticism: use of chromatic harmony
classical: most commonly, a period of western European music encompassing most of the eighteenth century and the beginning of the nineteenth century
coda: "tail," a few bars of music at the end of a song
coloratura soprano: the highest female voice category; vocal passages that require speed and agility
commedia dell'arte: a type of Italian theatre originating in the sixteenth century and featuring a series of fixed characters such as "Harlequin" and "Pierrot"
con bravura: "with energy"
con molto sentimento: "with much feeling"
con passione: "with passion"
consonant cluster: a group of two, three, or four consonants that are pronounced before or after a vowel
continuo Lied: a strophic German mid-seventeenth-century song with a continuo accompaniment
contralto: the lowest female voice category; an unusual voice type
contrapuntal: composed with the technique of counterpoint
coordination: in singing, when all the elements of the voice are working well together to produce a singer's optimal sound
counterpoint: literally "note against note;" independent musical lines that are related harmonically
countertenor: a male singer who sings exclusively in his falsetto register
da capo: "from the head;" song form in which there are three main sections (A, B, A) and the first section repeats
diaphragm: an important dome-shaped muscle in the human body that makes breathing possible and separates the thorax from the viscera
diction: the enunciation of speech sounds
diphthong: two consecutive vowel sounds
dissonance: two or more notes that have tension; the opposite of consonance
ditties: insignificant but "catchy" tunes
double consonants: two of the same consonants together that are pronounced with exaggeration and more emphasis than a single consonant, for example, "rr," "mm," "zz"
durchkomponiert: "through-composed," a German song form
dynamic: the volume of a song
elision: a characteristic of the French sung language; the omission of a sound at the end of a word for ease in the pronunciation of text
Empfindsamer stil: "sensitive style;" eighteenth-century German term to describe expression and sensitivity in music
espressivo: "with expression"
falsetto: a vocal register used by countertenors or other male singers
fermata: "stop;" a held note in a song
First Berlin School (1750–1770): a group of German composers active from about 1750 to 1770 who emphasized simplicity of form and poetry
Fisk Jubilee Singers: a groundbreaking gospel choral group from Fisk University in Nashville, Tennessee; the first ensemble to benefit commercially from performance of gospel
folk song: a song that is not attributed to a specific composer; a song passed through generations by aural traditions
fortissimo: "very loud"

Frankfurt group: a group of the British composers Norman O'Neill, Roger Quilter, Cyril Scott, and H. Balfour Gardiner who studied composition with Iwan Knorr in Frankfurt, Germany

frottola: an Italian secular song of the fifteenth and sixteenth centuries

key change: a harmonic shift from one key to another

glottis: the space between the vocal folds

guttural: a speech or sung sound produced from the throat

harmony: the structure of the musical language; the combination of notes that make up chords and move through progressions

hymn: from the Latin "hymnus," traditionally a song used to praise God and most often strophic in form

hyperfunction: oversinging

hypofunction: undersinging

Impressionism: term used to describe an era of late nineteenth-century painting and eventually encompassed literary, musical, social, and political meaning[1]

interlude: brief piano solo in between sung parts of a song

intervallic: the space or distance between two notes

IPA: International Phonetic Alphabet; an alphabet of symbols that represent speech sounds

key signature: flat and sharp signs at the beginning of a song that indicate the notes to be used in the song; a group of notes that indicate the key of a song

keyboard: a classification of instruments that includes the piano

legato: smooth and connected; in singing, moving from one note to another smoothly and uninterrupted

lento tranquillo: "slow and calm"

Neapolitan school: a group of seventeenth- and eighteenth-century Italian opera composers

neoromantic: "new romantic;" used in the twentieth century to describe a return to expression and tonality in song

La Scala Opera: the most famous opera house in Italy, located in Milan

Langsam: "slow" or "very slow"

larynx: the voicebox; the structure of the voice that includes the vocal folds

Les Six: a group of six French composers active for a few years in the early twentieth century (Auric, Durey, Honegger, Milhaud, Poulenc, and Tailleferre)

Lied: a German art song

Lieder: plural of Lied; German art songs

Liederjahr: "song year;" term for Robert Schumann's seminal year of composition, 1840, in which he composed around 250 songs

lute: a stringed instrument which flourished in Europe from medieval times to the eighteenth century[2]

lute songs: English song style of the sixteenth and seventeenth centuries; songs in which singers accompanied themselves on a lute instrument

maestoso, non troppo presto: "majestic, but not too much"

markings: a composer's specific instructions for musical expression written in the score

melismatic: several pitches sung on the same vowel

meistersingers: "master singers;" male German singers of the fourteenth to sixteenth century who sang unaccompanied songs

mélodie: a French song

melody: the part of a song sung by the voice

Metropolitan Opera: the most famous American opera house, located in New York City

mezzist: a countertenor who focuses on the mezzo-soprano repertoire

mezzo-soprano: a female voice category that is higher than the contralto and lower than the soprano

minnesingers: "love singers;" German male singers of the twelfth and thirteenth centuries who sang songs about courtly love

minstrelsy: an exploitative form of musical theatre that exaggerated real-life black circumstances and reinforced dangerous stereotypes during the nineteenth and twentieth centuries in America[3]

mixed vowel: two vowel sounds pronounced at the same time
monody: music that is made up of a single line
Moravians: a culture that originated in Germany and has a strong musical tradition
motive: a short phrase of musical material that is repeated throughout a composition
musical style: the combination of song elements that are particular to a specific composer
nasals: a classification of speech sounds made with partial use of nasal resonation
Neapolitan song: a popular Italian song of the nineteenth century
opera buffa: comedic opera
opera seria: serious opera
operetta: light opera perfected by W. S. Gilbert and Arthur Sullivan in the nineteenth century British theatre
orchestra: an instrumental ensemble that includes string, brass, woodwind, and percussion instruments
ornamentation: an embellished melody; additional notes added by performers that fit into existing melody and harmony
otolaryngology: a medical specialty focused on the ear, nose, and throat
Pachanga: a type of Cuban music evocative of dance rhythms
parallelism: a differentiation of texture [4]
pastourelle: a French song form with a pastoral theme
pharynx: the inside of the mouth and resonating area for the voice
phonation: the act of using the larynx to make spoken or sung sounds
pianissimo: "very soft"
polyphony: a musical composition with more than one part
prelude: in song, an introductory piano solo before the singer begins to sing
Psalm-tunes: early American tunes for worship using text from the psalms of the Bible
range: the notes between two defined pitches
recapitulation: returning melodic material
recitative: a type of vocal writing that is similar to patterns of speech
register: a defined vocal range in which all the notes have the same quality
resonation: the ringing of the voice
rolling chord: a chord structure played one note at time, usually from the lowest to highest pitch
romance: French song form immediately preceding the mélodie
Romanticism: a period of the nineteenth century that emphasized expression of self through artistic pursuits
Schubertiad: in the early nineteenth century, a musical evening of German Lieder performances in a private home or salon usually featuring the songs of Franz Schubert
score: printed music
secco: "dry"
Second Berlin School: a group of German composers including J. A. P. Schulz, J. F. Reichardt, K. F. Zelter, C. F. D. Schubart, and J. R. Zumsteeg that was active from approximately 1770 to the early nineteenth century and focused on folk-influenced music
Second Viennese School: a group of twentieth-century Austrian composers; Arnold Schoenberg, Alban Berg, and Anton Webern
serialism: a genre of music composition featuring series of notes and usually incorporating use of the 12-tone scale
single consonant: one consonant that should be pronounced quickly
solfeggio: a vocal exercise usually sung on a vowel
song arrangement: a song written from a preexisting melody
song cycle: a group of songs performed together that may be related thematically or musically
sopranist: a countertenor who sings soprano repertoire
soprano: a female voice category that is higher than the mezzo-soprano
spiritual: an original American song form that flourished during the time of slavery; songs created by American slaves from a combination of musical influences
Sprechstimme: "speech singing," vocal writing that incorporates traits of speech into song; a combination of speaking and singing featured by composers such as Arnold Schoenberg

squillo: "ring"
stile antico: "old style;" used throughout music history to describe new compositional traits applied to older forms and styles
strophic: a song form with repeated melodic material; verses in song
Sturm und Drang: " storm and stress," a German literary movement emphasizing extreme emotional experiences
subglottal pressure: the build-up of air below the glottis
substitution: acting technique that uses real-life memories and emotions in place of the character's memories and emotions
subtext: the thoughts and emotions underneath the text of a song
syllabic: a description of text setting; one note per syllable
symbolism: a literary movement in which an object represents a person or emotion
tempi: more than one tempo
tempo: "time;" the speed of a song
tenor: a male voice category that is higher than the bass voice
tenorino: a male voice classification; a high, light tenor voice
ternary: in three parts
tessitura: in song, the range of the voice where the melody is focused
through-composed: a song form without repeated music
timbre: the quality of the human voice
time signature: the meter of a song (for example, 3/4 = three beats per measure); marked on the staff at the beginning of a song and where the song changes meter
tonality: observance of a single tonic key as the basis of composition[5]
tranquillo: "quiet"
triplet: a group of three notes performed within the time for two notes, sometimes indicated with a slur marking
troubadours: early song writers and poets of France
tune-books: the earliest American song books
tunesmiths: early Americans who wrote songs in addition to having full-time careers in other professions
twelve-tone method: a method used in musical composition in which twelve notes are used in a series, or fixed order, per the composer
umlaut: symbol used in German text to indicate a mixed vowel, for example: Ü, ü, ö
vibrato: a measurable undulation of pitch and intensity in singing
visualization: an acting technique that includes visualizing, or seeing, images that support the emotional intent of a song
vivo: "lively"
vocal cords: paired muscles within the larynx that can vibrate and produce sound, also known as the vocal folds
vocal folds: paired muscles within the larynx that can vibrate and produce sound, also known as the vocal cords
vocal tract: the area from the lips to the top of the larynx; the part of the body in which the voice resonates
voice classification: a method of assigning a singer the appropriate vocal category for the voice
volkstümliches: classification of the eighteenth-century Lied before Schubert
wanderlust: German term to describe the desire and intention to "wander" and travel

Notes

1. AN INTRODUCTION TO SONG

1. Deborah Davis, "An Interview about Choral Music with Ned Rorem," *The Music Quarterly*, v. 68, no. 3 (1982): 390–397.

2. THE DEVELOPMENT OF SONG

1. Sandra Jean Graham, "Spirituals," *Grove Music Online*, www.oxfordmusiconline.com

3. THE ELEMENTS OF SONG

1. Manuel Garcia II, *The Art of Singing, Part I* (Boston: Ditson, circa 1855), 6.
2. Dan H. Marek, *Singing: The First Art* (Lanham, Maryland: The Scarecrow Press, Inc., 2007), 93.
3. www.jakeheggie.com

4. HOW TO LISTEN TO SONG

1. Anthony Tommasini, "Elisabeth Schwartzkopf, Opera Singer, Dies at 90," *New York Times* (August 4, 2006).

5. ITALIAN SONG

1. Jeffrey Dean, "Le Nuove musiche," *Grove Music Online*, www.oxfordmusiconline.com
2. Barbara Hanning, "Giulio Caccini," *Grove Music Online*, www.oxfordmusiconline.com
3. Helmut Hucke and Dale E. Monson, "Bel canto," *Grove Music Online*, www.oxfordmusiconline.com
4. Hucke and Monson, *Grove Music Online*.
5. Denis Stevens, *A History of Song* (New York and London: W. W. Norton and Company, 1960), 299.
6. Ruth C. Lakeway and Robert C. White, Jr., *Italian Art Song* (Bloomington and Indianapolis: Indiana University Press, 1989), 21.
7. Lakeway and White, *Italian Art Song*, 58–59.
8. Lakeway and White, *Italian Art Song*, 99.
9. Steven R. Miller, "Stile antico," *Grove Music Online*, www.oxfordmusiconline.com
10. Keith Horner, "Paolo Tosti," *Grove Music Online*, www.oxfordmusiconline.com
11. Lakeway and White, *Italian Art Song*, 201.

6. GERMAN LIEDER

1. Gustave Mathieu and Guy Stern, *Introduction to German Poetry: A Dual Language Book* (New York: Dover Publications, Inc., 1959), 9.
2. Mathieu and Stern, *Introduction to German Poetry*, 6.
3. C. Michael Hawn, "Baroque Corner: German Continuo Lied," *The NATS Bulletin* (1988): 33.
4. Mathieu and Stern, *Introduction to German Poetry*, 39.
5. Mathieu and Stern, *Introduction to German Poetry*, 67.
6. Gunter Meier, "Johann Rudolph Zumsteeg," *Grove Music Online*, www.oxfordmusiconline.com
7. James Elson, "Carl Loewe and the Nineteenth Century German Ballad," *The NATS Bulletin* (October, 1971): 16.
8. Robert Winter, "Franz Schubert," *Grove Music Online*, www.oxfordmusiconline.com
9. Winter, *Grove Music Online*.
10. Winter, *Grove Music Online*.
11. Ernest Newman, *Hugo Wolf* (New York: Dover Publications, Inc., 2012), 29.
12. Eric Sams, *The Songs of Hugo Wolf* (Bloomington and Indianapolis: Indiana University Press, 1992), 1–10.
13. Sams, *The Songs of Hugo Wolf*, 1.
14. Newman, *Hugo Wolf*, 25.
15. Paul Hamburger, "Strauss the Songwriter," *Music and Musicians* 12, no. 10 (1964): 14–35.
16. Mathieu and Stern, *Introduction to German Poetry*, 93.
17. Douglas Jarman, "Alban Berg," *Grove Music Online*, www.oxfordmusiconline.com
18. Kathryn Bailey, "Anton Webern," *Grove Music Online*, www.oxfordmusiconline.com
19. Vivien Schweitzer, "Lamenting a Rejection by the Boss's Daughter: Matthias Goerne Sings Schubert at Carnegie Hall," *New York Times* (March 6, 2014).
20. Schweitzer, *New York Times*.

7. FRENCH MÉLODIE

1. Denis Stevens, *A History of Song* (New York and London: W. W. Norton and Company, 1960), 29.
2. "Symbolism," *Grove Music Online*, www.oxfordmusiconline.com
3. Pierre Bernac, *The Interpretation of French Song* (New York: W. W. Norton and Company, 1978), 35.
4. Carl B. Schmidt, *Entrancing Muse: A Documented Biography of Francis Poulenc* (Hillsdale, New York: Pendragon Press, 2001), 209.
5. Schmidt, *Entrancing Muse*, 210.
6. Patrick O'Connor, "Reynaldo Hahn," *Grove Music Online*, www.oxfordmusiconline.com
7. O'Connor, *Grove Music Online*.
8. Anne Midgette, "Gérard Souzay, 85, a Baritone Revered for Art Song Repertory, Dies," *New York Times* (August 19, 2004).
9. George Loomis, "Did Dessay Say Adieu Past Manon? Mais Non, Perhaps," *Classical Voice North America* (March 11, 2014).

8. SONGS OF THE BRITISH ISLES

1. "Lute," *Grove Music Online*, www.oxfordmusiconline.com
2. Paul Griffiths, "Michael Dewar Head," *Grove Music Online*, www.oxfordmusiconline.com
3. Anthony Tommasini, "From Full-Voiced Opera to Subtleties of Art Songs," *New York Times* (December 4, 2000).
4. Allan Kozinn, "Bryn Terfel in an All-German Recital," *New York Times* (October 26, 1994).
5. John von Rhein, "Bryn Terfel's Artful Song Recital Captivates at Ravinia," *Chicago Tribune* (August 4, 2011).

9. AMERICAN SONG: PART ONE

1. John Ogasapian, *Music of the Colonial and Revolutionary Era* (Westport, Connecticut and London: Greenwood Press, 2004), 56.
2. Ogasapian, *Music of the Colonial and Revolutionary Era*, 57.
3. James Weldon Johnson and J. Rosamond Johnson, *The Book of American Negro Spirituals* (New York: The Viking Press, Inc., 1925).
4. William Francis Allen, Charles Pickard Ware, Lucy McKim Garrison, *Slave Songs of the United States: The Classic 1867 Anthology* (New York: Dover Publications, Inc., 1985; reproduced from the original 1867 version).
5. U.S. National Archives and Records Administration, *National Archives*, www.archives.gov
6. Susan Heller-Anderson, "Leontyne Price—Still the Diva," *New York Times* (February 7, 1982).
7. William J. Mahar, *Behind the Burnt Cork Mask: Early Blackface Minstrelsy and Antebellum American Popular Culture* (Urbana and Chicago: University of Illinois Press, 1999).
8. Mahar, *Behind the Burnt Cork Mask*.
9. Edited by Robert Santelli, Holly George-Warren, and Jim Brown, *American Roots Music* (New York: Harry N. Abrams, Inc., 2001), 37.

10. Santelli, et al., *American Roots Music*, 88.
11. J. Peter Burkholder, "Charles Ives," *Grove Music Online*, www.oxfordmusiconline.com
12. Eileen Southern, "Hall Johnson," *Grove Music Online*, www.oxfordmusiconline.com
13. Carol Kimball, *Song: A Guide to Style and Literature* (Redmond, WA: Pst...Inc., 1996), 245.
14. Maida Goodwin, *The John Duke Papers* (Northampton, Massachusetts: College Archives, Smith College, 1986).

10. AMERICAN SONG: PART TWO

1. William Bolcom, www.williambolcom.com
2. Mary Ann Feldman and Laura Greenwald Strom, "Libby Larsen," *Grove Music Online*, www.oxfordmusiconline.com
3. John Musto, www.johnmusto.com
4. NYFOS (New York Festival Of Song), www.nyfos.org
5. Thomas Hampson, www.thomashampson.com
6. Song of America, Hampsong Foundation, www.songofamerica.net
7. Corinna da Fonesca-Wollheim, "Dawn Upshaw Sings Crumb's 'Ancient Voices' at BAM," *New York Times* (September 12, 2014).
8. Kevin Berger, "For Dawn Upshaw, 'Winds of Destiny' Lead to Ojai," *Los Angeles Times* (June 5, 2011).

GLOSSARY

1. Jann Pasler, "Impressionism," *Grove Music Online*, www.oxfordmusiconline.com
2. "Lute," *Grove Music Online*, www.oxfordmusiconline.com
3. University of South Florida, Tampa Library Exhibit: Special Collections of African American Sheet Music
4. Robert Pascall, "Style," *Grove Music Online*, www.oxfordmusiconline.com
5. "Tonality," *Grove Music Online*, www.oxfordmusiconline.com

Bibliography

Abendroth, Wolfgang. *A Short History of the European Working Class.* New York and London: Monthly Review Press, 1972.

Allen, William Francis, Charles Pickard Ware, and Lucy McKim Garrison. *Slave Songs of the United States: The Classic 1867 Anthology.* New York: Dover Publications, Inc., 1985 (reproduced from the original 1867 version).

Bailey, Kathryn. "Anton Webern." *Grove Music Online,* www.oxfordmusiconline.com

Berger, Kevin. "For Dawn Upshaw, 'Winds of Destiny' Lead to Ojai." *Los Angeles Times* (June 5, 2011).

Bernac, Pierre. *Francis Poulenc: The Man & His Songs.* New York and London: W. W. Norton and Company, 1977.

————. *The Interpretation of French Song.* New York: W. W. Norton and Company, 1978.

Burkholder, J. Peter. "Charles Ives." *Grove Music Online,* www.oxfordmusiconline.com

da Fonesca-Wollheim, Corinna."Dawn Upshaw Sings Crumb's 'Ancient Voices' at BAM." *New York Times* (September 12, 2014).

Davis, Deborah. "An Interview about Choral Music with Ned Rorem." *The Music Quarterly,* v. 68, no. 3 (1982): 390–397.

Dean, Jeffrey. "Le Nuove musiche." *Grove Music Online,* www.oxfordmusiconline.com

Elson, James. "Carl Loewe and the Nineteenth Century German Ballad." *The NATS Bulletin* (October, 1971): 16–19.

Feldman, Mary Ann, and Laura Greenwald Strom. "Libby Larsen." *Grove Music Online,* www.oxfordmusiconline.com

Garcia II, Manuel. *The Art of Singing, Part I.* Boston: Ditson, circa 1855, 6.

Goodwin, Maida. *The John Duke Papers.* Northampton, Massachusetts: College Archives, Smith College, 1986.

Graham, Sandra Jean. "Spirituals." *Grove Music Online,* www.oxfordmusiconline.com

Griffiths, Paul. "Michael Dewar Head." *Grove Music Online,* www.oxfordmusiconline.com

Hamburger, Paul. "Strauss the Song Writer." *Music and Musicians* 12, no. 10 (1964): 14–35.

Hanning, Barbara. "Giulio Caccini." *Grove Music Online,* www.oxfordmusiconline.com

Hawn, C. Michael. "Baroque Corner: German Continuo Lied." *The NATS Bulletin* (1988): 32–47.

Heggie, Jake. "Jake Heggie Composer and Pianist." *The Official Website of Jake Heggie,* www.jakeheggie.com

Heller-Anderson, Susan. "Leontyne Price—Still the Diva." *New York Times* (February 7, 1982).

Horner, Keith. "Paolo Tosti." *Grove Music Online,*www.oxfordmusiconline.com

Hucke, Helmut, and Dale E. Monson. "Bel canto." *Grove Music Online*, www.oxfordmusiconline.com

Jackson, Bruce. (ed.) *The Negro and His Folklore in Nineteenth-Century Periodicals.* Austin and London: University of Texas Press, Published for the American Folklore Society, 1967.

Jarman, Douglas. "Alban Berg." *Grove Music Online*, www.oxfordmusiconline.com

Johnson, James Weldon, and J. Rosamond Johnson. *The Book of American Negro Spirituals*, New York: The Viking Press, Inc., 1925.

Kimball, Carol. *Song: A Guide to Style and Literature.* Redmond, WA: Pst...Inc., 1996.

Kozinn, Allan. "Bryn Terfel in an All-German Recital." *New York Times* (October 26, 1994).

Lakeway, Ruth C., and Robert C. White, Jr. *Italian Art Song.* Bloomington and Indianapolis: Indiana University Press, 1989.

Loomis, George. "Did Dessay Say Adieu Past Manon? Mais Non, Perhaps." *Classical Voice North America* (March 11, 2014).

Lowens, Irving. *Music and Musicians in Early America.* New York: W. W. Norton and Company, 1964.

"Lute." *Grove Music Online*, www.oxfordmusiconline.com

Mahar, William J. *Behind the Burnt Cork Mask: Early Blackface Minstrelsy and Antebellum American Popular Culture.* Urbana and Chicago: University of Illinois Press, 1999.

Marek, Dan H. *Singing: The First Art.* Lanham, Maryland: The Scarecrow Press, Inc., 2007, 93.

Mathieu, Gustave, and Guy Stern. *Introduction to German Poetry: A Dual Language Book.* New York: Dover Publications, Inc., 1959.

Meier, Günter. "Johann Rudolf Zumsteeg." *Grove Music Online*, www.oxfordmusiconline.com

Midgette, Anne. "Gérard Souzay, 85, a Baritone Revered for Art Song Repertory, Dies." *New York Times* (August 19, 2004).

Miller, Richard. *The Structure of Singing: System and Art in Vocal Technique.* New York: Schirmer Books, 1996.

Miller, Steven R. "Stile antico." *Grove Music Online*, www.oxfordmusiconline.com

Newman, Ernest. *Hugo Wolf.* New York: Dover Publications, Inc., 1966.

O'Connor, Patrick. "Reynaldo Hahn." *Grove Music Online*, www.oxfordmusiconline.com

Ogasapian, John. *Music of the Colonial and Revolutionary Era.* Westport, Connecticut and London: Greenwood Press, 2004.

Olson, Margaret. *The Solo Singer in the Choral Setting.* Lanham, Toronto, Plymouth, UK: The Scarecrow Press, Inc., 2010.

Roden, Timothy J. "Schumann and Chamisso: The Music and Poetry of Frauenliebe und Leben." *The NATS Journal* (May/June, 1988): 13–33.

Sams, Eric. *The Songs of Hugo Wolf.* Bloomington and Indianapolis: Indiana University Press, 1961.

Santelli, Robert, Holly George-Warren, & Jim Brown. (eds.) *American Roots Music.* New York: Harry N. Abrams, Inc., 2001.

Schenk, H. G. *The Mind of the European Romantics.* New York: Doubleday and Company, Inc., 1966.

Schmidt, Carl B. *Entrancing Muse: A Documented Biography of Francis Poulenc.* Hillsdale, New York: Pendragon Press, 2001.

Schweitzer, Vivien. "Lamenting a Rejection by the Boss's Daughter: Matthias Goerne Sings Schubert at Carnegie Hall." *New York Times* (March 6, 2014).

Southern, Eileen. "Hall Johnson." *Grove Music Online*, www.oxfordmusiconline.com

Stein, Deborah, and Robert Spillman. *Poetry into Song: Performance and Analysis of Lieder.* New York and Oxford: Oxford University Press, 1996.

Stevens, Denis. *A History of Song.* New York and London: W. W. Norton and Company, 1960.

"Symbolism." *Grove Music Online*, www.oxfordmusiconline.com

Tommasini, Anthony. "Elisabeth Schwartzkopf, Opera Singer, Dies at 90." *New York Times* (August 4, 2006).

Tommasini, Anthony. "From Full-Voiced Opera to Subtleties of Art Songs." *New York Times* (December 4, 2000).

U.S. National Archives and Records Administration, *National Archives*, www.archives.gov

Vennard, William. *Singing: The Mechanism and the Technic.* New York: Carl Fischer, Inc., 1968.

von Rhein, John. "Bryn Terfel's Artful Song Recital Captivates at Ravinia." *Chicago Tribune* (August 4, 2011).

Winter, Robert. "Franz Schubert." Grove Music Online,www.oxfordmusiconline.com

Index

Vogelweide, Walther, 90; Weinstein, Arnold, 215; Werfel, Franz, 115; Wylie, Elinor, 204
polyphony, 13
Ponselle, Rosa, 25
pop, 4
Porgy and Bess, 218, 220
Poulenc, Francis, 5, 9, 19, 27, 141, 145, 146
Presley, Elvis, 23
Previn, André, 59, 77, 219
Price, Florence, 198
Price, Leontyne, 27, 35, 190, 198, 207
Proses lyriques, 138
Prudhomme, Sully, 140
psalm-tunes, 19, 187
Puccini, Giacomo, 65, 69, 78, 79
Purcell, Henry, 14, 15, 58, 160
Purdy, James, 213

Queen Elizabeth I, 159
Queen Victoria, 164
Quilter, Roger, 92, 167

Ragin, Derek Lee, 78
range, 57
Ravel, Maurice, 144
Ravinia Festival, 218
Ravinia Steans Music Institute, 220
The Reasonableness of Regular Singing, 187
recitativo (recitative), 5
Reichardt, Johann, 92
resonation, 24
Respighi, Ottorino, 71, 72, 80
"Rêve d'amour", 136
rhythm, 57
Rilke, Rainer Maria, 90, 115
Rimbaud, Arthur, 141
Rochberg, George, 218
rock, 4
Roethke, Theodore, 214
romance, 18, 92, 133
romanticism, 30
Roméo et Juliette, 146
rondeaux, 132
Roosevelt, Eleanor, 190
Rorem, Ned, 4, 6, 19, 50, 76, 211
Rossini, Gioacchino, 17, 65, 69, 70

Roussel, Albert, 144
Royal Academy of Music, 163, 172, 173
Royal Chapel in Naples, 66
Royal College of Music, 164, 165, 167, 168, 169
Royal Northern College of Music, 173, 174
Royal Opera House Covent Garden in London, 80
Rückert, Friedrich, 90

Salieri, Antonio, 96
Salonblatt, 106
Salzburg Music Festival, 80
Sangiacomo, Elsa Olivieri, 71
"Sapphische Ode" Brahms, 106
Satie, Erik, 144
Sauguet, Henri, 144
Scarlatti, Alessandro, 60, 66
Schäfer, Christine, 116
Schein, Johann, 18, 91
Schneider, Maria, 60
Schiller, Friedrich, 90
"Schlagende Herzen", 109
Schmidt, Hans, 106
Schoenberg, Arnold, 18, 60, 113, 114, 116
Schubart, C. F. D., 92
Schubert, Franz, 2, 8, 9, 18, 22, 33, 38, 50, 53, 89, 92, 95, 96, 97, 99, 101, 107, 115, 116, 133
Schubertiad, 2, 97, 164
Schulz, J. A. P., 92
Schumann, Robert, 18, 33, 38, 39, 95, 101, 105, 116
Scott, Cyril, 167, 168
"Sea Fever", 168
Seagle Music Colony, 202
secco, 5
Sechs Lieder nach Gedichten von George Trakl, 114
Second Berlin School, 92, 97
Second Viennese School, 114
"See How They Love Me", 212
Seit ich ihn gesehen" from *Frauenliebe und leben*, 104
Senfl, Ludwig, 18, 91
Serenade for Tenor, Horn and Strings, 173
serialism, 18
Sense and Sensibility (film), 174

About the Author

Margaret Olson is an independent scholar and writer who has taught, studied, and performed song for many years. She has a special interest in American and British song and has performed these songs in diverse venues inlcuding the White House and State Department in Washington, D.C., the Walters Art Museum in Baltimore, Maryland, and at various colleges and universities. She has studied American art song repertory at the Aspen Music Festival with Arlene Shrut, Ned Rorem, and Paul Sperry.

She has been on the music faculties of the University of Tennessee, Morgan State University, Peabody Conservatory and Preparatory, and Georgetown University. She has taught music programs for the Washington National Opera Institute and Wolf Trap Foundation, among others. She is the author of *The Solo Singer in the Choral Setting* (Scarecrow Press) and has been published in academic journals such as the *Journal of Singing* and *Choral Journal*.

She holds a Doctor of Musical Arts degree in performance and pedagogy from the University of Iowa, and music degrees from the University of Maryland, College Park, and the University of North Carolina, Greensboro. Her song mentors are Geraldine Cate, Robert McCoy, Arlene Shrut, Darlene Lawrence, and Patrick O'Donnell.